VOICES
IMPERIAL ROME

VOICES OF IMPERIAL ROME

Guy de la Bédoyère

TEMPUS

First published 2000

PUBLISHED IN THE UNITED KINGDOM BY:

Tempus Publishing Ltd
The Mill, Brimscombe Port
Stroud, Gloucestershire GL5 2QG

PUBLISHED IN THE UNITED STATES OF AMERICA BY:

Arcadia Publishing Inc.
A division of Tempus Publishing Inc.
2 Cumberland Street
Charleston, SC 29401
1-888-313-2665

Tempus books are available in France, Germany and Belgium
from the following addresses:

Tempus Publishing Group	Tempus Publishing Group	Tempus Publishing Group
21 Avenue de la République	Gustav-Adolf-Straße 3	Place de L'Alma 4/5
37300 Joué-lès-Tours	99084 Erfurt	1200 Brussels
FRANCE	GERMANY	BELGIUM

British Library Cataloguing in Publication Data.
A catalogue record for this book is available from the British Library.

ISBN 0 7524 1497 6

Typesetting and origination by Tempus Publishing.
PRINTED AND BOUND IN GREAT BRITAIN

Contents

List of coin illustrations

1 Introduction
The Genius of the Roman People, as depicted on the reverse of a bronze coin struck for Constantius I between 297 and 305. At a time of change and insecurity the rulers of the Late Empire looked for symbols of Roman greatness to place on coins struck and distributed throughout the fragmenting Roman world.

2 Soldiers, brutality and valour
Brass sestertius of Trajan (98-117). During this emperor's reign Roman military success was taken to its ultimate extreme and the Empire reached its greatest extent.

3 Cities, circuses and crowds
Brass dupondius of Vespasian (69-79). Under Vespasian the most notorious of all Rome's monuments was begun: the Colosseum. Unlike his predecessors Vespasian recognized that the basis of his power lay with the Roman mob, and he was the first emperor since Augustus to die in his bed.

4 Decadence, cruelty and vice
Silver denarii depicting three of Rome's most outrageous emperors whose reigns were marked for their vicarious and random cruelty. From bottom right, anti-clockwise, they are Nero (54-68), Commodus (180-92), and Caracalla (211-17) with his formal name Antoninus Pius.

5 Corruption, swindles and double-dealing
The reverse of a copper as struck in 86 by Domitian (81-96) depicting Moneta, the personification of the Roman mint, with her scales.

6 Villas, relaxation and rest
Silver denarius of Hadrian (117-38). Hadrian's private villa at Tivoli, east of Rome, was the ultimate expression of the Roman rural retreat.

7 Provincials, foreigners and barbarians
Reverse of an as struck by Hadrian c. 119-22 depicting the province Britannia. Head hung, the personification of this remote and wayward province is shown as defeated and crushed. In reality the province was never conquered in its entirety and remained a permanent problem.

8 Disasters, omens and phenomena
Reverse of a silver denarius struck by Vitellius (69) in Spain in early 69. The legend
VICTORIA AVG is a declaration of his imperial military aspirations during the Civil War
of 68-9 though the omens were not in his favour and he lasted little more than six
months before he was killed.

9 Gods, spirits and demons
The Undefeated Companion Sun-god, as depicted on the reverse of a bronze coin
struck by Constantine I between c. 307-25.

10 Slaves, insurrections and masters
Reverse of a silver antoninianus struck by Philip I (244-9) bearing the legend AEQVITAS
AVG, 'The Fair Dealing of the Emperor', which contrasts directly with the reality of life
in the Roman world where slavery guaranteed total inequity.

Foreword

A number of years ago I purchased an edition of the poems of the Roman poets Catullus and Tibullus. I needed the texts for a book I was writing at the time. But I was particularly attracted to the second-hand copy which I had found. Inside the front cover is the bookplate of one Thomas Byrnand Trappes-Lomax. On the facing page Lomax had written in pencil, 'TBT-L 8th June 1917', and had added, perhaps as an afterthought, 'Prior to France 10th June'. It was moving to think that a young man chose a work of literature from the Roman world to read before he embarked on his way to one of the greatest tragedies of the twentieth century. Serving with the Scots Guards, Lomax was wounded twice on the Western Front but survived. Perhaps Catullus offered him some consolation and diversion along the way, though the poet himself would scarcely have ever had an idea where his works would one day find a willing ear.

Lomax belonged to a generation that took the classical world and its languages for granted as a part of its education. The wars which he and his kind took part in, and in which so many died, produced colossal changes in every aspect of society. One of those changes was in education. Latin and Greek now form a minimal part in the school curriculum and few schools offer it at all. Oddly, at the same time, there has been a proliferating interest in the ancient world, manifested in the large numbers of popular books and television programmes produced to feed an apparently insatiable fascination in a time when the worlds of men and myth seem to have been blurred. Archaeological excavations produce great public interest, and tours of ancient sites are more popular than ever before.

Remarkable though such monuments are, they seem often sterile, bereft of the men and women who walked the streets of the great Roman cities of Europe, North Africa and the Near East. The clatter of crowds and markets, the smells, laughter in the theatres, the banter and abuse of political rallies, the noise and horror of battle, and the bewildered shrieking of doomed animals in the circus — all this is lost from the ruins of places like Ephesus, Dougga, Verulamium, and even in the Eternal City herself. Excavation produces pottery and other artefacts, which sit silently on the shelves in stores and museums.

As we dig deeper into the physical remains of antiquity we seem at the same time to have become paradoxically distanced from the human beings who lived there. Not long ago a Roman coffin containing a young woman was opened to great excitement in London. She and her sarcophagus were indeed well-preserved. But we do not, and never will, know her name, where she came from and who she truly was. She remains an anonymous skeleton, a silent witness to her world accessed only through the presumptions and assumptions inherent in scientific and archaeological techniques. Instead it is through the histories, letters, literature, and inscriptions that we can really find a way into the minds of the Roman world and its people. What of course turns up is a world just like our own, where dignity sat side by side with decadence, creativity with corruption, and power with humility.

The Roman Empire stands head and shoulders above much of European history. It was the first great western state. Despite its problems, and the length of its death agonies, it lasted for centuries and straddled much of the known western world. As a time of great cities, centralised and regional government, law and order, military power, financial systems and industries, it has much to tell us about ourselves.

This book is therefore an anthology, a personal selection of some of the legacy of the Roman world, but in translation. The idea is scarcely original but I hope the treatment is. The vast majority belong to the days of the Empire, when the notorious personalities of the emperors and the vast extent of the Roman world provided contemporary writers with so much vivid material to draw on. However, I have also included a selection of texts either written under the late Republic, or which describe events in that tumultuous episode of change such as the account of the slave revolt led by Spartacus. Although each passage is individually introduced, the chapters are deliberately thematic and each text follows on from its predecessor.

Some passages, like Pliny the Younger's description of his villa, will be familiar because they are so important and unique that they could not be omitted. But many others will, I hope, be entirely new, having been trawled from the less-familiar pages of writers like Herodian or Sidonius or the papyri of Roman Egypt. Although a broadly chronological sequence is followed within the chapters the book is essentially topical, and seeks to reflect aspects of life that we will recognise. The essence of some of the original, and especially the sheer economy and neatness of Latin and Greek, has inevitably been lost but I have tried to retain the fundamental sense of immediacy. In our own intensely visual age it is all too easy to forget that it is through the words of men and women that the past really comes into our own lives. I'd like to thank Peter Kemmis Betty once more for his enthusiastic reception of the text and Anne Phipps of Tempus for seeing it through the press.

Most of all I hope this is a good read. The ancient writers knew that their stories and anecdotes made for gripping reading and I see absolutely no reason why they should not still be regarded in the same way. So, this book is as much about the scurrilous and outrageous as it is about military feats and religious worship and I have included as many tales as possible which have made me laugh, opened my eyes, or squirm with disgust. When it comes to epic scandal there is no match for Caligula, Nero and Elagabalus, and when it comes to wonder there is no equal for the underground fumes which poisoned everyone except eunuchs, or the eruption of Mount Vesuvius.

You may love or hate Rome but you cannot ignore her.

Guy de la Bédoyère, Eltham 2000

1 Introduction

'In my opinion nothing is more satisfying than that people should always want to know what sort of a person a man had been', observed Pliny the Elder, writing in the middle of the first century AD (*Natural History* XXXV.10). He was in the middle of describing the development of libraries in the Roman world and had grasped the essential truth that curiosity drives the human spirit. Pliny was a man whose life was dictated by an insatiable and voracious appetite for information. He was in every sense a product of a literate and cosmopolitan society, and concluded that, 'without doubt, of all the peoples of the world, the Romans are the ones who exhibit outstanding virtue' (VII.130). In love with archives and books himself, Pliny's great contribution to civilisation was to synthesise all that he came across into his own monumental *Natural History*. This epic compilation remained a rich resource throughout antiquity and into the early modern world. Even today his accounts of medicines, herbs, natural phenomena, animals, remarkable feats and remarkable men remain an unparalleled window on the ancient world.

Despite the vast quantities of artefacts and buildings surviving from antiquity the written word is the only way to access the past and understand it as a human experience. The Greek and Roman worlds were probably the first periods in the west when literacy spread amongst the masses to a greater or lesser degree, though how much remains a matter of some dispute. It became part of everyday life on coins, inscriptions, manufacturers' marks, signs and graffiti. In the barbarian provinces of the west, such as Britain and Germany, literacy, or any evidence for it, was all but non-existent until the Romans arrived. Roman accounts of the tribes before they were conquered are the only 'history' we have for their pre-Roman way of life. Their incorporation into the Empire was through the Latin language and Roman institutions.

Of course the degree of literacy in antiquity could not match the level it has reached in our own time, but it is obvious from finds of graffiti and other casual scribbles that some people from all classes came to use reading and writing in the course of their lives. Even if it remained a minority activity it is likely that almost everyone had access to someone who was functionally literate. Those who benefited from a formal education, which on the whole meant boys from more affluent backgrounds, learned as children to copy passages from literature and to produce their own compositions.

Such people grew up corresponding through letters, reading public inscriptions and electoral slogans, and owning or funding libraries which, as Pliny put it, 'put works of genius into public ownership' (XXXV.10).

But there were also countless trained secretaries, copyists, and clerks who were responsible for churning out vast quantities of legal and other official documents which covered trials, land disputes, imperial edicts and taxation amongst other things. Scattered remains of archives show that these could deal with anything from an order of food for a fort right up to letters from the emperor sent to a provincial governor. Then there were the ordinary soldiers, builders, potters, and other artisans who wrote their names or comments on their property or products, the remains of which lie scattered across the Roman world and beyond.

Part of the development of literacy resulted from the introduction, long before Roman times, of alphabet-based languages such as Phoenician and Greek. The Egyptians used a variety of forms based on visual representations of objects or sounds. Some Egyptian characters resembled their meaning. Thus, a hawk meant a hawk. But such a symbol could also be used to represent a syllable, a euphemism, or a single character or sound. The complexity of some of the symbols led to the creation of other scripts, using abbreviated forms of these characters. Egyptian ended up with three principal forms: formal hieroglyphic, and the shorthand versions of hieratic and demotic. It required a great deal of skill to command any of these forms of writing. This, together with a combination of religious and social restrictions, meant that literacy was an art practised by only a few and it was jealously protected.

Greek and Latin, like certain other languages, rely on a fixed number of characters, each of which represent single letters. Obvious though this may seem, it is easily forgotten that such a system also demystifies the art of literacy. With a small number of characters to learn it is relatively easy for most people to grasp a basic technique. Naturally, the words used and their meanings are altogether a different matter. But the result it that in a short time a person can come to recognise his or her own name, the name of an emperor, the name of his city, and those of the deities he or she worships. In short, alphabet languages are more egalitarian.

Greek and Latin were not the only languages spoken in the Roman world. Versions of Celtic were used in the west though it had no written form, and its survival in Welsh, Cornish, Gaelic and Breton shows that it continued in use beyond the collapse of Roman government. In the East, Egyptian survived into Roman times along with Aramaic and other languages, many of which have since vanished with the ages or merged seamlessly into later tongues. In Pompeii, Oscan, an ancient Italian language, appears amongst the city's graffiti, while Coptic preserved parts of the Egyptian language.

But Greek and Latin remained throughout the period the principal languages used in formal and public life, and often for private and commercial affairs. Thus Latin texts appear throughout West, and Greek throughout the East, even in Egypt and to a limited extent vice-versa. Thus Greek turns up in Britain on some Roman inscriptions.

For a person living in the Roman Empire, knowledge of Latin or Greek gave him or her the same access to learning, law, services and understanding that English and

Spanish do today in the United States. While it is almost certain that many people continued to use their local languages for day-to-day conversation, it is also true that these rarely manifest themselves in the record. Even where a bereaved husband called Barates buried his wife in Britain and recorded her details in his native Palmyrene this formed a secondary text to the Latin inscription above it. She, despite being explicitly described as a native of the British Catuvellaunian tribe, had an unequivocally Latin name, *Regina*, or literally 'Queen'.

The absence of many local languages is of course a loss for us. But it is also a benefit. Almost all of what we know about the Roman world is recorded in Latin or Greek. In contrast it was not unusual in the nineteenth century for non-literate cultures to be presented with an alphabet form of their language which would serve as a 'civilising' influence. In 1821 the North American Cherokee people were provided with an alphabet based on 86 characters to represent letters and syllables. Their use of this tool in their own courts and newspaper was regarded on one hand by whites as evidence of their integration, but it also served as a stimulus to self-expression, identity and resistance. That their alphabetic benefactor, Sequoyah, had a Cherokee mother and a white father is symbolic of its dual impact. For the Celtic-speaking tribes of the western Roman Empire, Latin was their only avenue to literacy and its liberating effects. Tacitus of course regarded this as a token of their enslavement to Roman ways. Even in the East, where languages such as Egyptian or Palmyrene existed in written form, Greek was as the principal administrative and commercial *lingua franca*. Josephus wrote his account of the Jewish war in Aramaic to begin with, for local circulation. However, as he says himself, it was necessary for him to translate it into Greek to make it available to other 'subjects of the Empire' in his effort to correct other accounts which he described as 'eulogies' or 'abuse'.

For us, the consequences lasted on into through the Middle Ages to our own time. With Latin and Greek serving as the main languages of the Christian churches, the surviving historical and other texts of the Roman Empire had a chance to survive. Copied by men who understood them much has endured to our own time in a form that we too can understand. The record is accessible to anyone prepared nowadays to spend time familiarising him or herself with just these two languages. One need only consider how many languages would be needed to understand the records of the same geographical territory today to appreciate how privileged we are (Arabic, English, German, Spanish, Hungarian, Romanian, and French to name but a few). It has also meant that for centuries the surviving texts have been printed and published, often in translation. Almost all the principal extant sources for history and society in the Roman world are available in some form, whereas anyone interested in exploring the laws and history of ancient Egypt or Persia would find the prospect rather more intimidating. But Rome has a more natural interest to most of us. This extraordinary world of cities and circuses, emperors and slaves, and villas and farms, leads directly into our own. At once it merges continuity with the beguiling fascination of, what seems to us to be, the remote and fabulous past but was in reality a world filled with heroes, villains, miscreants, and geniuses just like our own.

Literature in the Roman Empire

By the first century BC Rome was the pre-eminent power in the Mediterranean. Once Octavian took supreme power after the Battle of Actium in 31BC Rome was already effectively at the head of an empire which included Italy, Gaul, Greece, North Africa, and Asia Minor. Along with the burgeoning machinery of a complex state came the growth in records and documentation, which created the sense of Roman destiny. Augustus presented himself to the world as the restorer of the Roman Republic. He was in every real sense a monarch though he never called himself this. Most of his contemporaries willingly accepted this transition as an improvement over the chaos and civil war of preceding decades.   The Roman world was a stage on which the Roman ruling class, the senatorial and equestrian families, acted out their lives. Qualified by their wealth to hold all the most prestigious magistracies and other positions, they included intellectuals, statesmen, non-entities, moral derelicts and political opportunists. Like every élite before and since they sought a moral and ethical justification to their position and it was from this that Roman history and literature grew. Octavian, as Augustus, sought his legitimacy within the offices and privileges of the senatorial class. He always took care to tread a careful path as a 'first' (but not a tyrannical first) among equals'. One of the failings of many of his immediate successors, such as Caligula, was a failure to recognise the need to play the game. They had forgotten Augustus's claim to have 'restored' the republic and its offices. The drama of these political machinations was not lost on the historians of the age who were intoxicated by the literary potential of monsters like Nero.

The route to Rome's greatness was found in her traditions, which included Republican literature like the works of Cato. Central to the theme was an indulgent fantasy in Roman destiny and natural supremacy borne out of a primeval bucolic purity. Virgil and other poets like Propertius were encouraged to present Octavian's power struggle with Antony as a struggle to rid Rome of foreign enemies and restore her institutions and traditions. That this involved elevating Octavian to primacy, awarding him the name Augustus and accepting his unprecedented parallel tenure of various republican magistracies, seems to have been a deal the Roman people were prepared to accept. One might readily be forgiven for seeing more than a passing resemblance to the ludicrously romanticised German past trumped by the Nazis during the 1930s, and its fantasy of solidarity in the face of various 'foreign enemies'.

It would certainly be true that there was no more factual basis to Nazi ideas of Teutonic supremacy than there was to the Roman fantasy of a mythical rural paradise, their 'Age of Saturn'. But where the Romans were involved, this had as much to do with the fact that the records scarcely existed until the end of the third century BC. It was only by this time that the permanent destruction of Carthaginian power not only placed Rome firmly in the driving seat but also provided her with a scenario that needed an explanation. This did not result in a history that we would recognise as such, but it did begin to establish a literary tradition, and developed a literary and dramatic ritual that provided the Romans with an over-mantle of martial and mythical self-glorification. That the legendary founder, Romulus, had a name created out of the city's name and was said to be a son of Mars illustrates the convenient circular device of myth.

When Livy, the first serious Roman historian whose works are extant, wrote at the end of the first century BC it was obvious to him that the material he had available from most of Rome's earlier times was impossible to verify. He likened it to writing a history based on the eulogies heaped on former worthies by their families and acolytes. But even if he had a more acute sense of the inadequacy of such subjective accounts he nevertheless, like his contemporaries and successors, had little concern with writing a history based on firsthand research. This was largely because Roman literature, of which history was no more than an expression, occupied a ritual role within social circles. In the preceding century, Latin had become the medium in which the Roman literary tradition was firmly founded. Composing Latin prose or poetry for public or private readings was both an entertainment and an educational rhetorical expression of style and achievement. 'Roman history', such as it was, served for Augustus and his circle as classical myth served for the court painters of the English Restoration. It provided set piece dramas for heroes and villains and for which opposing speeches could be composed as literary devices and as moral instruction. The composer was applauded for his literary style, not his familiarity with the topography of such and such a battlefield. By the time that the Empire had come into being, historical literature had become an important component in consolidating and reflecting its natural lineage from the purity of Roman antiquity whose virtues the imperial state sought perpetually to revive.

As the Roman Empire developed and began to exhibit greater extremes in its rulers and nature of its rule, so the quality and diversity of Roman historical writing increased. In the first century BC Julius Caesar produced his own terse and factual accounts of his campaigns. Around the beginning of the second century Tacitus wrote the finest historical account that survives from the Roman world. In fact, a large proportion of what he wrote is not extant, but the parts which are do provide us with a brilliantly vivid account of most of the reigns of the first two-thirds of the first century AD. Nonetheless, Tacitus' works were exercises both in literary and allegorical style and they often lack precise detail, or contain contradictions and obscurities. His contemporary, Suetonius, produced a colourful account of the same period but by using an entirely different device. He composed individual biographies of rulers from Julius Caesar through to Domitian. These vivid records, which contain scurrilous gossip alongside important factual accounts of events, help flesh out some of the gaps in Tacitus but like so much of Roman history they focused on events and personalities in Rome often to the exclusion of all else. It must be remembered that men like Tacitus and Suetonius were essentially writing about their own peer groups. For them the Empire was simply the setting in which the emperors and the senatorial class played out their power games.

A provincial governorship was usually only of interest to Tacitus where that post played an important part in the rise and fall of a statesman or was integral to an event with significance for Rome. He was particularly impressed by military achievements. This is no better seen than in his account of his father-in-law, Gnaeus Julius Agricola, a unique piece of work, which supplies us with an extraordinary amount of detail for a single man's career. Agricola made his name with his monumental northern campaign in Britain during his governorship between c. 77-84 and Tacitus makes it possible to draw up a fairly precise chronology of events until the moment that Agricola left. Britain was a relatively incidental component to Tacitus in the sense that he was only really interested in it as a backdrop to Agricola. Had Agricola fought a war in Germany then that is where Tacitus would have written about. After 84 Britain falls almost silent in the historical record and, in spite of occasional passing references from other historians later, there is little that compares with Tacitus.

The survival of texts

One of the curious paradoxes of the Roman world is that, while lettering was routinely reproduced on coins through the engraving of coin dies, printing or any equivalent was never invented. There was no such thing as the book in the form we know it. Output was relatively small, and the number of copies few. The *Aeneid* of Virgil is about 64,000 words long, or about three-quarters of the length of this book. Caesar's *Gallic War*, is about the same length as the whole of this book. Texts were written by hand on scrolls of paper or papyrus, ultra-thin sheets of fine wood, or on potsherds. We can be sure that other perishables, such as cloth, were also used. While potsherds might survive, almost nothing else does.

In H.G. Wells's *The Time Machine*, the Time Traveller finds a shelf of books. Eager to grasp the learning gained in the centuries between his own time and the distant future in which he finds himself, the Time Traveller seizes a volume which turns to dust in his hands. Pliny the Elder said that 'our civilisation, or at least our written records, depend very largely on paper' (XIII.78-83). He described the various techniques, and even minimum standards laid down by Claudius, and was impressed by the durability of paper prepared with special adhesives and then flattened. He concluded that this should guarantee it would last 'a long time' and proudly recounted the documents he had seen with the autographs of the great men of the Republic such as the Gracchi, and Cicero. Unfortunately, it is no exaggeration to say that the very greater part of the written record of the Roman world has turned to dust like the books in the Time Traveller's hands. Private and public libraries, domestic and public archives have crumbled, been burned, lost or otherwise destroyed. Only the sands of Egypt or the waterlogged moorland of northern Britain have preserved any meaningful record (at least that found and recovered), and that is fantastically limited. Even these texts are rarely complete and when they are, often record little more than military rosters, stock lists, or the arcane details of an obscure lawsuit. The following account, which will make many readers wince, illustrates how ignorance, bigotry and small-mindedness could destroy in seconds material which had survived for centuries. Here, a monastic account recorded the excavations of the Roman city of *Verulamium* (St Albans) in search of usable building material for the eleventh-century abbey church.

In the days of Abbot Eadmar, while the excavators were exploring the walls deep down, they located the foundations of a huge palace in the centre of the ancient town. While being astonished at its scale they found an unknown book, with other smaller books and scrolls, in a recess resembling a cupboard in a wall. It had scarcely been affected by the passage of time. The writing and the words were too old to be comprehensible but they were beautiful and written clearly with initials and headings in gold. The book had boards of oak, and silk ties, which had kept most of their original strength and beauty. They found an ancient broken-down priest after looking far and wide for a long time. He was a learned man called Unwona who was highly-skilled in scripts and languages and he had no difficulty making sense of the book. In addition he also interpreted the other books in the cupboard. It was the writing used when *Werlamnescestra* [*Verulamium*] was still lived in. It was ancient British with some Latin...

In the first book Unwona discovered the story of St Alban, the first English martyr ... but in the others he found the prayers and rituals of the pagan citizens of *Werlamnescestra*. From these books he found that they favoured worship of Phoebus, god of the sun ...

The books containing demonic subject matter were discarded and burnt and only the one containing St Alban's story was kept ... When a translation in Latin had been transcribed, the original turned to dust.

Chronicles of the Monastery of St Alban, Lives of the Abbots of the Monastery of Holy Alban, Rolls Series 1876 I.24-8

It is impossible to be sure how accurate this account is. But it is likely at least to be representative of many similar incidents. Even the extant Four Gospels are the chosen survivors from a canon of evangelical literature, much of which was suppressed by the early church's censors. What we have instead are the copies of copies of copies of texts which lasted into the early medieval period and which the monastic copyists had the wit to transcribe.

By the time that printing became widespread in the fifteenth century and afterwards, a concerted effort was made by publishers to produce classical texts from the monastic manuscripts to satisfy the public demand for antiquity. At the time there was a common belief in the infallibility of certain antique authorities. Henri Estienne in sixteenth-century Geneva, for example, produced many texts. A copy of Estienne's 1572 edition of Plutarch's Lives was purchased by the English diarist and virtuoso John Evelyn (1620-1706) in Paris in 1651 while travelling in Europe. He added it to his sprawling library of classical texts, which he trawled for material to insert in his prolific writings. Like many of his contemporaries he tended to wonder at the works of ancient authors and accepted them with little critical sense. On 13 June 1662 his friend Samuel Pepys recorded,

Up by 4 a-clock in the morning and read Cicero's *Second Oracion against Cataline*, which pleased me exceedingly; and more I discern therein then ever I thought was to be found in him. But I perceive it was my ignorance, and that he is as good a writer as ever I read in my life.

The demand from people like Pepys and Evelyn guaranteed production, and thus preservation, of material which might otherwise have gone the way of other long-lost texts.

The randomness of this process is illustrated by the text of the poems of Catullus.

Gaius Valerius Catullus was another member of the first-century BC Roman ruling class, although he came from Verona. Nonetheless, the family counted Caesar amongst its friends but for all that Catullus himself is known almost exclusively from his poems. These are practically all known only from copies made in the fourteenth century of an older manuscript extant in the 1300s. This latter manuscript was lost not long after the copies were made. It is thus obvious that had the copies not been made then we would know little or nothing about Catullus at all. Tacitus wrote two major historical works, the *Annals*, and the *Histories*. The latter is known only from an eleventh-century copy made at Monte Cassino in Italy, and even then we only have the opening section which covers the civil war of 68-9. The remaining accounts of the reigns of Vespasian, Titus, and Domitian are lost. A similar precarious situation affected the transmission of the *Annals*, though rather more is extant. Unfortunately, the losses include the account of the reign of Caligula (37-41), and some of the early part of the reign of Claudius (41-7), as well as sections of the reigns of Tiberius and Nero.

Some of the gaps in Tacitus are filled by the history written by Dio Cassius (also known as Cassius Dio). Dio wrote in Greek but lived and worked in Rome during the late second and early third century. He was well-placed to produce an authoritative account of all Roman history from the very beginning up to the year 235. Unfortunately, the only complete section deals with the period 68BC to AD47, a period much of which, it must be said, is relatively well-recorded by others. But thanks to later writers like Zonara and John Xiphilinus who had access to the whole work before it was lost, the missing sections are partly made good in what is known as the Epitome of Dio Cassius. The result is an invaluable if imperfect record, happily reinforced and complemented by the history written by Herodian for the years 180-238. Also composed in Greek, this work has, extraordinarily, survived in its virtual entirety.

In contrast, Virgil's popularity was such that more assiduous efforts were made to preserve and copy his works. Not only do a relatively large number of manuscripts from the late Roman period exist (mostly of selected parts of his works) but many copies made at later dates from other early versions no longer extant. Imperfections exist in all the copies to a greater or lesser degree, often with attempts made across the centuries to correct texts. This, for example, afflicts the ninth-century text of Juvenal's *Satires*. But cross-referencing between various copies makes it possible to work which was the original, or most original (the archetype), and the family tree of copies. Sometimes, the recovery of papyrus fragments or other ancient documents makes it possible to confirm short passages or even to fill small gaps in the extant record. But this is extremely rare.

Generally speaking therefore, where literature is concerned we are left with material that has come down to us in an almost exclusively indirect form. We virtually never have the physical evidence of contemporary copies. There is no manuscript of Virgil or Tacitus that belongs to either author's own time. When it comes to inscriptions we have potentially unadulterated material, albeit brief, and in the same way the recovery of original documents may provide us with the same purity. This is an extremely important distinction and is one that provides us with an immediate connection with the past. The problem is the brevity and abbreviation. Official or private inscriptions tend to be short statements, and only rarely do they carry full transcriptions of more discursive manuscript originals. An example is Claudius' speech to the Gauls of 48. Recorded on a bronze tablet found in Lyons which in part survives (*ILS* 212), it can be compared with the version in Tacitus. It is clear that Tacitus, to some extent, rewrote and reordered the text for literary purposes and this is a sobering reminder to us that all Roman literary sources probably have similar shortcomings. However, it is of course equally impossible to verify the Lyons tablet apart from the fact that it has not been physically altered since it was carved. Sometimes, the heavily-abbreviated protocol of epigraphy can be cryptic but problems are more likely to come from the inscription being partly shattered or defaced. Even a small hole in the middle of a crucial text can occasion generations of academic debate about the original meaning.

In a different way, private documents are equally difficult to understand. Here the reason is likely to be the cursive hand used. Roman cursive handwriting was quite different from the Carolingian minuscule, developed under the Holy Roman Emperor Charlemagne (d. 814) and the lettering used in many of the monastic copies. Modern handwriting owes its origin to Carolingian minuscule, but Roman handwriting was more distinguished by its reliance on closely spaced vertical strokes. The letter 'e' was, for example, typically represented by two vertical strokes pointing upwards slightly towards each other. The letter 'm' was represented by four similar strokes. Closely-spaced, damaged and often incomplete, these documents are usually extremely difficult to transcribe and translate, not least because the ordinary Roman often showed him or herself to be almost as bad at Latin or Greek grammar and spelling as the proverbial schoolboy of later centuries.

Neither inscriptions nor documents are common. As a habit, erecting inscriptions seem to have been particularly popular amongst the military and some civilian settlements and then only at certain periods and in certain places. The early third century is a period which is relatively well-served but in practice this also means a great deal of ponderously-duplicated imperial titles. Official inscriptions of the first half of the second century are amongst the highest aesthetic quality but less common. But the record is highly scattered and very far from ubiquitous. Documents are very much rarer. It is sobering to realise how little we know about day-to-day affairs of a single household. Most of the Roman Empire has produced no record in the form of ordinary manuscripts at all. Egypt is the only province to have yielded anything approximating to a significant archive, and then just in the form of scattered papyrus documents gathered from places like Oxyrhynchus. They have yielded countless examples of private letters, bills of sale, land tenure agreements, complaints, wills, and tittle-tattle. But Egypt was an unusual place and what was true for there was not necessarily representative of anywhere else.

Graffiti, which can be described as casual jottings either for fun or to provide a note or record, are by contrast known almost everywhere. They provide the evidence for the popular growth in literacy. They are more likely to survive than other ephemeral forms of writing. But the recovery of painted slogans and other comments on the plastered walls of streets in Pompeii and Herculaneum show that, however many amphorae we may have which tell us their contents and where they came from, they only represent an infinitesimally small part of what once existed. By their very nature graffiti were not expected to last. Walls were repainted and plastered. One year's election daubings were rapidly buried beneath a layer of fresh paint and disappeared forever. Unfortunately, most surviving graffiti were written on portable objects like potsherds and their find-spots may be as far from their original homes as a modern landfill rubbish site is from the houses which provided the rubbish. More importantly, they are rarely dated. So their value to us is really quite limited. Graffiti from Roman Britain are amongst the best recorded but most are no more than individual letters or numerals which, frankly, tell us nothing really worth knowing. Those bearing coherent statements, slogans or other messages are unusual and even then, often cryptic.

In the end what we have is an unsatisfactory record but one which is better than nothing. The imagination and vigour of the monks who copied what they selected has provided us with a priceless archive. In the pages which we have, all human behaviour is laid out for us to see, with lives played out amidst the barbarity, horror, excitement and beauty of the Roman world. Tacitus, Suetonius, the Plinies, Herodian and others provide us with a path to some of the most vivid personalities and events the world has ever witnessed.

2 Soldiers, brutality and valour

The Roman Army was the Roman Empire. Even the word *imperator* means, literally, 'commander'. It came to mean someone with total power across the Roman world, as if our word for emperor was 'field marshal'. Throughout the Middle Ages and beyond, the writings of military leaders like Caesar or strategists like Frontinus were read eagerly by men such as Napoleon. For them the Romans proved the point that military discipline, planning and organisation were sure paths to absolute power. To pro-Romans in antiquity the proof was in the pudding and commentators like Josephus were simply overwhelmed by Roman military might.

The picture was not so straightforward. There were mutinies and Roman legions were quite capable of voting with their feet and money pouches in times of political crisis. More than one war saw Roman soldiers fighting one another. The army also changed across time. Caesar built up a hardy force of dedicated and disciplined troops. Around 150 years later Hadrian found a dozy frontier army growing plants and throwing dinner parties. In individual forts sickness and bad weather could confound the best-laid plans.

Firstly though, Roman army organisation needs a little explanation. At its core were the 5000-strong legions, manned by Roman citizens drawn from Italy, Gaul and Spain. There were never more than about 30 of these units, distinguished by a number and an epithet alluding to origins and past victories. Thus we have *XXX Ulpia Victrix* with a victory title based on Trajan's name, Marcus Ulpius Trajanus. Distributed across the Empire, the legions were almost all infantry, divided into cohorts made up of six centuries of 80 men. Legionaries did the engineering, the fort building, the surveying and so on. They engaged in relatively little combat.

The auxiliary units did most of the fighting. These were specialist units made up of provincials whose 25 years of service would lead to a grant of citizenship. They were maintained in cohorts of infantry or cavalry, or both, as appropriate to needs and their skills. These soldiers manned frontier forts, were paid less, and suffered more. Apart from these there were many more irregular or semi-regular units which were even more specialised and paid even less, usually without even the chance of citizenship. By the late Empire the distinctions between these various units had become more and more opaque and the legal advantages eroded through the universal grant of citizenship in the early third century.

Going to war

Cicero analysed the reasons for going to war. What he says provides us with the philosophy of war in a context where the exercise of power was seen simultaneously to involve responsibilities towards the conquered. He regarded war as a way of guaranteeing peace and security. Augustus would later justify what was transparently a civil war in his struggle against Mark Antony for supreme power as a war to defend and restore the Republic, peace and security. While we might refute Cicero's ideas, it is also true that we live in a time when war is potentially so comprehensively destructive that we can no longer contemplate it on an international scale. Interestingly though, when we do, we use the same justifications. Cicero's concept of responsibility to the defeated is also intriguing. It helps explain some of Rome's military success.

There are two ways of sorting out a disagreement, one by negotiation, the other by force, and since the first is a human characteristic, and the second of brutes, we must only use force when we are not able to use negotiation. So, the only reason to go to war is in order to live safely in peace. When victory is achieved, those who did not fight in a bloodthirsty or barbaric way we should spare. For example, our ancestors allowed the Tusculans, Aequians, Voluscians, Sabines and Hernicians to become full Roman citizens, but they burned down Corinth and Numantia. I wish Corinth had not been razed, but I believe there were special reasons for what was done, perhaps the advantageousness of its location, which might in the future have provided a temptation to go to war again. At the very least my view is that we should always try to achieve a peace that involves no trickery ....

We must be considerate to those whom we have defeated by force and also protect those who surrender and offer themselves up to the mercy of our generals, even though battering rams have battered their walls. Justice has been so conscientiously observed amongst our own people on this subject that those who have promised protection to districts or nations defeated in war become patrons of those places, according to our ancestors' customs....

But when a war is fought to gain the upper hand and its purpose is glory, it must be started for the same motives I outlined just before as the only morally acceptable reasons for going to war. Wars fought for glory as their purpose must be conducted with less harshness.

Cicero, *On Duties*, I.34-5, 38

Rome's mission

This must surely be one of the best-known passages from all Roman literature. It represents the imperial mission to control, improve and benefit the world. It is at once a statement of benign intent, a justification of ruthlessness and an assertion of the supremacy of a people. The lines come from the sixth book of Virgil's *Aeneid* and are addressed to Augustus. Virgil acknowledges the fact that other peoples might perform certain skills or activities better; in the end it is Rome's destiny to be in charge. Augustus was delighted by the composition and made sure it was published after Virgil's death. It provided a poetic version of the political, social, legal and moral justification for imperial Rome.

You, the Greatest, are he, the one who by delaying restored our state. Others, I am certain, beat out living bronze into more gentle lines, bring out in marble the appearance of life, plead causes better, mark out with the rod the track of the heavens and say when the constellations rise. Remember, Roman, to rule nations with absolute authority — this will be your vocation — to impose peace and law, to spare the subjected and defeat the arrogant in battle.

Virgil, *Aeneid*, VI.845-54

I set no boundaries in space or time for the deeds of the Roman people. I have given them unlimited power.

The words of Jupiter, given by Virgil, *Aeneid*, I.278-9

The army is the basis of liberty

The Roman Empire was built on its army. Augustus stated this from the outset. It was, as all men of power have claimed, the basis of liberty. This was a tradition observed by many military leaders afterwards who fancied themselves as latter-day Roman generals. As Virgil noted, the Romans had a divine right to unlimited conquest, awarded by Jupiter.

When I was nineteen I raised an army at my expense and on my own initiative, through which I restored the Republic's liberty, which had been oppressed by a tyrannical faction … I undertook civil and foreign wars throughout the world at sea and on land ….

Augustus, *Res Gestae*, 1, 3

THE ORGANISATION OF THE ARMY

Augustus reorganises the army

After the civil wars of the first century BC Octavian was triumphant. As Augustus Caesar he had supreme power and there was no longer a need for Romans to fight Romans, though the civil wars of the future would set the clock back in due course. The Roman army's chief purpose now was to defend the frontiers and control the provinces.

Augustus assigned the legionaries and auxiliaries from his military forces to the provinces, a fleet at Misenum and another at Ravenna to defend the Tyrrhenian and Adriatic Seas respectively. He used the rest partly to defend Rome and partly to act as his own bodyguard. He disbanded a unit of Calagurritani troops which had been part of that bodyguard until Antony was defeated, and another of Germans, which he had kept amongst the troops around him until the Varian disaster.

However, Augustus never allowed more than three cohorts to be in Rome at once, and those had no permanent fort. He sent the rest to winter or summer quarters in the towns round about the city. What is more, he restricted all the soldiers wherever they were to the same pay and allowance scheme, fixing the length of service and the rewards for finishing

it according to individual rank. This was to discourage them from being provoked into rebellion after their discharge by old age or poverty. Augustus set up a military treasury, paid for out of new taxes, so that money would always be available to pay soldiers their wages and rewards they were due.
Suetonius, *Augustus*, 49.1-2

A review of the army in the year 23
Despite the enormous size and importance of the Roman army very little in the way of administrative records survive. The disposition of the citizen legions and the provincial auxiliaries has had largely to be traced through the scattered stone inscriptions erected in and around forts and at other military buildings. Happily for us, the Roman army loved display and proudly recorded its achievements whenever it could. However, the record is far from complete and there is nothing to compare with this passage from Tacitus, one of the very few accounts of where the army was and how it was used. He is describing the situation in the year 23, the tenth of the reign of Tiberius (14-37) and shows how Rome used legionaries, auxiliaries and also a system of client kings or buffer states to secure the frontiers. This account predates the conquest of Britain in 43. Britain would never require less than three legions, as well as numerous auxiliaries, to hold her. It also predates the vicious civil war of 68-9 which led to the creation of other legions. Significantly, he abandoned any attempt to provide details about the auxiliaries on the grounds that they were in such constant flux that it would be futile.

Italy was guarded on both coasts by fleets at Misenum and at Ravenna, and where the coastline carries on round to Gaul by ships of war captured in the victory of Actium, and sent by Augustus with crack crews to the town of Forum Julium. But our main strength, numbering eight legions, was on the Rhine, as a defence against both Germans and Gauls. Spain, recently conquered, was held by three legions. Mauretania belonged to King Juba, who been granted it by the Roman people. The rest of Africa was garrisoned with two legions, and Egypt by the same number. Next, starting with Syria as far as the Euphrates, all the land covered in this vast sweep, was controlled by four legions, and on this frontier were Iberian, Albanian, and other kings, for whom our greatness was a protection against any foreign power. Thrace was held by Rhoemetalces and the children of Cotys. The bank of the Danube was held by two legions in Pannonia, two in Moesia, and two also were stationed in Dalmatia, which, due to the state of the region, were behind the other four, and were close enough to be recalled, should Italy suddenly need help.

But Rome was garrisoned by its own special soldiery, three city and nine praetorian cohorts, raised for the most part in Etruria and Umbria, or ancient Latium and the old Roman colonies. There were besides, in commanding positions in the provinces, allied fleets, cavalry and light infantry, of but little inferior strength. But any detailed account of them would be misleading, since they moved from place to place as circumstances required, and had their numbers increased and sometimes diminished.
Tacitus, *Annals,* IV.5

The secret of Rome's success

Around four   centuries later a Roman military historian called Flavius Vegetius Romanus, whose works we shall return to later, looked back to the Roman army of these early days. In this extraordinary organisation he found an explanation for the unparalleled success and power of Rome His book on Roman military techniques would survive antiquity. Its record of how the Roman army had operated at its zenith would prove a powerful influence over the warriors and generals of Europe and elsewhere. Vegetius provided an explanation for how the Romans had been able to overwhelm vastly more numerous enemies. This would be regarded as a useful precedent by the nineteenth-century imperialists, and also Adolf Hitler.

We can see that the conquest of the world by the Romans was due exclusively to their military training, garrison discipline, and experience in war. Otherwise, what possible chance would the very small numbers of Roman soldiers have had against the hordes of Gauls? How else could they have set out against the tall Germans, seeing how short they were? The men of Spain obviously outdid our men in quantity and physical strength. We Romans have never been as good as the Africans at deception, and we lacked their wealth. Everyone knows that the Greeks left us behind when it came to techniques and brainpower.

But in spite of all these we held the day through our choice of soldiers, and by teaching them (as I said before) in the arts of war, toughening them up through daily exercises, by familiarising them in advance with everything that can happen on the march and on the battlefield, and by ruthlessly punishing laziness ....

One ancient custom which survived, reinforced by edicts of the deified Augustus and Hadrian, was exercising infantry and cavalry three times a month on marches.... The foot soldiers were ordered to march fully-armed and equipped for ten miles using the military step, covering part of the route at a faster tempo, and then come back to their camp. Similarly the cavalry, also fully-equipped, divided up into troops carried out the same march, practising variously assaults and retreats. The soldiers did not carry out these exercises on flat open spaces. Instead both cavalry and infantry were obliged to go up and down hills and steep inclines...

In practice, the Roman legion is victorious because of the quantity of soldiers and the various machines. To begin with the legion is equipped with the hurling machines which no armour or shield can cope with. The routine is to have one *ballista* for each century, mounted on a carriage. To each *ballista* mules and eleven men are attached to look after loading and firing. The bigger the *ballista*, the further and more forcefully they hurl their ammunition. These defend forts and are also used on the battlefield behind the heavy infantry. Faced with their firepower, there is no enemy cavalry equipped with breast-plates or infantry with shields which can hold its ground. Normally there are fifty-five such mounted *ballistae* per legion.

Similarly, the legion has ten *onagri* (one per cohort). They are pulled, pre-loaded, on carts by oxen so that when the enemy makes an assault on the rampart, the fort can be defended with their projectiles and boulders.

Vegetius, *Military Science* I.1, 9, 27, II.25

Qualities of leadership

The leadership of Julius Caesar was legendary in the Roman army and illustrated what one man could achieve by imposing greater discipline on himself. Decades after his murder, Seneca recounted his qualities.

You'll also see the tolerance that man had for hardship. Walking at the head of his army he crossed the North African deserts. You can see that thirst can also be tolerated. Always wearing armour, tramping over a sun-baked plain, the remains of a thrashed army with no supplies, he was always the last to drink when they found water.
Seneca, *Letters*, 104.33

The Roman war machine in action

Vegetius looked back across the years, perhaps enviously, to the first century. This was when the Roman Empire was still expanding, despite military and problems and disasters (which we will look at below) and there was much for the military historian or strategist to admire.

An exceptional account from that period of the Roman army on campaign survives. During the reign of Nero (54-68), there was a revolt in Judaea. One of the leaders was Josephus, afterwards Titus Flavius Josephus. He was captured by the Romans but saw the way the tide was turning for Rome and told the then Roman commander, Vespasian, that he would become emperor. Vespasian liked what he heard and hung on to his prisoner. Within two years Josephus' prophecy had come true. Vespasian won the civil war of 68-9 and ruled from 69-79.

A quisling by any other name thereafter, Josephus continued to work for the Romans and he had a front-row seat to history in the campaign against the Jews run by Vespasian and his son Titus. Josephus produced the single most vivid account of the Roman war machine in action. He was anxious to make it clear that the Romans were successful because their organisation, planning and discipline was without parallel in the known world and that therefore the Empire and its breadth was inevitable. What comes across from his description more than anything else is a degree of regimentation and foresight which has influenced army commanders, dictators and opportunists ever since.

Nonetheless, as we shall see later, this picture of rigour and iron discipline is not reflected in the mutinies that occurred before and after, nor in some of the day-to-day documents which have survived from elsewhere in the Empire. Josephus had an agenda, part of which was watching his own back and presenting his patron to the world as the leader of the greatest imperial power ever seen.

Practice and preparation

Now, you cannot help but admire Roman forethought in providing themselves with domestic staff who were useful to them in ordinary daily life and also in war.

Actually, anyone looking at their whole military structure is forced to admit that their conquest of such a vast empire has been through valour, not just good luck.

They never wait for war to break out before handling weapons. Equally, they never sit around idly during peace, waiting to be spurred into action by a crisis. They have never laid down their arms, as if their weapons were part of their bodies, and nor do they wait for a declaration of war. Their military exercises are exactly the same as a real war. Every soldier practices his training daily, with great diligence, as if it was wartime.

This how the Romans can put up with the exhaustion of battles so easily. No amount of chaos disrupts their formations, terror cannot unnerve them, and heavy labour cannot exhaust them either. This means they always defeat others who lack their training. You might call their training bloodless battles, and their battles bloody training.

Building forts on campaign

Enemies of the Romans never have an opportunity to catch them unawares. When Romans invade enemy territory they refuse to fight until their camp is fortified in a way which is neither disorderly nor irregular. Moreover, the work is performed by organized gangs rather than the whole unit.

Where the ground is rough it is comprehensively flattened and then the site is laid out in a rectangle. To achieve this the army is followed around by numerous engineers carrying all the construction tools needed. The interior is marked out in preparation for the buildings.

Outside, the perimeter resembles a wall and is fitted out with regularly-spaced towers. In the spaces between the towers the Romans erect loaded catapults, spear and stone-throwers, and every other type of armament. A total of four gates are built, one on each side, suitable for supply animals to come in, and armed sallies to go out if necessary.

The fort is partitioned by accurately laying out streets. Officers' quarters are in the middle, and in their centre is the CO's headquarters which looks like a shrine. The whole thing looks like a boom town, with its market, labourers' huts, and places where officers of all ranks can sort out arguments and rows as and when they occur. It takes them less time to build the outside wall and the structures within than it does to think about it, thanks to the quantity and quality of the labour. If the fort needs it, a six-foot wide and six-foot deep perimeter ditch is dug all the way round.

Settling in

Once the fortifications are finished, the troops go to their barracks, century by century. Everything else outstanding is done with due attention to discipline and security. Timber, food and water, are carried in by the centuries detailed to do so as needed. No-one has breakfast or an evening meal as takes his fancy, but instead they all eat together. Trumpets sound to announce sleeping time, sentry duty, and reveille and everything is done according to orders.

When the sun comes up, ordinary soldiers report in their centuries to their centurion. The centurions assemble before their tribunes to salute them. The tribunes go with all the other senior officers to the headquarters where the CO, following the usual routine, supplies them with the day's pass-word and other orders to take back to the rest of the troops. This they carry out as if they were on a battlefield, snappily altering direction when required, and move forwards and backwards as one.

Striking camp

When the Romans are about to leave the camp, there is a trumpet call and every soldier goes straight to his appointed job. Once the call is given, the buildings are taken to pieces in an instant and everything made ready for departure. The trumpet calls the soldiers to be ready to march. The soldiers immediately load up the carts and mules with all the baggage and then take up their positions like sprinters waiting for the starting signal.

Next they burn the camp down to prevent an enemy taking advantage of it. They can easily build it up again if they need to. The trumpet sounds again for a third time to chivvy along any latecomers so that no-one is missing from the column. Next, the military crier, standing on the CO's right, asks the soldiers three times in their native language if they are ready to fight. They shout back three times, loudly and enthusiastically, that they are ready before the question is even finished. They shout with their right arms held high, in a warlike frenzy. Finally, they set off in disciplined order, every soldier holding his position in the column.

A soldier's equipment

A foot soldier is equipped with breastplate, helmet and a blade on either side of his body. The one on the left is much the longest, and the other is only nine inches long. The CO's bodyguard of picked infantry carry a lance and small round shield. The other centuries a javelin and long shield, saw, basket, axe, pick, and also a strap, crop-harvesting hook, chain, and enough food for three days. The infantry soldier resembles a baggage mule!

A mounted soldier has a long sword on his right hip, and a large pike in his hand, a shield held at an angle over the horse's flank. Next to this is a quiver with three spear-sized missiles with wide blades. They wear the same helmets and breastplates as the infantry.

The CO's bodyguards have the same equipment as all the other mounted troops. The legion at the head of the column is chosen by lot. That's that as far as Roman military organization on campaign and in camp and all the various weapons they use are concerned.

Never act on impulse

Everything is planned, and nothing is impulse, in battle. Planning comes before taking any action, the decision so made is final and everything done must be to that end. Consequently, the Romans rarely suffer setbacks and when they do, amends are easily made. As far as they are concerned a chance victory is less desirable than a failure following a plan, because such triumphs encourage men to trust in luck not judgement. On the other hand, despite the occasional setback forethought is the proper way to avoid making the same mistake. In any case, good things borne out of luck do the recipient no credit, but disastrous misfortune which destroy plans at least have the consolation that the preparations were competently made.

Discipline

Military training provides the Roman soldier not just with a resilient physique but also a resolute spirit. Fear lies behind some of the training because Roman military law means the death penalty for abandoning one's post, and also for a variety of petty crimes. The commanding officers invoke even more fear than the law does because by rewarding the good soldiers the punishments for bad soldiers seem even worse.

Roman troops are so completely obedient to their superiors they set a good example to Rome in peace. For the same reason they act as one on the battlefield, so tight are their formations, so adaptable their manouevring, their ears pricked up for orders, their eyes watching for signals, and their hands ready for the work to be done.

Consequently they act as quickly as they give ground slowly. There never has been a battle in which the Romans were fewer, outclassed by skill, in possession of disadvantageous ground or, for that matter, lacking in luck, something which is even harder for them to come by than victory.

The Empire

Considering that planning always comes before taking action, and those plans are executed by such an effective force, can there be any surprise that the Euphrates in the east, the Atlantic in the west and in the north the Danube and Rhine mark the boundaries of their Empire? You might almost say that the Romans are more remarkable than what they have conquered.

The whole point of the description above has been more to commiserate with Rome's vanquished enemies and to put off anyone from thinking about rebellion than it has been to flatter the Romans. It might also be useful to anyone interested in research and who is new to the subject to have inside knowledge about the Roman military machine. I have nothing more to say on the topic.

Vespasian on campaign

Anxious to invade Galilee in person, Vespasian left Ptolemais with his army set in the customary marching order. He ordered lightly-armed auxiliaries and archers to take the lead, and to fight off any enemy attacks while checking out woodland which might be hiding ambushes.

Following this vanguard came a column of heavily-armed Roman infantry and cavalry, and next came ten soldiers detached from each century carrying their personal equipment as well as the tools used for setting out the camp. Behind these came the road engineers who removed bends in the road, levelled the road surface, and cleared woodland, all so that the army would not be worn out by an exhausting march.

The personal effects and baggage belong to the CO and all the other officers came next, guarded by a strong body of cavalry behind which Vespasian rode with his picked escort of infantry, cavalry and spearsmen.

He was followed by the legion's own cavalry; every legion had its own 120-strong troop of cavalry. The next part of the column was led by the mules which carried the battering rams and other pieces of artillery. After these came the legionary commanders, the prefects commanding the auxiliary cohorts, and the tribunes, with their own bodyguard of selected soldiers.

The eagle standards, which stand at the head of every legion as the king and most fearless of all birds, came after these. To the Romans, the eagle symbolizes their empire and promises victory regardless of their enemies. These sacred talismans were followed by the trumpeters who were themselves followed by the main body of troops who march shoulder-to-shoulder in a six-man-wide column, supervised by a centurion to keep them in order.

Legionary servants came next, taking care of all the troops' baggage being carried by mules and other animals. Most of the mercenaries marched behind them while finally a rearguard shield of light and heavy infantry together with a solid troop of cavalry picked up the rear.

In this way, Vespasian arrived at the Galilee borders with his army.
T. Flavius Josephus, *The Jewish War*, III.3-6

Special tactics

The Roman army did not only excel in battle. It was familiar with all sorts of labour-saving ways of winning battles and breaking sieges, as the military historian Frontinus recorded, using examples from the days of the Republic as well as the early Empire.

Publius Servilius diverted the river from where the townsfolk of Isaura took their water, and in this way he forced them to surrender because of the thirst which followed.

In one of his Gaulish campaigns, Gaius Caesar deprived the capital of the Cadurci tribe of water, even though it had water all around it and numerous springs. He diverted the springs with underground channels, while his archers prevented anyone getting to the river.

While he was fighting in Nearer Spain, Lucius Metellus diverted a river course and made it flow down from a higher level on the enemy's camp, which was sited on lower ground. When the enemy panicked from the unexpected flood, he had them mowed down by troops whom he had positioned ready for ambush to this very end....

During a Sardinian campaign, Lucius Scipio, in order to bring out the defenders of a particular city, gave up the siege he had started, and made as if he was retreating with a detachment of soldiers. When the inhabitants all raced out to attack him, Scipio assaulted the town with the help of those whom he had hidden nearby.
Frontinus, *Stratgems*, III.7.1-3, 10.2

In the Parthian war in the latter part of his reign Trajan moved east from Antioch to the Tigris. In order to take Adiabene (equivalent to northern Iraq) on the far bank he had to cross the river in a land where no trees grew. Like the Allied troops crossing the Rhine at the end of the Second World War, he brought his boats with him.

When spring began Trajan hurried into enemy territory. Seeing as no timber suitable for building boats grows in the Tigris region, he had brought his own boats, built in the forests of Nisibis, to the river on carts. They were designed to be dismantled and reassembled easily. Bridging the river opposite the Gordian mountains was very difficult for him because the barbarians had taken up a position on the opposite bank to try to slow him down. But Trajan had a very large force of boats and troops, so a few of the boats were assembled very quickly while others were tied up next to them filled with foot soldiers and infantry. Meanwhile other soldiers raced about making as if to cross the river. These tactics

added to the barbarians' alarm at the sight of so many boats appearing in a woodless country and they gave in. So the Romans crossed over and captured all of Adiabene.
Dio Cassius, *Roman History*, LXVIII.26.1-3

Equipment

Although the fourth-century Roman army was an altogether different force from the army of the first and second centuries AD, it still made use of some well-established equipment. Describing the year 363 Ammianus Marcellinus recorded some of the artillery and siege-breaking equipment still in use. The lack of explosive firepower was made good, largely through the torque power released by highly-stressed rope windings, and by sheer force.

The ballista

First I will explain the design of a ballista. A long, strong, iron bar is fastened between two pillars and sticks out like a huge ruler. A squared post extends a considerable way from its smooth, curved, surface (which is highly polished in the centre), tied there with a large number of twisted ropes, and is hollowed out all the way along with a narrow channel. To this post, wooden rollers are firmly attached and next to one of them the man who aims the shot stands. With care he locates a wooden arrow with a substantial iron head in the groove of the projecting iron bar. When he has done that, muscular youths on each side rapidly rotate the rollers and ropes. Once the arrow-head is level with the outer ropes, it shoots off the ballista out of sight, driven by the force [in the ropes], and sometimes sparks fly off from the friction. Quite often, a fatal wound caused by the bolt is felt before anyone has time to see it.

The scorpion

These days the scorpion is called the wild ass. It looks like this. Two posts are cut from oak or holm-oak and then slightly curved, so that they appear to have humps. Next they are joined to one another [side by side] in the manner of a sawing machine and reasonably sized holes are drilled through on each side. Through these holes, strong ropes are tied between the posts holding the machine together and stop it flying apart. A wooden arm rises at an angle from the centre of these ropes and points upwards a bit like a chariot pole. It's lashed with ropes so that it can be pulled up or down. Iron hooks are attached to the top of this arm off which hangs a sling made from hemp or iron. In front of the arm is a large pad of goat's hair cloth packed with tiny bits of padding, lashed on with strong ropes. The whole assembly is placed on a turf mound or pile of sundried bricks because if heavy machine like this is put on a stone platform it breaks everything to pieces from the force, rather than its weight.

During a battle, a round boulder is deposited in the sling and four lads on either side rotate the arm, to which the ropes are attached, until the arm is bent almost horizontal. Then at last, the artillery officer, standing above, knocks out the bolt which secures the fastenings on the whole machine with a heavy hammer. At that moment the arm is freed and flies forward in one smart action and, hitting the soft pad, flings the boulder which crushes everything it strikes.

The machine is called the *tormentum* because all the force released comes from torque power, and a scorpion because it holds its sting up high. Nowadays it has been named an *onager*, because wild asses being chased by hunters throw boulders by kicking them backwards some way, which either crush their pursuers' chests, or shatter their skulls.

The ram

A tall fir-tree or ash is chosen and on the end a long and hard iron piece is attached. This looks like the projecting head of a ram and that's where the machine's name comes from. This tree is hung between beams bound with iron in a manner that leaves it suspended from the third beam like a pan hanging on scales. Then as many men as the tree accommodates pull it back and push it forwards with mighty blows to smash everything in its way, just like a ram charging and withdrawing. This force is compounded like repeated lightning strikes, so buildings are cracked and broken as their walls are pulverized. If this class of equipment is used with maximum effort, even the strongest cities are opened, and the siege ended, once the walls have been cleared of defenders.

Fire-darts

Fire-darts are a type of missile made like this: the shaft is made out of reed and between it and the head is an iron-band skin. It looks like the cleft staff women use to make linen thread. The underside is skilfully hollowed out with a number of openings and along this channel fire and inflammable substances are located. If the dart is fired from an excessively slack bow (because it will be blown out by being fired too fast) and gets stuck anywhere it will burn resiliently. Water poured on only makes it burn harder and there is no way of putting it out except by covering it with dust.
Ammianus Marcellinus, XXIII.4.1-9, 14

Artillery

Being made of perishables like timber and rope, artillery equipment does not really survive and indeed there is little direct evidence for its existence. Inscriptions from a remote outpost fort in northern Britain seem to record installations for artillery. The texts are enigmatic but the fort itself has yielded a large number of the rounded boulders which Ammianus describes being fired from the scorpion (*onager*). This text belongs to a time nearly 150 years before Ammianus wrote. The flowery imperial titles belong to the man better-known as Elagabalus.

For the Emperor, Marcus Aurelius Antoninus Pius Felix Augustus, in the year he was voted tribunician power for the 3rd time, in his 3rd consulship, with proconsular power and as father of the nation, the First loyal Antonine cohort of Vardulli erected this *ballistarium* [artillery platform?] from the ground up under the command of the emperor's legate of praetorian status, Tiberius Claudius Paulinus, and directed by the tribune Publius Aelius Erasinus.
RIB 1280 (High Rochester), for the year 220 under Elagabalus

The equipment described sounds impressive but, as Maximinus I found in 238 in the siege of Aquileia, it was highly susceptible against determined defenders with the right weapons (see below).

The grumbling of soldiers

Despite the views of people like Vegetius that the Roman army operated almost like a machine under the iron hand of discipline and an unparalleled training regime, the truth was that no-one could afford to take soldierly loyalty for granted. If their life sounds tough by our standards, it undoubtedly was and so, it seems, by theirs as well. In their ruthless and harsh existence, soldiers were perpetually preoccupied by their pay, and the punishments and extortion managed by the centurions. It became easy for them to believe that a rebellion and, perhaps, a new emperor would improve their lot. It would not be long before they realised that they alone held the power to make their dreams come true.

Augustus had no sooner died in the year 14 when a mutiny broke out amongst the soldiers stationed along the Danube in the province of Pannonia. It was quashed by Drusus, Tiberius' son but then the new emperor's nephew Germanicus found himself facing a repeat performance in Germany. Loyalty to the person of the emperor would be an ongoing problem, here exacerbated by a body of inferior troops conscripted after the catastrophe in the year 9 when three legions were wiped out (see below). The mutiny was an omen for the future, and a lesson to all generals.

About the same time, for the same reasons, the legions in Germany mutinied. They did this with a fury proportionate to their greater numbers, in the confident hope that Germanicus Caesar would not be able to endure the supremacy of someone else [i.e. Tiberius] and thus offer himself to the legions, whose strength would force the day.

There were two armies on the south bank of the Rhine. The upper army was commanded by Caius Silius, the lower by Aulus Caecina. Supreme command rested with Germanicus, then busily employed in assessing Gaul's tribute. Caius Silius' troops watched the uprising by others, unsure of their own sympathies. But the soldiers of the lower army fell into a frenzy, which started out amongst the men of the XXI and V legions, and into which the I and XX were also drawn. They were all quartered in the same summer-camp on the frontier in Ubian territory. When they heard that Augustus had died, the impressionable minds of the soldiers came under the influence of the rabble of slave recruits recently levied in Rome. Accustomed to easy living and frustrated by hardship, this lot filled the ignorant heads of the rest of the troops with the idea that the time had come for veterans to demand a discharge, for junior troops to have a pay rise, for everyone an end to their woes, and revenge for the cruelty of centurions.

It was not left to one man to speak in this way, as had Percennius among the Pannonian legions, nor was it in the ears of trembling soldiers, who were apprehensive about other and mightier armies. There was sedition here in many a face and voice. 'The Roman world,' they said, 'was in their hands. Their victories made the state great. It was from these soldiers that emperors received their title [Germanicus].'

Powerless leaders

Their commander did nothing to stop them, the sheer anger of so many soldiers having destroyed his nerve. In a sudden frenzy they rushed with drawn swords on the centurions, the traditional target of the soldiers' resentment and the first cause of savage fury. They threw them to the earth and beat them brutally, sixty to one, matching the number of centurions. Then tearing them from the ground, mangled, and some dead, they flung them outside the fortifications or into the river Rhine. They kept up their demands for one Septimius, who fled to the tribunal and was grovelling at Caecina's feet, until he was given up to meet his end.

Cassius Chaerea, who later won for himself a place in posterity by murdering the emperor Gaius Caligula [in the year 41], being then a youth of high spirit, cut a way through the armed and hostile mob with his sword. Neither tribune nor camp-prefect had authority any longer. Patrols, sentries, and whatever else was needed at the time, were organized by the men themselves. To the careful observer of military psychology, the most convincing evidence of widespread and intractable disaffection, was the fact that, instead of isolated incidents instigated by a handful, they were unanimous in their fury and equally unanimous in their composure, so uniform in consistency that one might have attributed it to their discipline ....

Germanicus takes charge

On hearing about the legionary mutiny, Germanicus went instantly to the troublespot, and met the soldiers outside the camp, eyes fixed on the ground, apparently full of remorse. As soon as he entered the fortifications, a babble of complaints became audible. Some men, seizing his hand under pretence of kissing it, thrust his fingers into their mouths, so that he might touch their toothless gums. Others showed him their limbs bent and bowed with age.

Germanicus ordered the crowd which stood near him, as it seemed to be completely disorderly, to organize themselves into companies. They replied that they would hear better as they were. The standards would instead be brought forward, he said, so that thus at least the cohorts might be distinguished. The soldiers obeyed reluctantly. Then beginning with a reverential tribute to Augustus, he moved on to the victories and triumphs of Tiberius, lingering to make special mention of his glorious achievements with those legions in Germany. Next, he extolled Italy's unity, Gaul's loyalty, and the complete absence of turbulence or strife.

Germanicus was heard in silence or with but just slight murmuring. As soon as he mentioned the mutiny and asked what had become of soldierly obedience, of the glory of ancient discipline, and asked where they had driven their tribunes and centurions, they all bared their bodies and taunted him with the scars of their wounds and the marks of the lash. Then, with one uproar, they spoke bitterly of the prices charged for exemption from duties, of their miserable pay, the severity of their tasks, with special mention of the rampart, the ditch, transporting fodder, timber of construction quality, firewood, and whatever other drudgeries were borne out of necessity, or imposed to prevent idleness in the camp.

The fiercest clamour came from veterans. Listing their thirty campaigns or more, they begged Germanicus to give relief to worn-out men, and not to let them die from the same hardships, but bring an end to such grinding service, and give them rest, safe from having to beg a living. Some even claimed the money left them by the Divine Augustus, with words of good omen for Germanicus. Should he wish to become emperor, they made it clear they were ready.

Germanicus threatens to commit suicide

Thereupon, as though he were becoming infected by their guilt, Germanicus leapt impetuously from the podium. The men barred his way with their weapons, repeating threats to use them if he did not go back. But Germanicus, protesting that he would die rather than be a traitor, pulled his sword from his side, held it aloft and was plunging it into his breast, when those nearest him seized his hand and held it by force. The remoter and most densely-packed part of the crowd, and this almost defies belief, some individuals coming close up to him, urged him to strike the blow. A soldier called Calusidius offered him a drawn sword, saying that it was sharper than Germanicus' own. Even in their fury, this seemed to them a savage act setting an evil precedent, and there was a pause during which Germanicus' friends hurried him into his tent.

There they discussed the possible remedies. Word reached them that the soldiers were preparing to send emissaries to persuade the upper army to join their cause; that the capital of the Ubii was marked out for destruction, and that hands stained by plunder would soon be brave enough to sack Gaul. The alarm was made more urgent by the information that the enemy was aware of the Roman mutiny, and would certainly attack if the Rhine bank were undefended. But if the auxiliary troops and allies were to be armed against the seceding legions, then a civil war would have broken out for sure. Severity would be dangerous; letting them get away with it scandalous. Either way the state faced a catastrophe.

Consequently, having weighed up all the options, they decided that a letter should be written in Tiberius' name, to the effect that full discharge was granted to those who had served in twenty campaigns; that there was a conditional release for those who had served sixteen, and that they were to remain in the army exempt from any duties except actually keeping off the enemy. Finally, the legacies which they had asked for, were to be paid twice over.

The soldiers capitulate

The soldiers realised this had all been improvised on the spot, and instantly pressed their demands. Discharge from service was quickly arranged by the tribunes. Payment was put off until they reached their respective winter quarters. The men of the V and XXI legions refused to leave the summer quarters they were in until the money was paid in full out of the purses of Germanicus himself and his friends. The I and XX legions were led back by their officer Caecina to the Ubian capital, marching in disgrace, since sums of money which had been extorted from the general were carried alongside the eagles and standards. Germanicus went to the upper army, and induced the II, XIII, and XVI legions to give him the oath of allegiance without delay. The XIV had hesitated [about mutinying] a little, but their money and the discharge were offered even without their demanding it.
Tacitus, *Annals*, I.31-37

Subsequently, the troops found a chance to wipe the slate clean when Germanicus took them deeper into Germany to wipe out tribes who thought that Augustus' death and the mutiny had rendered the Roman army powerless. See Military Atrocities below.

Roman setbacks

The Roman army was not perfect or invincible, despite what Vegetius had to say. The mutinies in the year 14 showed that discipline was not wholly effective. The disaster in the year 9 not only meant that second-rate recruits had been taken on but also showed how a professional modern fighting force could be annihilated by guerrilla warfare in hostile and unfamiliar territory. Deep in the heart of the Teutoburgian Forest in Germany, a force of three legions (XVII, XVIII, and XIX), and various auxiliaries under the command of Publius Quintilius Varus was wiped out.

It had been thought that Germany was well on the way to being romanized. However, the usual policy of educating the sons of tribal leaders in Roman military and political ways backfired. Varus provoked a rebellion when he over-enthusiastically imposed taxation and Roman justice, and was misled by artful German tribes who exploited his gullibility (see Chapter 7). One of the tribal princes, Arminius (who had served with the Roman army), led a rebellion at the head of the Cherusci. Varus set out against Arminius but was lured into the forest where he and his men were exterminated by the Cherusci. Three legions approximated to more than ten percent of the Roman legionary force. Although replaced in time, their numbers were never allocated again.

Augustus had only just wound up the war in Pannonia and Dalmatia, when, within five days after completing this task, sorrowful news arrived from Germany that Varus was dead, three legions wiped out, as well as the same number of cavalry troops, and six cohorts....

It was at this time that a noble youth called Arminius appeared, the son of a ruler called Sigimer of that people, who was brave in action, quick-witted, and much more intelligent that the average barbarian, showing in his eyes and manner the ardor of his feelings. Arminius was a young man who had constantly marched alongside our army in the previous war, earning the privileges of Roman citizenship, and the rank of an equestrian. He took advantage of Varus' laziness to perpetrate an atrocity, sensibly concluding that nobody is more easily cut off than the man who feels no fear, and that a sense of security often precedes a disaster. He shared his thoughts at first with only a handful, and then to more, telling and reassuring them that the Romans could be cut off by a surprise attack. Next he added action to his plans, and settled on a time for executing the scheme. Information about the attack was passed to Varus by Segestes, a German worthy of respect and high rank, but destiny would not be held back by warnings and had already clouded the Roman general's judgement. Indeed, heaven normally perverts the judgement of a man whose fortunes it has decided to reverse. Heaven lets happen by chance things which seem to be deserved, which is the tragic part of it, and what was an accident becomes something to blame.

So, Quintilius would not believe the information, believing that the trust in the goodwill exhibited by the Germans reflected his kindness towards them. After this warning there was no time for another. The circumstances of this appalling disaster, the like of which had not befallen the Romans in a foreign land since the calamity of Crassus in Parthia, I will endeavour to describe (as others have done) in my larger work. For the moment I can only lament the tragedy as a whole. An army, unrivalled for bravery, the cream of Roman soldiers in discipline, energy, battlefield experience, was brought, thanks to their leader's negligence, the treachery of the enemy and the cruelty of bad luck, into an utterly desperate situation. Here they had not even a chance of fighting their way out as they wished, some of them even being severely punished by Varus for using arms and showing a Roman spirit. Hemmed in by woods, lakes and enemy bands in ambush, they were completely cut off by an enemy they had previously slaughtered like cattle, over whom the Romans in their mercy or severity had always had the power of life or death.

Varus showed some courage when he died, though not in combat, for (like his father and grandfather) he ran himself through with his sword. Of the two camp-prefects, Lucius Eggius set as honourable a precedent for valour as Ceionius set for the basest action. After most of the army was dead, Ceionius recommended surrendering, preferring death by execution rather than in battle. Numonius Vala, one of Varus' legates, who had normally acted as a modest and well-meaning man, was now guilty of fearful treachery. Abandoning the infantry unprotected by the cavalry, he fled with the auxiliary cavalry and tried to reach the Rhine. Fortune took care of his crime because he did not survive his fellow soldiers left behind, but died while deserting. The savage foe mutilated Varus' half-dead body, decapitated it and took the head to Marobodus who sent it to Augustus. In spite of the disaster it was honoured with burial in the family tomb.

Gaius Velleius Paterculus, *Roman History*, II.117, 118-20

Germanicus finds the remains of Varus' army

When the news reached Rome Augustus was transfixed with horror. A few years later, in the year 15, Germanicus, nephew of Tiberius (Augustus' successor) and then in command of the army in Germany, came across the site of the carnage during a renewed campaign.

The Bructeri were burning their property when they were routed by Lucius Stertinius, commanding a detachment of light-armed troops sent out by Germanicus. In the middle of the carnage and plunder Stertinius discovered the eagle of the XIX legion which had been lost with Varus. The troops were then marched to the furthest frontier of the Bructeri, and all the territory between the rivers Amisia and Luppia was ravaged. This was close to the Teutoburgian Forest where the unburied remains of Varus and his legions were said to lie.

Germanicus was overcome with a passionate desire to pay those soldiers and their commander a last tribute. The whole of his army was moved to compassion by the thought of their kin and friends, and, indeed, of the calamities of wars and the lot of mankind. Having sent on Caecina in advance to explore secret forest-passes, and to raise bridges and causeways over watery swamps and treacherous plains, they visited the mournful scenes, with their horrible sights and associations. Varus's first camp with its wide spread and the layout for officers and standards clearly indicated the handiwork of three legions. Further on, the half-collapsed rampart and the shallow ditch suggested that that was where a shattered remnant of the army had taken its last stand.

In the centre of the area were bleached human skeletons, fallen as they fled, or stood their ground, strewn everywhere or piled in heaps. Nearby lay fragments of weapons and limbs of horses, and also human heads, prominently nailed to trunks of trees. In the adjacent groves were the barbaric altars, on which the enemy had executed tribunes and first-rank centurions. Some survivors of the disaster, who had escaped from the battle or from captivity, described how this was the spot where the officers fell. They told how over there the eagles were captured, where Varus was pierced by his first wound, where too by the stroke of his own ill-starred hand he found death himself. They pointed out too the raised ground from which Arminius had harangued his army, the number of gibbets for the captives, the pits for the living, and how in his exultation he insulted the standards and eagles.

And so now the Roman army on the spot, six years after the disaster, grieving and furious, began to bury the bones of the three legions. No soldier knew if he was interring the relics of a relative or a stranger, but looked on them all as kin and of their own blood, while their anger towards the enemy grew stronger than ever. Germanicus laid the first sod to start raising the tumulus, in this way offering a most welcome honour to the dead, and sharing also in the sorrow of those present.

Tacitus, *Annals*, I.60-62

Revenge for Varus

Germanicus and his troops decided it was pay-back time and set off after Arminius who retreated into wild and uncharted territory. Part of the force was led by Aulus Caecina Severus, governor of Lower Germany. Arminius set them the same trap and there was very nearly a repeat performance. Instead, however, it was Arminius who found that he had met his match.

The barbarians tried to break through the outposts and to throw themselves on the engineering parties. They harassed them by pacing around them and continually charging at them. There was a confused din from the men at work and the combatants. Everything was against the Romans: the place with its deep swamps, unreliable underfoot and slippery as they advanced, bodies weighed down with armour, and it was impossible to aim their javelins from the water. The Cherusci, on the other hand, were familiar with fighting in fens; they were physically huge, and had lances long enough to inflict wounds even from a distance. Finally, it was nightfall which saved the failing legions from a disastrous battle.

Their success left the Germans in fighting fettle. Without even taking a rest, they diverted all the streams rising from the slopes of the surrounding hills down into the land below. With the ground flooded this way, and the Roman fortifications finished so far being submerged, the soldiers found their work doubled.

This was Caecina's fortieth campaign as a subordinate or a commander, and, with such experience of success and peril, he had no fear. While he considered the possibilities for the future, he could come up with nothing apart from holding the enemy in the woods until the wounded and the more heavily-laden troops had moved on. Between the hills and the swamps there was a plain flat enough for a narrow line of battle. The legions had their assigned places: the V on the right wing, the XXI on the left, the men of I to lead the vanguard, and the XX to repel pursuers.

It was a restless night for different reasons. In their celebration the barbarians filled the valleys under the hills and the echoing glens with jolly songs or savage shrieks, while in the Roman camp there were flickering fires, broken exclamations, and the men lay scattered along the fortifications or wandered from tent to tent, wakeful rather than watchful. A ghastly dream appalled the general. He seemed to see Quintilius Varus, covered with blood, rising out of the swamps, and to hear him, as it were, calling to him, but he did not, as he imagined, obey the call; he even repelled his hand, as he stretched it over him.

At daybreak the legions, posted on the wings, from panic or perversity, deserted their position and hurriedly occupied a plain beyond the morass. But Arminius, despite being free to attack, did not rush them until the Roman military equipment was stuck in the mud and the defences. The soldiers were in chaos all around it, their units in confusion, and each soldier selfishly looking out for himself and not listening to orders.

Arminius ordered the Germans to charge, shouting again and again that here was another Varus and legions caught in the same trap. As he spoke, he cut through the column with some picked men, inflicting wounds chiefly on the horses. Staggering in their blood on the slippery marsh, they shook off their riders, scattering everyone who was in their way and trampling over those who fell down. The fight was at its fiercest around the standards which could neither be held up against the battery of missiles, or set up in the muddy ground.

As Caecina was fighting to hold the position he fell from his horse, which was run through under him. He was being hemmed in when the first legion threw itself in the way. The enemy's greed helped him, because they abandoned the killing in order to gather the spoil. As evening approached, the legions struggled on to open and firm ground.

But this brought no end to their misery. Fortifications had to be built and materials sought for earthworks. The army had lost most of its tools for digging earth and cutting turf. There were no tents for the ordinary ranks and no comfort for the wounded. As they shared their food, fouled with mud or blood, they spoke gloomily about the ominous darkness, and the one day of life left to so many thousands of men.

By chance a horse, which had broken its halter and wandered wildly in fright at the uproar, overthrew some men into whom it crashed. As a result there was a terrible panic because it was thought the Germans had burst into the camp and they all rushed to the gates. Most made for the main gate because it was furthest from the enemy and the safest one to escape from. Caecina made sure there was no reason for the alarm but his authority, requests and even force, had no effect on stopping the soldiers. So, he threw himself on the ground at the gate and, at last, this appeal to their pity (because they would have had to clamber over their general's body) stopped the panic. Meanwhile the other officers convinced them it was all a false alarm.

Once he had assembled the soldiers at the headquarters, and ordered them to listen to him in silence, Caecina reminded them of the urgency of the crisis. He told them their safety lay in their arms, to be used with care. They should stay within the fort until the enemy came closer in the hope that they could storm them. At that moment there should all break out and in that way they might reach the Rhine. On the other hand, if they fled they would face more forests, deeper swamps and a vicious enemy. If they were victorious glory and fame would be theirs. He dwelt on everything that was dear to them at home, everything that testified to their honour in the camp, without any allusion to disaster. Next he handed over the horses, beginning with his own, of the officers and tribunes, to the bravest fighters in the army, without favouritism, that these first, and then the infantry, might charge the enemy.

There was as much restlessness in the German army with its hope and eager longings, and the arguments amongst its chiefs. Arminius advised that they should let the Romans leave their position, and, when they were on their way, surprise them once more in swampy and difficult ground. Inguiomerus, whose advice was rather more bloodthirsty (which the barbarians welcomed) was all for assaulting the defences because, he said, it would be easy to storm the Romans and as a result there would be more prisoners and the loot would be in good condition. So, when the sun came up they filled up the ditches, built crossings, and poured over to seize the top part of the parapet. This was where the defenders were thinnest and apparently paralyzed with fear.

Once the Germans were well inside the defences the signal was given to the cohorts, and the horns and trumpets sounded. Instantly, with a shout and sudden rush, our men threw themselves on the German rear. They taunted the Germans that there weren't any woods or swamps here — they were on equal ground. The sound of the trumpets, the flash of equipment, had all the more effect for being unexpected. The enemy had only considered the prospects of an easy fight against a few, half-armed, men. Now their elation at their success was matched by how unprepared they were for a setback. Arminius, who was unhurt, and Inguiomerus, who was severely wounded, fled from the battle. Their followers were slaughtered, as long as our fury and the light of day lasted. It was not till night that the legions returned. Despite the fact that they suffered from more wounds as well as the shortage of supplies, they found strength, healing, sustenance, everything indeed, in their victory.

Tacitus, *Annals*, I.63-68

Agricola's campaigns in Britain

Far away in Britain between the years c. 78-84, the governor Gnaeus Julius Agricola was putting Roman military discipline and order to the test. On campaign in the north, he seems to have been engaged in trying to conquer the whole island once and for all. For the tale of his efforts, we have the account by his son-in-law, Tacitus. We can never be sure how accurate this is, but it remains one of the very few detailed records of the Roman army at war on the edge of empire. In the third year of the campaign, about 81, the prospects looked excellent despite the weather and conditions.

The third year of Agricola's campaigns opened up new tribes, our ravages on the native population being carried as far as the Taus, being the name of an estuary [probably the

Tay]. This struck such terror into the enemy that they did not dare attack our army, harassed though it was by violent storms; and there was even time for fort-building. Our experienced officers observed that no general had ever shown more judgement in choosing suitable positions, and that not one fort established by Agricola was either stormed by the enemy or abandoned by surrender or running away. Sorties were continually being made, because these positions were secured from long sieges by a year's supply of food and stores.

   Thus winter brought no emergencies, and each garrison could take care of itself while the confused and demoralized enemy, used to making good summer losses by winter successes, found itself pushed back in summer and in winter.

Tacitus, *Agricola*, 22

Agricola taken by surprise

Agricola was not perfect and his campaign shows that, regardless of the organisation of the Roman army, local conditions could compromise everything, something that plenty of modern armies have had cause to appreciate. No war ever goes according to plan and unpredictable circumstances will dictate the sequence of events. No amount of technology, hardware and back-up can make good the vicissitudes of the weather. Agricola nearly lost the whole war in a single night when one of his two legions was caught unawares. Tacitus paints it as a victory, even to the extent of claiming that the Roman victory would have brought the whole campaign to an end had the escaping Britons not been able to hide in the swamps and forests. It is plain nonetheless that the Roman army was far from perfect. This was a very close-run thing.

Fearing that the greater enemy numbers and their knowledge of the terrain might allow them to trap him, Agricola divided his forces into three divisions, and advanced. When the enemy soldiers found this out, they suddenly changed their plan, and with their whole force attacked the IX legion, identified as the weakest, in the middle of the night. Cutting down the Roman sentries, who were asleep or terrified out of their wits, they burst into the camp. The battle was in full flow inside the camp. Agricola, whose scouts had told him which way the enemy was marching and had kept close on their track, ordered the fastest amongst his cavalry and infantry to attack the rear of the assailants, and then the rest of the army would shortly raise a battle-cry.

   Soon Agricola's standards were glinting in the rising sun. A twin peril thus terrified the Britons, while Roman courage was rallied. Feeling confident of their safety, they now fought for glory. In their turn they rushed to the attack, and there was a furious conflict within the narrow passages of the gates till the enemy were routed. Both Roman armies did their best; one for the glory of saving the day, the other to prove that the help had not been needed. If it had not been for the marshes and forests sheltering the fleeing Britons, this victory would have ended the war.

Tacitus, *Agricola*, 25-6

THE EMPIRE FOR SALE

Civil War in 68-9

The conditions that led to the mutinies in Pannonia and Germany in the year 14 could have told anyone the way the future would go. Nero's reign (54-68) was marked by his profligacy, greed, autocracy and megalomania. Despite beginning well the reign was a miserable end to the Julio-Claudian dynasty. A vicious civil war followed in the year 68-9, during which time three short-lived emperors struggled to buy the army's loyalty.

To begin with, although Nero's death was initially welcomed by jubilant outbursts, it provoked mixed emotions, not only in Rome amongst senators, ordinary people and the city garrison, but also amongst the legions and their commanders. The reason was that the secret of empire had been exposed: an emperor could be made in other places besides Rome.
Tacitus, *Histories*, I.4

The scene was set for the Roman army to divide amongst its various candidates.

The army of Upper Germany loathed their commander, Hordeonius Flaccus. Old age and lameness meant he was laid-up. He wasn't brave and he lacked authority. While the troops were at ease he could not control them. Once they were angry, his ineffective control only made them more infuriated. For a long time the soldiers of Lower Germany had no commander who had held the consulship, until Galba sent them Aulus Vitellius, son of the Vitellius who had held the post of censor and the consulship three times. He seems to have inherited enough prestige from his father's honours. In Britain, the army stationed there had no grievances. In fact there were no other legions during all the chaos of civil war which caused less trouble. This was either because they were further away and separated by the sea, or perhaps because they had learned in repeated campaigns to keep their hatred for the enemy . There was quiet in Illyricum …. The East remained, for the moment, undisturbed.
Tacitus, *Histories* I.9-10

Every soldier has his price

Fortunately for the Empire, the outcome was a victory for Vespasian. His dynasty began well but ended badly with the reign of his second son Domitian (81-96). Nonetheless it was characterized by growing provincial stability. The reigns of Nerva, Trajan, Hadrian, Antoninus Pius and Marcus Aurelius were widely regarded in late antiquity as the most settled time in the Roman Empire. Apart from Aurelius, none had natural sons and adopted the best man for the job. It worked extremely well. Marcus Aurelius however bequeathed the Empire to his highly unsuitable son Commodus. His murder in 192 was followed by a steady decline into instability in which the Roman army showed that it would elevate anyone stupid enough to offer them ludicrous wage increases.

As time wore on Augustus' pay scheme had proved a generally reliable system. In the first century AD the legionaries received 225 silver denarii a year, with around half being deducted for living costs and other expenses. The auxiliary troops received varying amounts less, depending on which unit they belonged to. From time to time imperial handouts were made to curry favour with the soldiers either in the form of grants or bequests. Erratic pay, extortion and poor conditions had led to the mutinies of the year 14, so, unfortunately, the Roman army was no less susceptible to the prospects of a pay increase than any other army.

Generally speaking, none of these would-be emperors lasted longer than it took for someone else to produce a better offer. In the decades and centuries to come it proved possible for many a man to buy himself into the race to become emperor. First up was Pertinax, a stickler for discipline, whose strictures provide an interesting clue to how the Rome garrison was accustomed to conduct itself in the streets of the imperial capital.

The soldiers were ordered to bring an end to the insulting way in which they treated the people, and they were forbidden to carry axes or to hit passers-by.
Herodian, *History of the Empire*, II.4.1

For this tactless attempt to introduce reasonable behaviour, Pertinax was also rewarded with being murdered by the city garrison. They had no patience with tradition, even though Pertinax's measures had proved popular with everyone else (not surprisingly, considering the kind of hazard passers-by had been suffering).

While most people were living in a contented way under an efficient administration, the Praetorian garrison alone had grown distressed about what was going on and yearned for the disorderly, booze-fuelled chaos under the tyranny [of Commodus] when they had been able to intimidate and extort. So, they conspired to get rid of Pertinax whom they regarded as a complete pain.
Herodian, *History of the Empire*, II.5.1

Didius Julianus joins the auction

Next up was Didius Julianus who found himself bidding for the Empire in competition with the prefect of Rome, Sulpicianus. The news that that Pertinax was dead reached Didius Julianus while he was in a 'drunken stupour' (according to Herodian, II.6.6) which indicates his level of suitability for the job; unfortunately, it was a presage for the future.

Didius Julianus was given to being both greedy for cash and a profligate spender, as well as being keen on the idea of a revolution. Consequently, Commodus had exiled him to his home city of Milan. When Didius heard that Pertinax had died, he rushed to where the Praetorian Guard was camped and made offers to the soldiers while he was standing at the camp gates, in exchange for power over the Roman world. What came next was a thoroughly reprehensible affair Rome did not deserve. Rome and her Empire were auctioned off just as if they were in a sale room or market. The murderers of the emperor were the sellers and the buyers were Sulpicianus and Julianus. They competed with each other, one inside the camp, the other outside.

Gradually they elevated their bids to 5000 denarii per soldier. A few of the troops would let Julianus know, 'Sulpicianus is offering this much, how much more can you offer?' Then to Julianus, 'Julianus is promising this sum, can you beat him?' Sulpicianus, being in the camp and also prefect of Rome, as well as offering 5000 denarii first, ought to have won. However, Julianus started raising his bid, no longer by small increments, but by 1250 denarii at once, yelling out the sum at the top of voice and showing the figure on his fingers. Transfixed by this outrageous offer, the soldiers (who were worried that Sulpicianus might avenge Pertinax, as Julianus had suggested to them) took Julianus into the camp and made him emperor.

Dio Cassius, lxxiv.11.2-6

This time was the beginning of when the nature of the troops was tainted, and they developed a wicked, insatiable greed for cash and had no respect for their rulers.

Herodian, *History of the Empire*, II.6.14

Septimius Severus offers a pay-rise

Didius Julianus in fact never came up with the cash. He lacked the funds and instead he paid up only seven and a half denarii per man. Consequently he was lucky to have lasted as long as 98 days before he followed the hapless Pertinax. The winner of the civil war that followed was Lucius Septimius Severus (193-211), who dealt with his rivals in a duplicitous manner (see Chapter 5). He took steps to thank his troops appropriately when he reached Rome.

Once he had been up to the Temple of Jupiter and finished the religious ceremonies, Severus returned to the palace and handed out a vast quantity of money to the people in celebration of his victories. He also gave a very significant amount to the soldiers together with many other privileges which they had not enjoyed previously, for example a pay-rise (which he was the first to award), permission to wear the insignia of equestrian rank, and the right to reside at home with their wives. All of these are normally believed to be the absolute antithesis of military discipline. Undoubtedly, Severus was the first to undermine the severe frugality of the military diet, their obedience when confronted with tough conditions, and their orderly respect for their generals, by teaching them a greedy hunger for wealth and inveigling them into an effeminate lifestyle.

Herodian, *History of the Empire*, III.8.4-5

Caracalla buys loyalty

In the vain hope that he had established a long-lasting dynasty, Septimius Severus left the Empire to his two sons, Caracalla and Geta. Severus died in York and Caracalla moved fast.

After the death of his father, Caracalla went to the Praetorian fort and moaned there to the soldiers that his brother was organizing a conspiracy against him. So he had his brother murdered in the imperial palace, ordering that his body be cremated immediately. He also said in the fort that his brother had been preparing to poison him and had been disrespectful to their mother. He gave thanks in public to the people who had murdered Geta; indeed he even awarded them a bonus for being so loyal to him.

Nevertheless, some of the soldiers at Alba were furious when they heard about Geta's death, and all declared they had sworn allegiance to both Severus' sons and should maintain that allegiance to both. Then they closed the fort gates. Caracalla was not admitted for a long time, and then not until he had pacified them, not only by slating Geta and by bringing charges against him, but also by huge sums of cash, by means of which, as usual, the soldiers were placated.

Aelius Spartianus, *Antoninus Caracalla*, II.4-8

Macrinus fails to impress the troops

The self-indulgent troops of the early third century were even less impressed by self-indulgent emperors, perhaps out of jealousy. Macrinus was a nobody from the province of Mauretania who rose to become commander of the Praetorian Guard in Rome under Caracalla after serving in the imperial household. When Caracalla was murdered in 217 Macrinus' men declared him emperor. He began to enjoy himself before a conspiracy by Caracalla's relatives made sure he was chased away and killed.

Macrinus regularly indulged in mime shows, dancing and all artistic performances. In the meantime he ignored state business. His habit was to go out wearing brooches and a belt and covered with gold and gems. Roman troops don't think much of this type of extravagance, apparently regarding it as more appropriate to barbarians and women. So, when they saw him, they thoroughly disapproved and were furious at the way Macrinus conducted himself because they thought it too decadent for a soldier. Remembering Caracalla's disciplined military way of life by comparison, they condemned Macrinus' extravagance. They were also cross because, while they were still bivouacking in far-off places, sometimes even living on poor supplies and not coming home despite the fact that things were apparently peaceful, they saw that Macrinus was living in the lap of luxury. In this state of discontent, and harshly criticizing him among themselves, they yearned for any excuse to get rid of this bone of their contention. After only one year of the easy life as emperor it was obviously inevitable that Macrinus would lose the empire and also his life, just as soon as luck supplied a small, trivial, excuse for the soldiers to get what they wanted.

Herodian, *History*, V.2.4-6

Severus Alexander secures his popularity

The reign of Severus Alexander (222-35), great-nephew of Septimius Severus, was one of the more stable periods of the third century. Towards the latter part of his reign he found the Empire faced by threats from the Sassanid ruler Ardashir in the East, and from the Germans in the north. The campaign in the East in cold weather at high altitude left many frostbitten, and added to deaths from battle and disease.

When he got back to Antioch, Severus Alexander was easily restored to health in the invigorating atmosphere of that city with its abundant supply of water after the bone-dry drought in Mesopotamia. He tried to restore the troops' morale and calm their anger with a generous handout of cash, which he thought was the only means of restoring his popularity amongst them.
Herodian, *History of the Empire*, VI.6.4

The scheme, in the long-term, backfired. The problem with buying loyalty was that it was essential to keep on buying it, and the price tended to go up. The soldiers were angered by Severus Alexander's decision to pay the Germans off with a bounty and the influence, they felt, his mother wielded over him.

From their point of view, Alexander had shown no inclination to take the honourable course of prosecuting a war, instead preferring to go chariot-racing and take it easy, when he should have marched off to punish the Germans for their insulting audacity…

In addition to their natural tendency to rebellion, the soldiers considered the state the Empire was in to be annoying, because of the long time Alexander had been emperor, and no longer lucrative because all his handouts had dried up.
Herodian, *History of the Empire*, VI.7.10, 8.4

MILITARY ATROCITIES

The Roman Empire was only one part of a world in which life was cheap, slavery was routine, and military power was decisive. The wars of the ancient world were horrific affairs in which prisoners were either killed, sent to be killed somewhere else, or enslaved. Killing old people, women, and children was routine. We may look on appalled but it takes little to realise that we, too, live in an age when these things have, and still do happen. Europe in the twentieth century has exhibited the same or worse levels of barbarity, and so have Africa and the Far East. In the following examples, Roman historians described some of the most notorious occasions on which Roman soldiers showed what they were capable of, and often justified the actions on political or military expediency.

Caesar's revenge at Avaricum

During Caesar's war of conquest in Gaul, the inhabitants put up a fierce and determined resistance against the Romans. In the year 52BC, Caesar besieged Avaricum (Bourges) but found himself and his forces under threat from the Gaulish leader, Vercingetorix. With his own supplies now at risk, it was vital for Caesar to break in. He took advantage of a downpour to distract the defenders and his troops took advantage of the task to settle a score.

The enemy, being alarmed by the suddenness of the attack, were dislodged from the wall and towers. They drew up, in form of a wedge, in the market place and the open streets, with the idea that, if an attack should be made on any side, they should fight with their line drawn up to receive it. When they saw no-one coming down to the level ground, and the enemy extending themselves along the entire wall in every direction, fearing that every chance of flight would be cut off, they cast away their arms, and sought, without stopping, the most remote parts of the town. A group was then slain by the infantry when they were crowding upon one another in the narrow passage of the gates; and another lot having got outside the gates were cut to pieces by the cavalry: nobody was worried about plunder.

In this way, worked-up by the massacre at Cenabum and the exhausting siege, no-one was spared: the old, women, or children. Finally, out of all that number, which amounted to about forty thousand, scarcely eight hundred, who fled from the town when they heard the first alarm, reached Vercingetorix in safety.

Caesar, *Gallic War*, VII.28

Atrocities in Germany

Soon after the mutiny on the death of Augustus in 14 the legionaries had the opportunity to make amends for their indiscipline (see above). Their behaviour when Augustus died had given the German tribes a chance to believe their troubles were over. They were wrong. Not only were atrocities supposed to suppress resistance but it was also a mechanism for Roman troops to restore their confidence and exult in their own glory even if that meant, as Tacitus uncritically observed, killing people of both sexes and regardless of their age.

Even then, the mood of the soldiers remained savage with a burning desire to set out against the enemy to make amends for their madness. They felt that that the spirits of their companions would only be appeased if they exposed their own wretched bodies to honourable wounds. Germanicus took advantage of their enthusiasm and, once he had built a bridge over the Rhine, sent across it 12,000 legionaries, 26 auxiliary cohorts and eight cavalry wings whose discipline had been unaffected by the mutiny.

All the time that we had been mourning the death of Augustus and were then distracted by the mutiny, the Germans had been loitering nearby and thoroughly enjoying the situation. But the Roman column on a forced march cut their way through the Caesian forest and the frontier started by Tiberius. Camp was made on the frontier with front and rear secured by fortifications and flanks defended by timber barricades. Then they explored some gloomy forest roads and spent time discussing which one to take: the well-known short route, or the difficult and unexplored one but which the enemy had left unguarded. The latter was chosen but otherwise everything else was hurried up because the scouts had reported the Germans were engaged in a night of celebrations, games and banquets.

Caecina [governor of Lower Germany] was ordered to advance with light-armed cohorts and clear a path through the forest. The legions followed at a reasonable distance. Bright starlight helped them on their way to the Marsi villages where small detachments of soldiers were distributed around the enemy. Even then the enemy were lying around on beds or tables without any fear or any guards around their camp, so total was their carelessness and chaos. Indeed, they had no idea that there might be a war but this was not peace — just the languid and careless ease of half-drunk people.

So that the scope of the devastation could be widened, Germanicus divided his enthusiastic legions into four columns and devastated a 50-mile wide area of the country with fire and sword. Neither age nor sex earned any pity. Everything was levelled, whether it was sacred or profane and including the temple of Tamfana, as it was called, the most important religious centre for those tribes. Not a single one of our soldiers was wounded as they cut down the half-asleep, unarmed or scattered enemy. The slaughter roused the Bructeri, Tubantes, and Usipetes, who occupied the forest passes through which our troops had to return. Germanicus heard about this and he set off, ready to march or fight. The column was headed by some of the cavalry and auxiliary cohorts. Next came the I legion, and, with the baggage in the middle, the XXI legion closed up the left, and the V, the right flank. The XX legion closed the rear, and, after its soldiers were the rest of the allies.

Meanwhile the enemy made no move until our army was passing through the wood. Then they made some light skirmishing attacks on the front and flanks before their whole force was flung on the rear. The light-armed cohorts were thrown into disarray by the dense mass of Germans until Germanicus rode up to the troops of the XX legion, and shouted loudly that this was their chance to expunge the mutiny, 'Forward, and move fast to turn your guilt into glory!' This stoked up their courage, and in one burst they broke through the enemy, and forced them back with great slaughter into the open country. Simultaneously the troops from the front of the column came out of the woods and dug the fortifications for a camp. After this their march was uninterrupted, and the troops, grown confident with their recent success, and putting the past behind them, were placed in winter-quarters.

Tacitus, *Annals*, I.49-51

Later on, in Britain, the death of a tribal king would provide an opportunity for unprecedented military corruption leading to horrific brutality on both sides (see Chapter 5).

Romans against Romans

This was no more than the Romans were prepared to do to each other. In the year 69, during the Civil War, the legions loyal to Otho met those of Vitellius on the fields of Bedriacum. It was a vicious affair.

Vitellius then directed his course to Cremona, and after witnessing the gladiatorial display put on by Caecina, he had a whim to visit the plains of Bedriacum and to look over the scene of the recent victory. It was a hideous and terrible sight. Less than 40 days had passed since the battle, and there lay mangled corpses, severed limbs, the rotting carcasses of men and horses; the soil was saturated with gore, and, what with levelled trees and crops, the desolation was horrific. No less disgusting was the stretch of road which the people of Cremona had strewed with laurel leaves and roses, and on which they had raised altars, and sacrificed victims as if to greet some barbarous despot, but what gave them so much pleasure now would bring about their ruin.

Valens and Caecina were present. They pointed out the various positions on the field of battle. They showed how from one point the columns of the legions had rushed to the attack; how from another the cavalry had charged; and how, from a third position, the auxiliary troops had turned the flank of the enemy. The tribunes and prefects extolled their individual achievements, and mixed together fiction, fact, and exaggeration. The ordinary troops also turned away from the marching line with joyful shouts, and recognized the various scenes of conflict, and gazed with wonder on the piles of weapons and the heaps of slain. There were some indeed whom this sight moved to thoughts of the mutability of fortune, to pity, and to tears. Vitellius did not look away. He did not shudder to see the unburied corpses of so many thousands of his countrymen. On the contrary, in his exultation and in his ignorance of the fate which was closing in on him, he actually instituted a religious ceremony in honour of the local gods.

Tacitus, *Histories*, II.70

The destruction of Jerusalem

During the siege of Jerusalem in the year 70 the population suffered horrific privations from starvation while the Roman army under Titus worked steadily to find a way in. When they finally broke through the revenge for the long wait was at fever pitch and little seems to have been learned from other provinces.

Now in full control of the walls, the Romans put up their standards on the towers. Singing and clapping, they celebrated the victory after a war that had ended far more easily than it had begun. Although it seemed too good to be true, the last wall had been breached without a single man being lost. They were confused when they found no opposition. They rushed into the streets clutching their swords, cutting down mercilessly anyone who came near them, and burned down the houses of anyone who had hidden inside for protection along with everyone and everything inside. Many houses they plundered, and as they hunted for booty, they came across whole families dead and rooms packed with people who had starved to death. Appalled by what they saw, they left with nothing.

Any sorrow they might have felt for those who had died like that was not matched by what they felt for the living. The soldiers ran their swords through every man they found and blocked the narrow streets with dead bodies, flooding the city with so much gore that the blood extinguished many of the fires. When the sun set the killing ended, but during the night the fire took over.

On the 8th day of Gorpiaios the sun rose on Jerusalem ablaze. Jerusalem had suffered so many troubles, that if she had been the subject of as many favours from the day she was founded she would have been the envy of the world. This was a city which had done nothing more to deserve such an awful fate apart from producing the generation which caused her downfall ....

Titus ordered that only armed men who were still resisting were to be killed, and everyone else to be captured alive, because the soldiers had had enough of killing. But in addition to those included in the orders, the sick and old were also executed. Men in the prime of life, of possible use, were rounded up in the Temple and confined in the Court of the Women. Titus instructed one of his freedmen to guard them, and his friend Fronto to make a decision about each man, depending on what he deserved. The men who had been involved in planning rebellion and terrorism gave each other away so Fronto put the

whole lot to death. He selected the handsomest and tallest young men for the triumphal procession. Of those who were left, anyone over seventeen was clapped in chains and sent off to hard labour in Egypt. At the same time, enormous numbers were given away by Titus to the Roman provinces to die in theatres from the sword or be killed by wild animals. Anyone under seventeen was sold. Eleven thousand prisoners died of hunger in the time that Fronto was dividing them up, some because the guards hated them so much they would not let them have any food and others because they would not take it when it was offered. Either way, there was not enough food to feed so many mouths.
Josephus, *Jewish War*, VI. 400ff.

How to deal with a 'gang of thugs'
By the fourth century the Roman Empire was under enormous threats from all sides. Decades of civil war, murdered emperors and economic insecurity had led to the early medieval world of the fourth century where oppressive legislation was used to keep people in their places of work, and the Empire was run by an increasingly top-heavy bureaucracy. The tribal peoples of northern Europe kept up a sustained battering ram. In the year 370, there was yet another incursion.

A horde of Saxons broke out, and after surviving the perils of the sea moved very fast towards the Roman frontier, having gorged on slaughtering our people.

After fighting, a truce was called in which hostages would be exchanged. But the Romans planned to double-cross the Saxons.

Infantry were sent in secret and laid an ambush in a lonely valley, from where they could attack the Saxons as they passed with as little trouble as possible. But the outcome was rather different from what had been hoped for. Excited by the sound of the approaching Saxons, a few of the men raced out before the time set. When they suddenly appeared, the barbarians made a terrible noise, and while the Romans were sorting themselves out, they were forced to retreat.

In a little while though, the Romans halted and got back into formation. Invigorated (as well as they could be) by the precariousness of their situation, they had no choice but to fight. However, after suffering terrible losses, they were put to flight. They would have all been killed had not a unit of armoured cavalry, positioned for the same reason in another place by a road to cause the barbarians trouble as they passed by, heard their screams of terror and raced to their aid.

At that point the battle became more heated and the Romans with renewed courage pressed on the Saxons from all directions, surrounded them, and with drawn swords killed the lot. Not one was in a position to go home, not one was allowed to escape the killing of his companions. While some righteous people will judge this incident as treacherous and hateful, on reflection they will not think it wrong that a destructive gang of thugs was destroyed when at last there was a chance to do so.
Ammianus Marcellinus, XXVIII.5.5-7

MILITARY WORKS

Quite apart from its military power the Roman army was a superlative engineering force. Unfortunately, few accounts of how much of the work was carried out exist. The great frontiers in northern Britain, Hadrian's Wall and the Antonine Wall, were amongst the most complex military systems ever built, involving walls, ditches, ramparts, forts, fortlets, signal towers and bridges as well as roads and other facilities. Yet, we know almost nothing at all about how these vast projects, unique in Roman history, were organized. Instead, understanding the Walls relies almost entirely on archaeology. Where written accounts exist, they can record buildings which otherwise leave no trace.

Building bridges

In the middle of the first century BC Julius Caesar recorded the techniques he used to cross the Rhine in a classic description of military engineering.

Caesar .... had resolved to cross the Rhine; but to cross using ships he decided was not safe enough, nor did he consider it consistent with his own dignity or that of the Roman people. Therefore, although the greatest difficulty in forming a bridge was presented to him, due to the width, rapidity, and depth of the river, he nevertheless believed that it ought to be attempted by him, or else his army should be not led across.

Caesar devised this bridge design. He joined a pair of piles together two feet apart, each a foot and a half thick, sharpened a little at the bottom, and with a length proportionate to the depth of the river. After he had, using rafts, sunk these into the river, and fixed them at the bottom, and then driven them in with rammers, just off the vertical like a stake, but bending forward and sloping to match the direction of the river flow. He also placed two others opposite to these, 40 feet beyond lower down the river, fastened together in the same manner, but angled against the force and current of the river. What is more, both these were kept firmly apart by beams two feet thick (the space which the binding of the piles occupied), laid in at their extremities between two braces on each side.

As a result of these being in different directions and secured on opposite sides, so great was the strength of the work, and such the arrangement of the components, that the more the water crashed against the bridge, so the parts were held together all the tighter. These beams were bound together by timber laid over them, in the direction of the length of the bridge, and covered over with laths and hurdles. As well as this, piles were driven into the water obliquely, at the lower side of the bridge. These, serving as buttresses, and connected to every part of the structure, took the force of the stream. There were others also a little way above the bridge, so that if the barbarians sent tree-trunks or boats down the river to wreck the bridge, the buffers might limit the force of such impacts and prevent it from being damaged.

Within ten days after the timber began to be collected, the whole work was completed, and the whole army led over...
Caesar, *Gallic War*, IV.17-18

Trajan's bridge

Caesar's bridge was made of timber and thus by definition unlikely to last for very long. One of the most celebrated military building projects was Trajan's bridge over the Danube, erected in the year 104. It was intended that the bridge would allow his army into Dacia (now Romania) from the province of Moesia (equivalent to Bulgaria and the eastern part of the former Yugoslavia), and remain a means of guaranteeing rapid transit of Roman troops into the newly-conquered territories in times of emergency. But disagreements over its military suitability and Hadrian's general policy of giving up remote territories meant that it was soon rendered functionless, though it remained a monument to Roman engineering genius. It seems to have consisted of masonry piers connected by a wooden superstructure.

Trajan built a stone bridge across the Danube for which no praise is enough. This exceeded all his other achievements, outstanding though they were. This bridge has twenty piers, each of which is 150 [Roman] feet [44.3 metres] high from the foundations and 60 feet [17.7 metres] wide. These piers stand 170 feet [50.3 metres] apart and are joined by arches. So how could anyone not be astonished at the money spent on them, how each was erected in a river that was so deep, had so many currents, and on so soft a bottom?

The fact is, of course, that diverting the river was impossible at any point. I have mentioned the river's width, but it is not always as narrow as this. In some stretches it is two or three times as wide, but the part where it becomes narrowest and is the most suitable in the area for bridging has the width described. But thanks to the river being narrowed as it comes down here from a great expanse, and then widens up again, means that here it is much deeper and more turbulent. This characteristic must be taken into account when considering how difficult the bridge was to construct. So this is another achievement which shows how great Trajan's projects were, in spite of the fact that the bridge is of no value to us. This is because now only the piers stand, by which alone there is no way of crossing. It is as if their only purpose was to show that human ingenuity can achieve anything.

The reason Trajan had the bridge erected was because he feared that one day the Danube might freeze and a war might break out against the Romans on the far bank. He wanted to be able to get across to them this way. But Hadrian took the opposite point of view and thought that barbarians, having dealt with the guards, would find this a convenient way to get into Moesia so he had the superstructure taken away.
Dio Cassius, *Roman History*, LXVIII.13.1-6

Hadrian's Wall

Hadrian's Wall in Britain, which remains one of the most important relics of the Roman world, was built in the early 120s. Despite the scale of the project this is the sole Roman literary record of the event.

And so, having reformed the army in the manner of a monarch, he set out for Britain, and there he corrected many abuses and was the first to construct a wall over a length of 80

miles, which was to force apart the barbarians and the Romans.
Aelius Spartianus, *Hadrian*, XI.2

Hadrian's Wall had been in use for only a generation or so when Antoninus Pius (138-61), shortly after his accession, ordered a new frontier.

Through his legate Antoninus Pius waged many wars. For example, through the legate Lollius Urbicus, he defeated the Britons and built another wall, of turf, having driven back the barbarians…
Julius Capitolinus, *Antoninus Pius*, V.4

Roman siege tactics defeated by wits

However invincible the Roman army and its siege machines might appear, against a determined and resourceful foe they were potentially useless. Maximinus I (235-8) was a soldier emperor, given power by his army after the murder of Severus Alexander, and one of a sequence of disastrous appointments that invariably ended in bloodshed.

Maximinus I was a competent soldier, and, after crushing mutinies in the Rhine garrison, he also settled the Rhine and Danube frontiers. This looked promising until the Senate sided with the governor of Africa who was declared emperor as Gordian I after a revolt against exploitation in Africa (see Chapter 5). Gordian committed suicide after a reign of only a few weeks when his son was killed in battle, but the Senate had already committed itself to him. In Gordian's place they elevated two of their number, Balbinus and Pupienus in 238. Maximinus I marched on Italy to force his hand but was delayed while besieging Aquileia in northern Italy, and found his military skills faced with a considerable challenge.

The people of Aquileia flung down a barrage of boulders from the walls, and brewed up a mixture of pitch, oil, sulphur and bitumen which was poured into empty pots with long handles. The moment Maximinus' army came close to the city walls, the compound was ignited and poured out like a shower of rain on the attackers. As it was poured out the pitch mixed in with all the other substances spreading through all unprotected limbs and covered the body. Soldiers ripped off their scalding cuirasses and the rest of their armour because the metal had become red-hot while the leather and wooden components were shrinking and bursting into flames. Consequently there was the sight of troops who looked like prisoners of war, having torn all their clothes off and thrown away their weapons. All this had been caused by scientific ingenuity, not military skills.

The outcome of this incident was that many soldiers went blind, or they suffered disfiguring burns on their faces and hands, or other exposed parts of their bodies. The Aquileians also fired torches, fitted with arrow-heads and drenched in pitch and resin, at the siege engines which were being taken up to the city walls. The arrows were fired off once they were burning and stuck fast into the engines, causing them to burst into flames without any trouble at all.
Herodian, *History of the Empire*, VIII.4.9-11

As it turned out, there was no serious prospect of the Aquileians giving up for want of supplies either. Careful preparations meant they were well stocked while Maximinus' army had already desecrated the general area and instead found itself running out of supplies first. Worse, the roads to Rome were blockaded. The soldiers were entirely fed up with the situation so they followed the usual practice and killed Maximinus and his son. Gordian III, the grandson of the former governor of Africa, was elevated to the purple.

MILITARY LIVES

Life on the frontier

If life was hard for ordinary soldiers, it could be convivial for some of the officers and their families, even on a far-flung frontier in Britain where border warfare was commonplace. Here a commanding officer writes to a fellow for a loan of hunting equipment around the years 92-103.

Flavius Cerealis to his own Brocchus, greetings.
Brother, if you care about me I am asking you to send me some traps .... the parts repaired very strongly.
Tab. Vindol., II.233 (Cerealis commanded the IX cohort of Batavians at Vindolanda; Aelius Brocchus commanded another, unknown, unit at a fort called *Briga*, also unknown)

Meanwhile, Brocchus' wife was organising her birthday party and inviting Cerealis' wife to attend.

To Sulpicia Lepidina of Cerealis, from Severa
Claudia Severa to Lepidina, greetings.
On the third day before the Ides of September [11th], sister, for the feast-day of my birth I ask with great pleasure that you make sure that you come to ours making my occasion all the more delightful by you turning up if [you can?].
   Best wishes to your Cerealis. My Aelius and little boy send their best wishes. Sister, I will expect you. Farewell and hail sister, my beloved soulmate, and I hope this device will have an effect.
Tab. Vindol., II..291

Hadrian puts an end to easy living

In the early second century Hadrian (117-38) toured the Empire and was not always impressed by what he found. He subscribed to the imperial military principle of being prepared for war but found his troops were enjoying the easy life. Having visited Gaul he moved on to the German provinces, which held the vital garrisons strung out along the Rhine.

Hadrian travelled to the Gaulish provinces, and came to the relief of all the communities with various acts of generosity. From there he went over into Germany. Though he wanted peace rather than war, he kept the soldiers in training as if war was about to break out. He inspired them with proof of his own powers of endurance, and actually led a soldier's life amongst their number. Following the example set by Scipio Aemilianus, Metellus, and his own adoptive father Trajan, he happily dined outdoors on such camp-fare as bacon, cheese and vinegar.

So that the troops might put up more willingly with the increased harshness of his orders, Hadrian bestowed gifts on many and honours on a few. For he re-established the military discipline, which, since Augustus' time, had grown slack through the laxity of his own predecessors. He regulated, too, both the duties and the expenses of the soldiers, and now no one could get a leave of absence from camp by dodgy methods, for it was not popularity amongst ordinary soldiers but worthy actions that recommended a man for appointment as tribune.

Hadrian inspired others with his own military example. He would walk as much as 20 miles fully-armed. He cleared the camp of banqueting-rooms, porticoes, grottos, and shady garden retreats, and generally wore the roughest clothing. He would have no gold ornaments on his sword-belt or jewels on the clasp, and would barely put up with having his sword furnished with an ivory hilt. He visited the sick soldiers in their quarters, and chose locations for forts.

Hadrian promoted to centurion only those who were tough and of good reputation, and appointed as tribunes only men with full beards or who were old enough to give to the authority of the tribuneship the full measure of prudence and maturity. He allowed no tribune to accept a present from a soldier, banished luxuries everywhere, and, finally, improved the soldiers' arms and equipment.

Furthermore, as far as length of military service was concerned, he issued an order that no one should violate ancient tradition by being in the service at an earlier age than his strength warranted, or at a more advanced one than common humanity permitted. He made it a point to familiarise himself with the soldiers and to know their numbers.

In addition to this Hadrian made sure he knew exactly what was in the military stores. The receipts from the provinces he examined with care in order to make good any deficit that might occur in any particular instance. But more than any other emperor he made it a point not to buy or maintain anything that was not serviceable.

Aelius Spartianus, *The Life of Hadrian*, X-XI.1

Fops in the Antioch garrison

Later in the second century, on the other side of the Roman world, little had changed despite Hadrian's reforms. The Antioch garrison seems to have been manned by fops and dandies.

Fronto to Lucius Verus

You took command of an army demoralized by high-living, decadence, and a long time taking it easy. The Antioch soldiers had got used to spending time applauding theatrical performers and were more usually found in bar gardens than in their ranks. There were shaved and groomed riders, but horses were scruffy from neglect. A soldier with a hairy leg or arm was a rare sight. On the whole the troops were better dressed than they were equipped to the extent that a thoroughly good chap and stickler for traditional discipline, Pontius Laelianus, was able to tear up the cuirasses of some of them with his fingers. He came across horses with cushions for saddles, and on his instructions the little pommels on them were cut open and feathers plucked out of the cavalry saddles as if they were geese. Hardly any of the soldiers could leap up onto their horses. The remainder pulled themselves up clumsily by kicking up from their heels, knees or thighs. Only a few could fling their spears a long way, most just chucked them about without any skill or strength as if they were toys. Gambling was everywhere in the fort. They slept all through the night, or if they were on watch they slept over cups of wine.

Fronto, *Letters*, XIX

A soldier's death in Britain

Northern Britain, like many remote provincial areas of the Empire was never entirely controlled. Agricola's conquests were given up, and despite subsequent campaigns it was Hadrian's Wall which really came to mark the end of the Empire in the north. Despite this remarkable fortification, centuries later soldiers were still being killed by incursions from beyond.

To the good spirits of the afterlife, Flavius Fuscinus, retired centurion, lived for 55 years. To the good spirits of the afterlife, Flavius Romanus, military record clerk, was killed in the fort by the enemy when he was 35 years old.

Tombstone from Ambleside, Cumbria, *JRS* liii (1963), 160, no. 4. Datable on style to the third century or later.

Military careers

Individual military careers were recorded across the Empire on career inscriptions or tombstones. These show how soldiers could spend their working lives almost anywhere in the Empire, transferred and moved about as necessary. For men of ability there was the chance to see the world and fight in wars almost anywhere while gradually accumulating enough personal prestige to rise to high office in great cities.

Titus Pontius Sabinus was an equestrian who commanded an auxiliary unit of Pannonians and Dalmatians. From here he progressed into the legions where he served in various centurion posts before finally becoming an imperial procurator in Gallia Narbonensis. His tombstone gives us enough information to fix his career in the reigns of Trajan and Hadrian.

Titus Pontius Sabinus, son of Titus, of the Palatina tribe, prefect of the First mounted Cohort of Pannonians and Dalmatians (Roman citizens), military tribune of the VI legion Ferrata, having been decorated with a ceremonial spear on the Parthian expedition by the deified Trajan, a standard and a mural crown, centurion variously of XXII legion Primigenia, XIII Gemina, senior centurion of III Augusta, commander of 1000-strong detachments from VII Gemina, VIII Augusta, and XXII Primigenia on the British

expedition, tribune of the III cohort of Vigiles, tribune of the XIV Urban Cohort, tribune of the II Praetorian Cohort, senior centurion II [meaning unknown], procurator of the province of Narbonensis, magistrate, priest and city patron.
ILS 2726, from Ferentini, Italy

Like Pontius Sabinus, Aemilius Iuncus was an equestrian who built up a prestigious portfolio of military positions which finally led to his procuratorship of Asia, one of the richest provinces of the Empire. One might equate it with the prestige of rising to a major administrative post in California.

[Aemilius] Iuncus, prefect of the First cohort of Pannonians, tribune of the Fifth cohort of Gemellans (Roman citizens), tribune of the X legion Fretensis, prefect of the ala of Gallic veterans, decorated with a ceremonial spear and a mural crown by the Emperor Trajan in the Parthian War, procurator of Cilicia and Cyprus, judge of Alexandria in Egypt, procurator of the province of Asia ….
Inscription at Ephesus, Turkey (recorded by the editor), *Smallwood* 246

Far from home

A raw Egyptian recruit to one of the Roman military fleets writes to his family after arriving in Italy at the port of Misenum. He has been given a new name and his expenses.

To Epimachus at Philadelphia from his son Apion.
Deliver to Julius, secretary, this letter from Apion for forwarding to his father Epimachus, at the camp of the First cohort of Apameni
Apion to his father and master Epimachus, many greetings.

First I give prayers for your good health, and that you may always be rich and well, together with my sister and her daughter, and my brother. I thank the lord Serapis that when I was in danger at sea, he saved me immediately. When I arrived at Misenum I received from Caesar three gold coins for the costs of the journey.

All is well with me. Lord and father, I ask you now to write a letter to me. Tell me first how you are, secondly how my brother and sister are, and thirdly allow me to pay due respects to your handwriting, because you taught me well and consequently I hope to be promoted quickly, if the gods wish it.

Give many good wishes to Capiton, my brother and sister, Serenilla, and my friends. I have sent you a picture of me via Euctemon. My [Roman name] is Antonius Maximus, in the company called Athenonica.

I give prayers for your health…
SP No. 112, second century

Another misses his mother

Deliver to Taesis at Karanis, from her son Apollinaris at Misenum
Apollinaris to his mother and lady Taesis. I pray for your health before everyone. I am well, and pray humbly to the gods here for you. Mother, I want you to know that I reached

Rome in good health on the 25th day of the month Pachon, and was posted to Misenum. But so far I do not know the name of my unit because at the time I wrote this letter I had not left for Misenum.

So, mother, I beg that you look after yourself and not to fret about me because I have come to an excellent place. Do please write to me about how you, my brothers and all the people there, are doing. I'll write to you whenever I find a messenger and I will never be slow to do so.

Best wishes to my brothers, and Apollinaris and Karalas and their children. I greet Ptolemaeus and Ptolemais and her children, and Heraclous and hers. I greet everyone who knows you, by name. I give prayers for your health.
SP No. 111, second century

Promotion

A *beneficiarius*, was a soldier detached from normal duties and assigned to the personal staff of an officer. Here one such *beneficiarius* uses his position in a legion in Egypt to seek a post for his dear friend. This form of personal approach and appeal was a fundamental means of advancement throughout Roman society, civil and military, as it has been ever since.

Greetings to Julius Domitius, military tribune with the legion, from Aurelius Archaelaos, his beneficiarius
Once before I recommended my friend Theon to you, Sir, and now again. I beg you to regard him as if he were me. He is certainly a man who deserves your affection. He has left his people, property and business and followed me. Out of his care for me, I have been protected by him through everything. So, I beg you therefore to admit him to your presence. He can tell you everything about our affairs. Whatever he said about me … I have loved the man … Sir, may you and yours be happy and prosperous for a long time. Look at this letter, Sir, and imagine that I am speaking to you. Farewell.
SP No. 122, second century

Family connections could be decisive. They were certainly worth mentioning.

You prove how much you think of me by the delicate way in which you have asked me to transfer the military tribunate, which I secured for you from the distinguished senator Neratius Marcellus, to your kinsman Caesennius Silvanus. From my point of view I would have been very pleased to see you in the post, but I shall be just as pleased if Silvanus is obliged to you for the position. If someone has believed a man to be worthy of promotion, in my view it is illogical to hold it against him for having the right to demonstrate loyalty to his own people, considering that this gives him more of a good name than any official post.
Pliny the Younger to Suetonius Tranquillus (the historian), *Letters* III.8

Stationed at the ends of the earth

The poet, Juvenal, seems to have served in the Roman army. In one of his Satires he describes far-off Britain, while an inscription from Aquincum in Italy, apparently naming the same man, records that he served as the tribune of the First cohort of Dalmatians in Britain. In this excerpt Juvenal seems to be recalling his time at the ends of the earth.

Indeed we have advanced our armies beyond Ireland's shores to the just-captured Orkneys and the Britons with their short nights.
Juvenal, *Satires*, II.159-61 (and *ILS* 2926)

Off sick

Day-to-day records of Roman military affairs are practically unknown. This document from Vindolanda in northern Britain, dating to around the end of the first century, shows that the nominal strength of a unit might be severely compromised for a number of reasons.

On the fifteenth day before the Kalends of June [18 May] the full complement of the First cohort of Tungrians, which the prefect Julius Verecundus commands, is 752 men, including six centurions.

Amongst these are absent:
The governor's guards at the place where Ferox is in charge: 46
At Coria [Corbridge] 337 (including 2 centurions)
At London [number lost]
At [...] 6, including a centurion
At [...] 9, including a centurion
At [...] 11
At [...] 1, 45
Total away: 456

Those who remain present: 296, including 1 centurion

Out of this number:
Sick 15
Wounded 6
Those with inflamed eyes 10
Total of these: 31

Leaving fit and strong: 265, including 1 centurion
Tab. Vindol., I.154

THE ROMAN MILITARY LEGACY

Learning from the glorious past

The power of the Roman army steadily waned throughout the days of the Empire. Once Hadrian made the frontiers technically permanent, the legions and auxiliary units found themselves guarding the borders of the Empire or taking part in the increasing numbers of civil wars, especially during the third century. By the fourth century the great days of the legions were over. This was a time of demoralised second-rate frontier troops eking out their lives in decaying garrison forts, while crack units of cavalry were despatched to help fend off barbarian incursions. In the middle of all this the late military historian Vegetius looked back at where the rot had set in.

Circumstances dictate that we try and list the types of weapons with which recruits were either armed or protected. But the ancient customs have been completely abandoned, for, although the example set by Goths, Alans, and Huns has been very useful for cavalry weapons, infantry continued to be unprotected. From the time when Rome was founded, right up to the reign of the late Gratian (367-83), infantry were equipped with cuirasses as well as helmets. But when field training was abandoned thanks to negligence and laziness, the equipment — which the soldiers rarely put on — became regarded as heavy. So, first they asked the emperor to stop issuing cuirasses, then helmets. Consequently, fighting with unprotected bodies and heads against the Goths, our soldiers were frequently wiped out by numerous archers.

Even after numerous disasters, when many cities were destroyed, none of these troubles led to the restoration of either cuirasses or helmets. Therefore, men who are unprotected in battle, and thus susceptible to injury, do not think of fighting, but of running away. What else can the foot archer do, without cuirass or helmet, unable to hold a shield at the same time as his bow? What should the various standard-bearers do in battle, wielding spears with the left hand, leaving their heads and bodies exposed?

But a cuirass and helmet seem heavy to an infantryman who perhaps rarely trains with or handles arms. But daily use isn't unduly tiresome, even if he is weighed down. The point is that those who cannot tolerate the effort required to carry traditional defensive equipment could, with their unprotected bodies, be wounded or killed. And, more importantly, they could be captured or betray the state by running away. As long as they evade training and effort, they are dishonourably cut to pieces like animals.

Why else would people in the old days have called the infantry army a wall, if it hadn't been for the way the javelin-armed legionaries behind their shields, positively shone with cuirasses and helmets? Even archers were equipped with armlets on the left arm. The shield-carrying infantry, however, in addition to cuirasses and helmets, resorted to iron greaves on the right shin. The combatants in the first line (called *principes,* in the second *hastati,* and in the third *triarii*) were equipped in this way. But the *triarii* were used to kneeling down behind their shields, in case they were wounded by incoming missiles when standing. When necessary, as if refreshed, they attacked the enemy more forcefully. This turn of events, when the *hastati* had crumbled and the *triarii* stood firm, is known to be a tidy victory.

But in the old days there were infantrymen called *levis armaturae* — slingers and light missile-armed troops — who were specifically placed on the flanks and with whom the battle traditionally began. The fastest and most experienced of these were selected (and there were many who didn't make the grade) who, if necessary, were used to passing between the front lines of the legion, so that the battle line remained steady. It remained the custom until recently that all soldiers were familiar with the 'Pannonian' *pilleus* of skins. This was kept on so that a helmet would not seem heavy to a man who was always wearing some sort of head-gear.

The infantry army was associated with the missiles known as *pila* which had a fine triangular iron point of nine inches or a foot at the end. When stuck in a shield, it could not be pulled out. Aimed expertly and strongly a *pila* could easily pierce a cuirass. Weapons of this type are now rare in our own time. Barbarian infantry who use shields are particularly associated with *bebrae*, carrying two or even three into battle. In addition, where missiles are concerned, a soldier must always advance with his left foot because spinning projectiles thrown in this way are more powerful.

But when it comes 'to the *pila*', as the saying goes, and fighting is hand-to-hand with swords, then soldiers must advance with their right feet. In this way both their flanks are protected from the enemy, so that they are not wounded, and so that the right hand is nearer and able to deliver a blow. Consequently it remains true that recruits should be taught about and protected by all kinds of ancient weaponry. It is vital that, with an armoured head or chest, he should be more keenly courageous in combat, and not fear being wounded.

Vegetius, *Military Science*, XX

3 Cities, circuses and crowds

The essence of Roman society was based on the city. Rome herself was often known as simply *Urbs*, 'the City'. Throughout the Empire a host of mini Romes acted as provincial or regional capitals. Each one had its forum, its basilica, temples to Capitoline Jupiter and the imperial cult, theatres, townhouses, brothels, bars and public lavatories. The town senate was modelled on the Roman senate and elected its local magistrates as Rome elected her consuls, tribunes, aediles and quaestors. In the eastern Empire urban life was already well-established and cities of Greek origin like Ephesus in Asia found themselves embellished with Roman additions. Today, the ruins of Ephesus are largely those of the second century. In the western Empire, urban life was more of a novelty. Where necessary towns were founded and built to conform to a general Roman theme. In Britain, a new province, towns scarcely existed at the time of the Roman invasion in 43. Under Vespasian (69-79) and later emperors, urban development in Britain seems to have proceeded apace, almost certainly as a result of direct imperial policy to promote Roman town life in the furthest corner of the Empire. Vespasian, builder of the Colosseum, seems to have had a particular appreciation of the value of appeasing the urban mob with facilities and entertainment.

Exploring the Roman world today means finding infinite varieties on the same themes. Pompeii and Ostia in Italy, Thuburbo Majus and Dougga in North Africa, Arles and Nîmes in Gaul, and London and Cirencester in Britain — all contained familiar Roman urban features. Anyone from the Roman period would have recognised facilities and the layout. Like all cities, Roman cities provided heaving concentrations of humanity. This was the world of the street mob, circus crowds, amphitheatre riots, noisy baths, corrupt officials, disorganisation, petty rivalries, thieves and vagabonds.

Choosing a place for a city

The following general principles should be applied for a fortified city. The first is choosing a very healthy location. Such a place will be high and not misty or frosty and in a temperate zone rather than being hot or cold; it should also not have any marshes nearby. This is because when morning breezes blow towards the city at sunrise, if they bring with them marsh mists which have mixed in with them the poisonous breath of animals that live in the marsh, then that gets drawn into the bodies of the inhabitants and makes the place unhealthy. Also, if the town is on a south or west-facing coast it will be unhealthy. This is because during the summer the southern sky gets hot at sunrise and like fire at midday while a western coast gets warm after the sun has come up, is hot by midday and is all aglow by the evening. Such variations in heat, and the cooling down afterwards, harm people living in such places.

Vitruvius, *On Architecture* I.4.1-2

ROME

Strabo's Rome

Strabo's geography covered much of the Roman world. His description of Rome dates to the early years of the reign of Tiberius. He found the city in a remarkable state, recalling Augustus' own claim (Suetonius, *Augustus*, 28.3) that he had found the city made of brick and left it one of marble. It is worth appreciating that Strabo's description preceded by generations many of the most famous buildings of Rome (for example the Colosseum, some of the imperial palaces, the Forum of Trajan and the Baths of Caracalla). Few cities today have such an impact, but perhaps the central part of Washington DC with its parade of official, neo-classical, public buildings overlooked by the US Capitol is the closest.

The reason the Greek cities are believed to have done so well is because of the happy choice their founding fathers made, with respect to the beauty, impregnability, closeness to a port, and the quality of the land. But Roman prudence was more concentrated on aspects which the Greeks practically ignored, such as paved roads, building aqueducts and sewers. In fact the Romans paved roads, cut passages through hills, and filled in valleys so that freight can be transported on carts to the ports. Sewers, arched with worked blocks, are big enough in some stretches for actual hay carts to pass through whilst the aqueducts yield so much water that it could be said rivers flow through the city and its sewers and practically every house is equipped with a water supply and copious fountains.

You might say that the men of old spent little time turning Rome into a thing of beauty. But their successors, and especially those of today, have at the same time embellished the city with a great number of wonderful objects. Pompey, the divine Caesar and Augustus with his children, friends, wife and sister, have outdone all the others in their enthusiasm and generosity in these adornments. Most of these can be seen at Mars Field which complements artistic beauty with that of nature. The size of the area is astonishing, with enough room for chariot races and equestrian events without obstruction. Crowds exercise with ball games in the circus, or on the wrestling compound. The buildings around, the greenery covered with herbage all year round, the summit of the hills beyond the Tiber, extending from its banks in a panoramic effect, present a sight which the eye only reluctantly abandons.

Near Mars Field is another one, surrounded with columns, sacred groves, three theatres, an amphitheatre, and superb temples. All are close to one another and are so marvellous that it would seem futile to go on to describe the rest of Rome. For this reason, the Romans regard it as their most sacred place and have erected funerary monuments to illustrious men and women. The most astonishing of these is the 'Mausoleum', close to the river, which consists of an earthen mound on top of a white marble foundation and is covered with evergreen plants. On the very top is a bronze statue of Augustus Caesar and inside the mound are the burial urns of himself, his family and his friends. Behind it is a large arboretum with lovely walks. In the centre of Mars Field is the place where this ruler was cremated. The spot is surrounded by a double wall, one of marble, the other iron, and inside poplars have been planted.

If after that you go on to visit the Forum, which is just as packed with basilicas, porticos and temples, you will see the Capitol hill and the Palatine hill and the stately works that beautify them, and Livia's piazza. Each one makes you forget the one you saw before. Such is Rome!

There is a constant need for wood and stone for the ceaseless construction work in Rome. This is caused by frequently collapsing houses, and because of the fires and house disposals which never seem to let up. These disposals are a kind of deliberate demolition, each owner knocking down his house and then rebuilding as the fancy takes him. To this end the huge number of quarries, forests, and rivers in the region which provide the materials, offer superb facilities.

Augustus tried to save Rome from these dangers and instituted a band of freedmen who would be ready to help put fires out. To prevent houses collapsing he ordered that new houses built alongside public streets should not be more than seventy feet high. But these precautions must have been abandoned apart from the facilities provided to Rome by the quarries, the forests, and the easy transport.

Strabo, *Geography*, V.3

Road rage and muggings

Astounding though Rome may have been to a visitor, it was also a picture of urban chaos. Strabo might have described a place like Washington but for others it was more like New York, Cairo, Bombay or Rio de Janeiro. Packed with swarms of people, merchants, visitors, traffic, it was noisy, congested and reeked of industry, tanning, cooking and smoke. Juvenal provides an altogether different account of this side to Roman city life. This was turmoil where the rabble controlled the streets while road rage blustered and people were run over by traffic. At one moment he was knocked out of his way by a rich man in his litter, and then by a crowd of people running for a handout of food accompanied by individual cooks equipped to keep the goodies hot for their masters. At home, staff busy about their duties are unaware their master has been run over by a cart carrying marble and is even now trying to pay his way across the Styx to the Underworld.

How can you possibly sleep in lodging houses? Who but the rich get a night's sleep in Rome? That is the root of the chaos. Wagons crossing narrow streets, drivers swearing when they get stuck, would make sleep impossible for a Drusus or a seal-calf. When a rich man has a social engagement, the rabble gets out of his way as he is carried over their heads in a huge Liburnian litter. He can read, write or sleep as he goes along, because the litter's closed window encourages sleep.

However we hurry he will get to his destination first because we're blocked by the crowd in front and by a dense mass of people shoving us from behind. One bloke sticks his elbow into me and another a sedan-chair pole. My head is whacked by a wooden beam by one man, and by a wine barrel held by another. My legs are caked with mud. Soon huge feet trample me from every direction and a soldier plants his hobnailed boot firmly on my toes.

Now look at the cloud of smoke rising from rushing crowd as if they were on their way to a free handout. There are a hundred guests and each one has his own cook. The general Corbulo would hardly have been able to bear the weight of all the big pots and equipment which that tiny slave is carrying along with his head held high, fanning the fires as he scurries along.

Freshly-repaired clothes are ripped in two. Along comes a huge fir-tree log swinging about on a cart and then a second one bearing a complete pine-tree. Towering overhead, they threaten people. If that axle breaks under its load of Ligurian marble and tips a collapsed mountain on top of the rabble what's going to be left of their bodies? Who'll identify the limbs and the bones? Like his soul, a poor man's crushed body will just disappear.

Meanwhile back at home, entirely unawares, people are washing up, blowing the fire with puffed cheeks, clattering over greasy flesh-scrapers, replenishing oil jars and laying out towels. While each one is absorbed busily in his own job their master is already sitting on the riverbank, a new arrival, shuddering at the sight of the ferryman. He's got no money to pay his fare and thus no chance to cross the murky river, the poor wretch.

Now look at the danger night brings. Look how far down from that teetering roof a potsherd has to fall every time some broken or leaky jug is flung out of the window. Look how it smashes onto the pavement and makes a dent. Death waits in every open window you pass by at night. You could be thought a fool for not considering the prospect of a sudden accident, if you go out to dinner without making a will. You can only hope, and make a feeble prayer in your heart, that all they will do is pour the contents of their slop-pans over you!

The drunken bully who luckily failed to kill his enemy spends the night in agony, just like Achilles mourning the death of his friend, lying first on his face, then on his back. He'll get no rest any other way because some men can only drop off after a fight. But however reckless that fellow is, however buoyed along with wine and a young man's hot blood, he goes out of his way to avoid the one wearing a red cloak with a gaggle of attendants whose torches and bronze lanterns tell him to back off.

But for me, whose normal escort home is moonlight, or the weedy light of a candle I carefully nurture, the bully has no respect. Listen to how the fight starts — if you can call it a fight when he does all the hitting and I just get hit. The bloke blocks my way and tells me to stop. I have no choice but to obey. What else can you do when a lunatic, far stronger than you, attacks you? 'Where are you from?' he shouts, 'whose sour wine and beans have you been eating? Which shoe-mender have you been out with eating leeks and boiled sheep heads. What, squire, nothing to say? Answer me or I'll kick your shins. Tell me where you hang out. Where's your manor?'

Whether you try to say anything, or creep off silently, it makes no difference. He'll beat you up anyway, and then in his fury, mug you for cash. Such are the liberties he takes that he accuses you of pounding him into a pulp and begs to be allowed to get home in one piece!

That isn't all there is to be scared of. When your house is closed, and your shop locked up with bar and chain, and everything is quiet you'll be robbed by a burglar, or perhaps a street thug will wipe you out quickly with cold steel. Whenever the Pontine marshes and Gallinarian forests are patrolled by an armed guard, all these types flee to Rome for refuge. Our furnaces and anvils groan under the forging of fetters. That's what most of our iron is used for nowadays, and you'd be right to worry that soon there'll be none left for ploughshares, hoes or mattocks. You'd say the ancestors of our forefathers were happy, and happy the days of yore when the Kings and Tribunes saw a Rome where one jail was enough. Juvenal, *Satires*, III.232-314

An ordinary day in Rome
In this epigram, Martial describes a day in Rome starting with the morning visits by clients to their patrons. The Caesar described here is Domitian (81-96).

The first hour and the next wear out those engaged on formal morning greetings. The third occupies the strident advocates. Rome extends her various hardships until the end of the fifth, the sixth offers peace to the exhausted. The seventh will be the end. The eighth to the end of the ninth is enough for the wrestlers with their shiny skin. The ninth orders us to shatter the heaped-up couches. The tenth hour, Euphemus, is that of my writings, when you take the trouble to lay out the sacred feast and good Caesar is relaxed with heavenly nectar and holds his frugal drink with his great hand. Admit these jokes then! Our Thalia is frightened to step freely to go to a morning Jupiter.
Martial, *Epigrams*, IV.8

The mark of status
Vitruvius the architect here indicates how a townhouse should match the station of its owner. He starts by pointing out that the clients did not need high-status houses.

Men of everyday fortune do not need entrance courts, tablina or atriums built in grand style, because such men are more apt to discharge their social obligations by going round to others than to have others come to them. Those who do business in country produce must have stalls and shops in their entrance courts, with crypts and granaries, store-rooms, and so forth in their houses, constructed more for the purpose of keeping the produce in good condition than for ornamental beauty.

For capitalists and farmers of the revenue, comfortable and showy apartments must be constructed, secure against robbery. Advocates and public speakers need handsomer and more roomy apartment to accommodate meetings. This because men of rank who, by holding offices and magistracies, have social obligations to their fellow-citizens. Lofty entrance courts in regal style, and very spacious atriums and peristyles, with extensive plantations and walks are appropriate to their dignity. They also need libraries, picture galleries and basilicas, finished in a style similar to that of the great public buildings, since public councils as well as private law suits and hearings before arbitrators are very often held in the houses of such men.

Vitruvius, *On Architecture*, VI.5.2, trans. Morris Hickey Morgan

A special day in Rome: the Triumph

After the fall of Jerusalem in the year 70, there was a triumph through the streets of the Eternal City herself. Although this was a military procession, the display was a ritual consolidation of Rome's might, associated with the person of the new emperor and his dynasty. It helped establish Vespasian as undisputed master of the Roman world but it was important to achieve this in Rome where the mob could see and approve their new master. The procession is most noticeable for its brutal climax: the public execution of the Jewish leader and the celebration of his death.

Carrying on with his interrupted journey to Egypt, Titus took the quickest route across the desert, arriving at Alexandria. He had resolved to go to Rome by sea. As he was accompanied by two legions, he sent each of them back to where they had come from. The V legion he sent to Moesia, and the XV legion to Pannonia. He ordered that the leaders of the prisoners, Simon and John, along with seven hundred men, picked from the rest for their stature and looks, be sent to Italy without delay as he had decided to display them in his triumph.

The voyage to Italy went ahead as planned and Rome greeted him as warmly as it had Vespasian. For Titus, however, the occasion was all the more glorious because his father emerged to receive him, and the crowd's greatest joy was when they saw all three, Vespasian, Titus and Domitian, together. Only a few days had passed when they decided to have a single triumph in honour of their separate achievements, even though the Senate had voted them one each. The victory parade was publicized in advance. Not one person out of the city's vast population stayed indoors: everyone went out to find somewhere to watch from even though it was standing-room only, with just enough space left for the parade to pass along.

While it was still dark, the soldiers marched out in their centuries and cohorts under their various commanders and took up their positions near the temple of Isis, not by the gates of the upper palace, because that was where the victorious commanders had spent the night. As soon as the sun rose, Vespasian and Titus emerged, wearing the laurel crowns and the traditional ancient purple robes and went to the Portico of Octavia. It was there that the Senate, the senior magistrates and the equestrians were waiting for them. A tribunal with ivory chairs placed on it had been set up in front of the colonnades, where Vespasian and Titus, unarmed and wearing only silk clothes and wreathes of laurel, proceeded to sit. At that moment the soldiers gave a great acclamation, each and every one of them bearing witness to their valour. Vespasian accepted their acclamations and although they were far from finished, he gave them a signal for silence. Once everyone was quiet he stood up and, covering most of his head with his cloak, he offered the usual solemn prayers followed by Titus who did the same.

When the prayers were over, Vespasian made a short speech to everyone before sending all the soldiers off to the traditional meal which victorious generals put on. Then he withdrew through the Triumphal Gate where they had their first food of the day. Then they put on their triumphal costumes and offered sacrifices to the gods on either side of the gate. Then they returned to the triumphal procession to march through the theatres where they could be seen more easily by the crowd.

It would be impossible to provide descriptions of the various shows which did them justice, being magnificent in every imaginable way, either as artistic works, rarities of nature or in their range of riches. Just about every treasure, priceless wonders from many different countries, that has fallen into the lap of those favoured by fortune came together that day, thus displaying the vast territories of the Romans. There was a huge amount of silver, gold, and ivory fashioned into all sorts of shapes, which looked more like a river running past than a triumphal procession. Wall hangings were carried along, some in the rarest shades of purple, others embroidered with vividly realistic portraits executed by Babylonian artists. There were transparent precious stones, some set in gold crowns and others mounted differently, in such quantities that we realised how foolish we had been ever to think them rare!

The procession included images of the gods, remarkable for their largeness and their quality of style, each one made from costly materials. Many different types of animals were led along, each one adorned in the proper style. Every feature of the procession was accompanied by a large group of men wearing clothes coloured with the true purple dye, interwoven with gold. Those who had been picked to take part in the actual procession were decked out with the most magnificent and remarkable ornaments. As well as these, one could see that even most of the prisoners were decorated while the variety and quality of their costumes concealed any sight of physical deformity.

However, the most remarkable sight was the way in which the moving displays were constructed. Anyone seeing them could not help worrying that those carrying them would not be able to support them, so enormous were they. Many were built to a height of three or four storeys, while their decoration was the occasion of delighted amazement. On many of them there were gold carpets, and fittings made of wrought gold and ivory. A series of tableaux showed the stages of the war in a very realistic series of scenes. Here there was a peaceful countryside laid to waste, then units of the enemy killed, men fleeing and being taken into captivity. There were walls of great height and strength wrecked and thrown down with machines, the strongest defences overwhelmed, cities with battlements and strongly defended completely defeated. Then soldiers pouring through the fortifications, everywhere filled with killing, the enemy holding up their hands in defeat when they could resist no more, the burning of temples, and houses demolished with their occupants still inside. Then, with total desolation and misery everywhere, the rivers flowing through a land on fire instead of countryside and providing drink for men and beasts. These were the things the Jews themselves said they had undergone during this war. The art and skill of these magnificent representations provided those who had not seen them for themselves with a chance to see what those events had been like. Every stage had the commander of the each captured city placed on top, posed in the manner he had been when defeated. Ships followed behind. As for the other spoils of the war, they were there too in vast quantities.

But the greatest display was of the spoils seized in the temple of Jerusalem: a gold table weighing several hundred pounds, the candlestick also made of gold but of a different design to the one we use. The central shaft is attached to a base, with small branches running out of it to considerable length rather like a trident. Each one has a brass lamp at its end. There were seven of these, reflecting the importance of the number to the Jews. Last of all, came the book of Jewish Law. Following this there was a large group carrying images of Victory made either all out of gold or silver. Behind came Vespasian with Titus after him. Domitian rode alongside them, dressed magnificently, on a splendid horse.

This procession came to an end at the temple of Capitoline Jupiter. When they reached it they stood still because it is an ancient custom of the Romans to remain so until someone brings news that the enemy commander is dead. This commander was Simon, son of Gioras, who had marched in the parade. Now, with a rope around his neck, he was pulled along to the traditional spot in the Forum where his minders beat him up. Roman law requires that those condemned to death for their misdeeds be executed on this place. When his death was announced everyone let out a great acclamation, and they began offering the sacrifices they had consecrated. Once the usual prayers had been offered and favourable omens noted they returned to the palace. Some spectators were entertained at the imperial feast while for everyone else arrangements had been made for them to celebrate at home. This was a feast day for the city of Rome, commemorating the victory won by her army over the enemy, the end of civil discord and the dawn of a new hope for future prosperity and happiness.

Josephus, *The Jewish War*, VII.3ff

Losing the spirit of the Saturnalia

Whatever our feelings about how the true spirit of Christmas has been lost, the fact remains that the mid-winter celebration was a pagan festival with its origins lost in the remote past. It lasted for a whole week, beginning on 17 December, and marked the shortest days of the year in feasts, indulgences, over-eating and fun. Seneca, who might as well be moaning that Christmas seems to come earlier every year, was thoroughly fed up with how the whole month seemed to have been given over to the festival.

It's December but despite that all Rome is at fever-pitch! Unrestricted festive fun at the state's expense has been given free licence. The row of preparations on an enormous scale is reverberating everywhere. It all creates the impression that the Saturnalia holiday is different from the average working day. But there is now no difference at all, to the extent that the man who once said December used to be just a month but is now a year long was spot-on in my view.

Seneca, *Letters*, 18.1

BATHS

Romans and baths must be the most familiar of associations in our minds. Roman bathing establishments existed in all shapes and sizes and in all places. At the high end were the colossal public baths of Rome like the Baths of Caracalla and the Baths of

Diocletian (part of which is extant as a church). After them came a multitude of commercial bathing establishments dotted around towns of all types, while the wealthier townsfolk of course had their own bath suites.

At Pompeii, the forum baths sat close behind the temple of Jupiter at the north end of the forum while a larger establishment, the Stabian baths, were only a few metres away from the south-east corner of the forum. An inscription found outside one of the nearby gates testifies to another. Further baths existed elsewhere in the town. The reason for the large number was the important role that baths played in Roman urban social life. The closest modern equivalent is the sports club with facilities like a swimming pool, a gymnasium, restaurant and bar. Naturally, they were heavily dependent on slave labour to maintain the plumbing, stoke up the heat and provide massage and oiling services.

Building baths

Baths of course needed maintenance. What had once been provided by a wealthy man at his own expense might easily fall into disrepair. During the reign of Trajan, the city of Prusa found itself with a derelict public baths. They seem to have taken their problem to their governor, Pliny, with the suggestion that money connected with the olive-oil trade be used to help pay for it. It is not entirely clear whether this was money normally used to distribute olive-oil, or money earned from it. It is interesting that imperial permission was apparently required.

Pliny to Trajan

Sir, the citizens of Prusa have a bath, which is ruinous and ancient. And thus they highly esteem a new one built. As for me, you seem able to indulge their request. Of course, money will be available, from which it is to be built. First of these are the funds I have now begun to demand and recall from private citizens; next, they are willing to bequeath the olive-oil money to contribute to the bath project; a work which the splendour of your times and the city's dignity seem to require.

Trajan to Pliny

If the erecting of a public bath will not be too great a charge upon the people of Prusa, we are able to indulge their request; provided, however, that no new tax be levied for this purpose, nor any of those taken off which are needed for essential services.
Pliny the Younger, *Letters*, X.23-24

A city benefactor and servant

Pliny himself donated funds in his will to provide baths at his home town of Como, recorded on an inscription which survives in a fifteenth-century copy of what remained of the text. The text also lists his various other posts. Although they include military positions, a number were offices in Rome concerned with the maintenance and administration of the city. Pliny thus provides a mirror for thousands of other men whose lives were spent in public service, and on whom the machinery of the Roman urban system depended.

Gaius Plinius Secundus, son of Lucius, of the Oufentina tribe, and who was [consul], augur, propraetorian legate with consular power for the province of Pontus [and Bithynia, having been sent there in accordance with the senatorial decree] by the Emperor Trajan who himself was victor over Germany [and Dacia and also father of his country], curator of the bottom and banks of the Tiber [and sewers of Rome], prefect of the treasury of Saturn, prefect of the military treasury, [people's tribune], imperial quaestor, commissioner for Roman equestrians, military tribune of the III legion Gallica, [magistrate on the board of ten], left according to his will public baths which cost [. . .], and an extra 300,000 sesterces to fit them out, with a further 200,000 sesterces put out to interest for their maintenance . . . He also willed 1,866,666 and 2/3 sesterces to support 100 of his freedmen and afterwards an annual dinner for the townsfolk . . . Similarly, when he was alive, he provided half a million sesterces to care for the boys and girls of the city, and 10,000 to maintain the library . . .
CIL.v.5262, ILS 2927, early second century

Bathing at Pompeii

It is easy to forget that the ruins of Pompeii, a city stopped in time in August 79, contain all the usual evidence for a settlement in a state of perpetual renewal and change, and with a mixture of buildings and establishments which were new and old.

The Baths of Marcus Crassus Frugi. Sea water and sweet [fresh] water bathing. Januarius, freedman.
Inscription from Pompeii, reused in a shrine. CIL x.1063, ILS 5724, undated, but perhaps late first century BC.

The chief magistrates, Caius Uuilius, son of Caius, and Publius Aninius, son of Caius, put out to tender the building of a sweat room and a scraping room, and the rebuilding of the porticoes and exercise yard, according to the decurions' decree, from the money they were required by law to spend on games or public buildings. They were in charge of the work and they approved it.
Inscription from the Stabian baths at Pompeii. ILS 5706, about 70BC.

Inconsiderate bathers

Baths also provided sources of irritation to people attempting to work nearby, unless they had become immune to the row. This extremely well-known passage tells us how Seneca dealt with the problem.

My dear Lucilius,
Peace and quiet is not quite as essential to study, if that's what you want to do, as you might think. I am surrounded here by every type of racket (my apartment overlooks the baths). Just imagine all those sounds that make you loath being able to hear. I hear the groans as the he-men pump iron and throw those heavy weights all over the place. Either they are really putting their backs into it, or just shamming. If for instance there's a lazy chap who's satisfied with a straightforward massage I can hear the slap of a hand on his shoulder (you

can tell the difference between a flat slap and a hollow one). If a ball player comes up and starts yelling out his score — then that's me finished. Pile on top of that the row of some cheeky so-and-so, a thief being caught, and one of those blokes who likes singing in the bath, as well as those who dive into the pool with giant splashes of water. That's as well as those with the loud voices. Think about the skinny plucker of arm-pit hair whose yells are so resonant that everyone notices him except when he's getting on with his work and making someone else yell for him. Now add on the medley of noise from drink sellers, sausage, pastry and hot-food vendors, each hawking his goods with his own individual cry.

You might say that I must be made from iron, or deaf, if my concentration isn't disturbed by that racket of discordant row all around, considering that non-stop morning greetings were sufficient to do for that Stoic, Chrysippus. Nevertheless, I say with certainty that this barrage of noise has no more effect on me than the sound of the sea or running water…
Seneca, *Letters*, 56.1-2

THEATRES AND CIRCUSES

Imperial entertainments

An important way in which the emperor ritually consolidated his popularity with the Roman mob was to put on elaborate shows in the amphitheatre and circus. The importance of these events in Roman life is underlined by their frequent portrayal on daily objects like pottery and mosaics, while the ruins of Pompeii have yielded dozens of graffiti referring to them. Events in the arena were the ultimate in Roman mass entertainment. To put on lavish shows was prestigious. To experience them was to participate in excitement, and to flirt with loyalties and rivalries. The crowd loved to indulge in them, and the emperors were happy, or obliged, to indulge the crowd. But they were essentially urban activities, as the vast arenas at Rome itself, El Djem in Tunisia or Arles in Gaul testify. These were where spectacles could be organized and a vast crowd was part of that, though naturally of course we cannot really tell if these vast stadiums were routinely filled to capacity. Like some modern experiments in mass entertainment, provision may have outreached demand. To some extent there was a kind of ritual in human sacrifice. That slaves and prisoners-of-war were put to death in this way was a consummate expression of absolute power and cultural supremacy. The death of exotic animals was another perspective on the extent of Roman rule: however bizarre or exotic a beast, it could be brought to Rome and done to death.

The shows were certainly popular. With each emperor determined to outdo his predecessors, the shows became progressively more and more indulgent, with thousands of wild animals and captives being put to death in public. It seems impossible to believe that even excitement at the thought of a chase could survive such grotesque overkill (for want of a better phrase). Apparently not, though some Romans thought that the situation had become ludicrous, even in the first century BC, long before the coming of the Colosseum. It is interesting to see how little sense of sympathy there was for the victims, even amongst the critics. Their perception of the problem seems to have been how it affected the spectators and their boredom. This led to more and more turgid excesses while the crowd became more and more languid.

But what possible pleasure can there be for a cultivated man when either a feeble human body is torn to pieces by a powerful wild animal, or a magnificent beast is run through with a hunting spear? And even if all of that was a sight worth beholding, you have seen them many times. For me, as a member of the audience, there was no novelty. On the last day were the elephants, and on that occasion the rabble and people were very impressed, but they showed no joy. In fact, it seems to have produced a sense of compassion and a sensation that the huge animal has a special relationship with man.
Cicero, *Letters*,7.1

Violence forsakes skill

A century later, Seneca had done his best to enjoy a gladiatorial show but was appalled at how the redeeming factors of skill and judgement, as he perceived them, had been replaced with gratuitous violence (even by Roman standards). We might be appalled but there is always an uncomfortable feeling that were such shows put on today they would still pull a certain sort of crowd.

I happened to stop off at a lunchtime show, hoping to enjoy myself with some wit and relaxation, where a man's eyes can rest at the sight of the death of their fellow men. It was just the opposite. The fights that used to take place were merciful by comparison. Now any mucking about is set aside and this is just plain murder. The fighters wear no armour, and their entire bodies are exposed to blows — and none of these are wasted. Many in the crowd prefer this to ordinary matched pairs and even to those laid by special demand. Why not? There aren't any helmets or shields to fend off the weapons. What's the point of armour or skills? Such things just hold up the dying.

In the morning men are hurled to lions and bears. At midday the men are thrown to the crowd. The latter demand for the killed to be thrown to those who will kill him in turn, and they hold back the winner for another butchering. The outcome for those who fight is death. The fighting is conducted with fire and sword. The following goes on during a gap in the arena proceedings: 'but one was a highwayman and he murdered someone.' So what? He deserves to suffer this way because he killed somebody but what you have done to deserve the right to watch it? 'Kill him, lash him, burn him. Why is he running at the other's weapons like a coward? Why isn't he keener on killing? Why isn't he keener on dying? Beat him forward to score his wounds. Make them offer each a bare chest and trade blows on them.'

When there's an interval in the proceedings, 'let's have some killing in the meantime, just to make sure something's going on!'
Seneca, *Letters*, 7.3-5

Nero livens up proceedings
Seneca was Nero's tutor. His pupil found new ways to liven up public entertainments.

Nero put on many shows of different types: the *Juvenales*, chariot races at the circus, theatrical performances and a gladiator display. At the first of these he even had old senators, and ancient matrons, participate. For the circus games he set apart the equestrians from everyone else, and even set chariots pulled by four camels against one another. At the theatrical performances he laid on for imperial eternity (which he ordered to be called the *Ludi Maximi*), parts were taken by men and women chosen from the senatorial and equestrian classes. One well-known equestrian, riding an elephant, rode down a tightrope. A Latin play called *The Fire*, by Afranius, was put on in which the actors were permitted to cart off furniture from the burning house and keep it. All sorts of gifts were thrown to the people every day. Amongst these were a thousand birds daily of all varieties, various foodstuffs, chits for grain, clothing, gold, silver, gemstones, pack animals, and even trained wild beasts. Finally, there were even ships, town blocks, and farms.

These performances Nero watched from the top of the stage. At the gladiator show, which he threw in a wooden amphitheatre built in the Mars Field district in less than a year, he had no-one killed including criminals. But he did force 400 senators and 600 equestrians, some of who were affluent and of excellent repute, to compete in the arena. Even those who battled with wild animals and carried out the various service duties were senators and equestrians.
Suetonius, *Nero*, 11-12

Nero's Golden House gives way to the Colosseum
The fall of Nero and the coming of the Flavians spelled the end of the days of the temporary wooden amphitheatres. Under Vespasian, most of Nero's notorious Golden House was demolished and a colossal permanent stone amphitheatre erected in its place as a pointed populist gesture of defiance towards the excesses of the Julio-Claudians. Called the Colosseum after the vast statue of Nero that stood on the site (later adapted into a statue of the Sun) it was dedicated by Titus and is of course still extant. Suetonius and Dio recorded the opening of the new amphitheatre, and Martial recounted what the site had once been, a house almost as big as Rome itself.

Titus outdid all his predecessors in munificence. At the dedication of the Amphitheatre, and the baths which had been swiftly knocked up next door, he threw the most splendid and expensive gladiatorial display. He put on a fake sea battle in the old naval showground where he also put on a gladiatorial display, showing 5000 wild animals of all types on just one day.
Suetonius, *Titus*, 7

Titus also provided things that would be of practical use to the people. From up high he would hurl down small wooden balls which had various inscriptions on them. One would state a type of food, another clothing, another a silver or even a gold vessel, horses, pack-animals, cattle, slaves and so on. The people who caught them were supposed to take them to the gift distributors, from whom they received whatever had been named.

Once he had finished all these shows, and cried bitterly on the final day so that the crowd were able to see him, he did nothing else that was of any consequence.
Dio Cassius, *Roman History*, LXVI.25.5, 26.1

Here, where the radiant Colossus sees the heavens from closer, and in the middle of the road towering scaffolds rise, the hateful halls of a vicious ruler shone; indeed, one house only stood in the whole of Rome. Here where the mass of the conspicuous and honourable Amphitheatre is erected, the stagnant pools of Nero were. Here where we wonder at the baths [of Titus], a very swiftly-built gift, a tyrannical domain stole homes from the poor. The most distant part of the palace came to an end where the Claudian colonnade stretches out its widespread shade. Rome is restored to her old self, and all which is the delight of the people under your rule, Caesar, was once that of a single lord.
Martial, *On the Spectacles*, 2, published in the year 80 to coincide with the opening of the
   Colosseum

The wonder of the amphitheatre
In this epigram, Martial describes how a late arrival at the amphitheatre might be bewildered at the sight of a naval battle in the arena, and not realise that what was underwater had a moment ago been dry land and would be again just as quickly.

Whoever you are, latecomer from faraway shores seeing this view of the sacred show for the first time, so that this naval battle with its ships and the waves for seas doesn't deceive you: just a moment ago dry land was here. You don't believe me? Watch, while the seas exhaust Mars. In a short space of time, you will be saying, 'just a moment ago, the sea was here!'
Martial, *On the Spectacles*, 24

Pompeii riot
Oddly, some provincial towns had been equipped with masonry amphitheatres at earlier dates than Rome. Pompeii was one such place. In the year 59 a riot exploded at the amphitheatre when rival supporters from Pompeii and a neighbouring town called Nuceria gathered. Anyone who believes that modern soccer violence is entirely attributable to the tabloid press and the decadence of our age needs to think again.

A trivial beginning led to frightful bloodshed between the inhabitants of Nuceria and Pompeii, at a gladiatorial show put on by Livineius Regulus, who had been expelled from the Senate as has been noted [this earlier reference is lost]. With the customary unruly spirit of people from country towns, they started off by hurling abuse at one another. Then they moved on to stones and finally weapons, the advantage resting with the Pompeii crowd, where the show was taking place. The outcome was that a number of maimed and wounded Nucerians were brought to Rome, while others lamented the deaths of children or of parents. The emperor entrusted the judicial hearing on the matter to the Senate, and the Senate passed it to the consuls. When the case appeared again before the Senate, the inhabitants of Pompeii were forbidden from having any more such public gatherings for ten years, and all their illegal associations were dissolved. Livineius and the others, who had set the riot off, were punished with exile.

Tacitus, *Annals*, XIV.17

Supporters

The Pompeii riot resulted from the kind of aggression we see in our own time at other sporting events though, happily, deaths are rare. Team, or clan, rivalry was particularly important in Roman sport and entertainment. But not all Romans were captivated by such loyalties. Pliny the Younger thought it an infantile way to behave, but found peace and quiet in a city deserted by the rabble which had disappeared off to the circus. Those who go shopping on Cup Final day often find exactly the same convivial solitude.

To Calvisius Rufus

All this time I have spent amongst my notes and papers in delightful peace. 'How on earth', you ask, 'is that possible in Rome?' Well, these are the days of the races, a form of spectacle which has never done anything for me. Nothing new and never different, once is enough. So, I am all the more astonished that so many grown men, just like kids, have a mania for watching galloping horses and charioteers time after time.

However, if the speed of the horses or the skill of the men attracted them, it would not be irrational. Now they support and love a team strip for its own sake, and if the colour was changed in the middle of a race, they would change their enthusiasm and support and suddenly relinquish their drivers and horses, whom they recognise from far off and shout their names. Such popularity and importance in one worthless garment; and here I'm not considering the rabble, because the garment is more valuable, but certain serious men. When I consider them, sitting down frozen solid by this futile activity, so wanting of fulfilment, I take pleasure in the fact that their pleasure is not mine. And during the days in which I happily organised my work amongst my books, they lost through the most idle of activities. Farewell

Pliny the Younger, *Letters*, IX.6

Here a fanatical supporter of circus teams seeks assistance from a malevolent deity in North Africa.

I swear to you, demon, whoever you are, and I ask you from this hour, from this day, from this moment, that you persecute and kill the horses of the Greens and Whites, and that you kill the drivers Clarus, Felix, Primulus, and Romanus, and squash all the breath out of them. I swear to you through he who releases for the opportunity the god of the sea and the skies... [there follows a reference to the night, the Ocean and the Tiber].

ILS 8753, from North Africa

A personal appearance by the emperor

To add to his catalogue of personal excesses and decadence, Commodus (180-92) was obsessed with his prowess in the amphitheatre and his skills with weapons. He presented the Roman public with an unprecedented opportunity, one which they were reluctant to miss. Not surprisingly, Commodus had pushed his luck, and he was murdered on the last day of the year 192.

Casting aside all inhibitions, now Commodus ordered that public spectacles be celebrated, promising that at them he would kill all the wild beasts with his own hands and take on the strongest young men in gladiatorial bouts. From all over Italy and adjacent provinces people gathered in Rome, as word spread, in order to see something they had never watched or heard of before. The main talking point was Commodus' marksmanship and how he made sure he never missed with either spear or bow. Although he was taught by the best Parthian archers and Mauretanian spearsmen, he was more skilled than the whole lot.

Finally the day of the show dawned, and the amphitheatre was crowded out. In order that Commodus could spear the beasts in safety from above and not risk any personal injury from being too close, a special raised area was built for him, thereby showing off his skill but not his bravery. He brought down deer, gazelles, and other such beasts (except bulls) by chasing them as they fled and, with a well-timed shot at the moment they bolted, he stopped them dead where they were. He speared lions, leopards and other big cats from above by racing round the pen. The shot was always fatal and no one ever saw him take a second one. He caught the animal with a strike through its head or heart as it bolted. That was all he aimed for, with his spear only hitting an area on the animal's body that would wound and kill it outright.

Types of wild animals, which we had only admired in pictures before and now saw for the first time, were transported in from all over the world for Commodus to kill. They came from India and Ethiopia, from the north and the south. The whole lot, and any formerly unknown, were placed on show in Rome for the people to see while Commodus slaughtered them.

It was generally accepted that Commodus' marksmanship was remarkable. One time, for example, he used arrows fitted with crescent-shaped heads to shoot at ostriches from Mauretania (birds which are capable of incredible speed because they run so fast and fold back their wings). Commodus lopped their heads off at the tops of their necks with his arrows so that they continued racing about as if they were unharmed, even when the arrow, slicing past, had cut off their heads. On one occasion, when a leopard had bolted out and attacked a victim ordered into the arena, Commodus speared it with a javelin the moment before it savaged the man. The leopard died, the man was saved: Commodus had stopped the edge of the leopard's teeth with the edge of his spear. One other time a hundred lions were set loose from the underground cages and Commodus wiped the lot out with exactly a hundred spears. The carcases were laid out in a long line, where they had fallen, so that everyone could count them at ease and observe that not one extra spear had been used.

For the moment, Commodus remained fairly popular with the rabble despite the fact that his behaviour, courage and marksmanship aside, was inappropriate for an emperor.

But when he raced into the arena in his bare skin, wielding his weapons for a gladiatorial bout, the crowd were ashamed at the sight of a Roman emperor of noble descent (whose father and ancestors had celebrated great victories) now bringing disgrace on his position with a comprehensively degrading display instead of taking up arms against barbarians and justifying himself to the Empire.

It was easy for him to defeat his opponents in gladiatorial bouts, just by wounding them, because they regarded him as emperor instead of a gladiator, and allowed him to win. But he became so deranged that he refused to remain in the palace any more and intended to move out and live in the gladiatorial barracks.

Herodian, *History of the Empire*, I.15.1-8

Benefits of circus casualties

Celsus wrote an extensive encyclopaedia at the beginning of the first century AD. Only the sections on medicine survive. Much of its content is remarkably accurate and valuable but he was pragmatic and brutal about the disadvantages of having to rely on dissecting corpses to find out how the human body worked. Even when beginning on a man who was still alive meant killing him before accurate observations could be achieved.

Only when a man dies are his chest or insides opened to the view of the killer doctor and these are therefore those of a dead, not a living, man. So consequently the doctor is just acting as a murderer and learns nothing about our insides as they function when we are living. But if anything can be seen while he is still breathing, a lucky break can mean those treating him get to observe it. Occasionally, a gladiator in the arena, a soldier in battle, or a traveller attacked by highwaymen, is wounded so that some part of his insides is exposed …

Nor, as some say, is it cruel that by executing criminals, and then only concerning a few, we ought to find cures for innocent people for all time.

Celsus, *On Medicine, Prooemium*, 43, 26

Chariot race

This passage provides a graphic description of a chariot race. Written by Sidonius in the middle of the fifth century, it shows that the popularity of the races which Pliny the Younger so despised had scarcely diminished in more than 300 years.

The various badges, white, blue, green, and red, all shine brightly. The hands of attendants hold the horses' heads and bridles and, using knotted ropes, force the manes into hiding. All the time they work up the horses, enthusiastically cheering them on with encouraging pats and cranking them up to a blissful madness. There, in the pens, those beasts chafe themselves by rubbing up against the restraints while a blast of vapour belches out from between the posts. Before the race has even started the field they have yet to enter is filled with their pants. They push, pull, hang back, resist, fury, leap, grow terrified and terrify others. Their feet are constantly in motion and without cessation they batter against the hardened wood.

At last the bugler with a loud blast calls the impatient teams out and sends the chariots off onto the track. Bolts of lightning, Scythian arrows, shooting stars, the gale of lead bullets from Balearic slings: none of these have ripped the air apart as quickly. The earth subsides beneath the wheels and the air is fouled by the earth thrown up behind. While they hold the reins the charioteers also use the whip. Now they lean forward prone over the chariots, charging along, to hit the horses' shoulders but leave their backs unscathed. With the charioteers lying down so you'd find it hard to say whether they were supported by the pole, or by the wheels!

Just like something soaring out of sight into the sky, you've now passed the open section of track to be hemmed in by the stretch packed with vehicles, into the middle of which the long central barrier protrudes with its low walls. Once the furthest turning post has released you, your partner overtook the other pair who had overtaken you. That meant that, according to the circuit regulations you had to take the fourth, outer, path. The pair now in the middle tracks were placing all their hopes on the first man being compromised by his horses heading for the seating area by moving too suddenly to the right. That would leave room on his left where he could be overtaken by a chariot on the near side.

All this time you're bent over with the sheer force of keeping a tight hold on your team's reins and using your exceptional skill to save them (wisely) for the seventh lap. The other drivers are busy holding on and yelling. Sweat pours off the charioteers and the speeding horses all over the track. Spirits are stoked up by the raucous cheering from opposing supporters. Competitors, men and horses alike, are warmed by the race and frozen with fear.

This is how they make the first circuit, the second, the third, and the fourth. But on the fifth the man out front couldn't take the pressure from those just behind him any more. He swerved his chariot to one side and as he conceded first place he discovered that his team was worn out. By now the second half of the sixth circuit was over and the crowd were shrieking out for the prizes to be awarded. Your rivals were carelessly tearing up the track in front of you, believing there wasn't any threat from you. Suddenly, you tightened up the horse harnesses, tensed your chest, got your feet firmly into position in front, and pulled back on the horses' mouths just as fiercely as that ancient charioteer who pulled Oenomaus along with him to make Pisa shudder with fear.

At this moment you harassed the first of your opponents while he tucked into the turning post taking the shortest route. He could no longer keep his horses in order on the right track as they lost control in their plunge forwards. You overtook him just by holding position and smartly reining back as he passed you out of control. Your other opponent was enjoying the cheers from the crowd and moved over too far to the right near to the spectators. After taking no notice for far too long he turned back, whipping his horses on, as you undertook him. Then without taking any care he overtook you again and, believing his colleague was already in front, shamelessly flung himself sideways making for your wheel. His four horses fell down, and all their legs became tangled up in the wheels. The twelve spokes were in total confusion until there was a cracking noise from the mess and the turning rim of the wheel smashed the tangled hooves. Then the driver, the fifth victim, was thrown out of his chariot. It fell on top of him resulting in a pile of destruction and his brow was soiled with blood as he lay.

At that moment the shouting started up again in a riot of noise not matched by Lycaeus with its cypress trees or the forests of Ossa, however much countless hurricanes assault them. This was a resonant roar that not even the sea of Sicily, whipped up by the south wind, can produce, nor even the Dardanelles whose deeps are a barrier to the Bosphorus. Then the just emperor ordered that the palms receive the addition of silk ribbons, and the gold necklaces crowns. The defeated in their shame were awarded rugs of multi-coloured hair on his orders.

Sidonius, *Poems*, XXIII *To Consentius,*323-427

Building a theatre

The Roman theatre had its origins in the Greek theatre, but was an altogether more elaborate structure. Conventionally a semi-circular auditorium, the Roman theatre audience faced a large stage with an elaborate architectural back screen consisting of multiple tiers of columns and arches. Few survive in this form, but the theatre at Aspendus in Turkey is an excellent example of the type. Not surprisingly, building a theatre was a complicated business as the inhabitants of Nicaea in Bithynia discovered to their governor's disquiet.

Pliny to Trajan

Sir, The citizens of Nicaea are building a theatre, which, though it is not yet finished, has already exhausted, as I am told (because I have not examined the accounts in person), more than ten million sesterces. What makes this even worse is that I fear it has been wasted. Either thanks to the foundation being laid in soft, marshy ground, or the light and friable stone, the walls are subsiding, and are cracked from top to bottom.

So, it deserves your consideration whether the best plan is to carry on the work, or stop it completely, or rather, perhaps, whether the wisest plan would be to demolish it completely because the foundations and buttresses intended to hold it up look more expensive than solid to me. A number of private citizens have agreed to build theatre facilities out of their own pockets, some promising to build the portico, others a gallery around the auditorium. But, these plans cannot be put into operation, as the main building, which needs finishing first, is now at a standstill.

The Nicaeans are also rebuilding their gymnasium (which was burned down before I arrived in the province) on a much larger scale. They have already gone to considerable expense and I fear it may have been to no purpose. The building is irregular and badly proportioned, and the current architect, admittedly a rival of the one who was on the project at the beginning, says that the 22-feet thick walls are not strong enough to hold up the superstructure. This is because the core is filled with rubble, and the walls have no brick facing.

The people of Claudiopolis are also digging out, rather than building, a vast public bath in a hollow at the foot of a mountain. The funds appropriated to pay for this project come from the cash which those honorary members you were pleased to add to the senate paid (or will pay, when I ask them to) for their admission.

Therefore I am concerned public money in Nicaea and your generosity to Claudiopolis (infinitely more valuable than mere money) will be abused. I must ask you to dispatch an architect out here to look at both the theatre and the bath. This is so that he can consider, in view of the money already spent, whether it would be better to finish them off as they are, or redesign one and abandon the other, depending on what seems necessary. If not, we may pour more money down the drain trying to make good what has already been paid out.

Trajan to Pliny

What ought to be done about the theatre, which has been begun at Nicaea, you will best determine and decide in person on the spot. It is enough for me to be informed, which conclusions you come to. With reference to the specific components of the theatre which are to be built at private expense, you will see those promises fulfilled when the main body of the building of which they are to be part, is finished.

Those wretched Greeks love a gymnasium; perhaps they were too ambitious in their scheme at Nicaea. They will have to make do with one able to fulfil their needs. I will leave it entirely up to you to advise the people of Claudiopolis about their baths, which it seems they have placed in a very inappropriate location. There is no province without men of skill and ingenuity so you cannot possibly need an architect unless you think the quickest way is to find them in Rome, when normally they come here from Greece.
Pliny the Younger, *Letters* X.39-40

A dedication of a new theatre stage in far-off Britain

Very few inscriptions survive in Britain which record public buildings. This is in spite of the fact that most Roman towns in this distant island are known to have had Roman public buildings of sorts. Either the inscriptions have not survived or, as seems more likely given the dominance of military and religious inscriptions, they were not so frequently displayed as elsewhere in the Empire. Nonetheless, at *Petuaria*, probably in or near a town now known as Brough a local aedile paid for a new stage for the theatre and proudly announced his munificence to the townsfolk.

In honour of the divine house of the Emperor Caesar Titus Aelius Hadrianus Antoninus Augustus Pius, father of the nation, consul for the third time, and to the spirits of the emperors, Marcus Ulpius Januarius, aedile of the settlement at *Petuaria*, presented a stage … at his own expense.
RIB 707, from Brough-on-Humber

AQUEDUCTS

From the beginning of the imperial period aqueducts were important components in prestigious public building projects. Augustus and Agrippa built several in Rome, and Claudius built one and completed another, which had been begun by Caligula but left unfinished. These channels brought the water from higher sources making use of natural contours, and artificially elevated courses, to bring it down into the city.

Other cities around the Empire followed suit but this was not always straightforward. Nonius Datus was a surveyor, retired, who had served with the III legion *Augusta* in North Africa. In the mid-second century he was asked by the procurator via the legion's commander to come and help sort out a problem with a water tunnel being cut through a mountain to carry water to the city of Saldae in Mauretania Caesariensis on what is now the Algerian coast. Not only does the story show what could be attempted in the Roman world, but also the dependence by civil authorities on the expertise afforded by the army. It is also a rare personal account by the kind of person usually ignored by Roman historians.

I set out and en route I was attacked by highwaymen. I was stripped bare and wounded. I escaped with my companions and came to Saldae. I met the procurator Clemens who led me to the mountain where they were in despair over a tunnel of suspect workmanship. They thought it would have to be abandoned because the tunnel digging had penetrated deeper than the mountain was wide.

It was obvious that the digging had veered off course, to the extent that the upper tunnel had gone to the right (that is, south), while the lower tunnel had gone to the left (that is, north). Consequently the two ends were out of alignment and were adrift. The upper tunnel is the part which admits the water, the lower is the part which discharges it. I organized a work contest between the fleet troops and auxiliaries when I was allocating the work so that they would know who was doing what. In this way they joined up at the point where the mountain was cut through ….

ILS 5795, said to be c. 153 (excerpt only)

Hot water

Aqueducts are almost synonymous with our concept of Roman urban life, together with roads and sewage. Enormous arched structures straddled the landscape, suspending a covered channel many metres above miles of farmland, and then over houses and streets within the city. Unfortunately, it seems that a lot of water never reached the city. Investigating this, Sextus Julius Frontinus, appointed to control the aqueducts of the city in the year 97, found that people were helping themselves. Many had even permanently plumbed themselves into the system. Frontinus recorded this in his treatise on aqueducts which otherwise provides largely dry technical information.

I have no doubt that many people will be astonished that, based on our measurements, the quantity of water turned out to be much greater than imperial archives record. This can be explained by the mistakes made by those who incompetently calculated each of these aqueducts in the beginning. But I cannot believe that it was a fear of summer droughts that caused them to be so far off the mark, because I made my own measurements in July and found that the over-measurement was consistent in every aqueduct for the rest of the summer. Whatever the reason is, we have discovered that 5000 *quinariae* [a unit based on pipe diameter] were lost, while the quantities awarded by the emperor are limited to the quantities recorded.

Here is another inconsistency in this form: one measure is taken at the source, another (much smaller) at the reservoir, and a third (the smallest) where it is distributed. The dishonesty of the water-men is responsible for this, they who have been found siphoning water from the public supply for personal use. But many landowners, alongside whose fields the aqueducts run, take a feed from the supplies, which is how private citizens watering their gardens cause the aqueducts to run dry.

On this type of crime, Caelius Rufus [d. 48BC] said all that needed to be said in his speech called 'Concerning Water'. If only we were not suffering every day, through law-breaking, these crimes which are committed just as blatantly now as they were then. We've located irrigated fields, shops, even upstairs flats, and finally brothels, equipped with fittings to guarantee a constant supply of running water ....

Damage frequently occurs thanks to the law-breaking of squatters who damage the channels in various ways. To begin with they fill the space around aqueducts with buildings and trees which, under an edict of the Senate, should remain open. Trees cause the most damage because their roots break through the top as well as the sides. In addition they lay village and country roads over the aqueducts themselves. Then they prevent anyone coming to make repairs from getting near the aqueducts.

Frontinus, *The Aqueducts of Rome*, II.75-6

Abandoned aqueducts

Like most public building projects, the provision of aqueducts was regarded as important and prestigious. Presented with the impressive remains of aqueducts it is easy to overlook the problems that were involved in getting them built at all. Appalling amounts of wasted money were discovered by Pliny at Nicomedia while investigating the abandoned aqueduct projects.

Pliny to Trajan

On an aqueduct, Lord, the Nicomedians had spent 3,318,000 sesterces which was given up while incomplete, and then demolished. Then they paid out 200,000 sesterces on another. This also has been abandoned so that, having spent so much money on nothing, they must incur further expense in order to have a water-supply.

I myself have visited the pure spring from which it seems water could be brought on an aqueduct (as the original plan was) if it is not to come only to the lower and level parts of the city. There remain only a very few arches, but the squared-off blocks from the earlier project could be used in the new arches. It seems to me that part of it should be built with brick because it is cheaper and easier.

But first it is essential that an architect or someone else qualified to build this sort of water-supply is sent by you so that it does not suffer the kind of setback which happened before. I will add just this, that the usefulness and beauty of the work will be worthy of your times.

Pliny the Younger, *Letters*, X.37

Trajan to Pliny

Attention must be given to supplying the Nicomedians with water. I truly believe you will apply yourself to this matter in the appropriate manner. But by heaven at the same time the affair needs your diligence to find out whose fault it is that the Nicomedians have spent so much money up to now. There may be those who have lined their nests by

starting the aqueduct and abandoning it. You will tell me what you find out.
Pliny the Younger, *Letters*, X.38

CITY MAINTENANCE AND ADORNMENT

Maintaining Rome and other cities

Rome of course was in a perpetual state of flux. What stands today is all that remains of a continuous cycle of new buildings, repairs, demolitions and replacements. By the reign of Hadrian (117-38) many early imperial public structures needed renovation or rebuilding. As an architect, Hadrian was particularly interested in the opportunity this provided. He built extensively in Rome and elsewhere throughout the Empire. Some of the resulting structures were amongst the most prominent buildings of the ancient world. The most remarkable is the Pantheon, a vast domed rotunda, which is extant in Rome to this day. Following his own general policy, Hadrian restored the structure's original dedication (in this case by Agrippa). He also restored and adapted the colossus of Nero.

Hadrian erected some sort of building and put on public games in almost every city …. In Rome, he restored the Pantheon, the voting enclosure, the Basilica of Neptune, a multiplicity of sacred buildings, the Forum of Augustus, the Bath of Agrippa. All these he dedicated in the names of their original builders. He also built the bridge bearing his name, a tomb on the Tiber's banks, and the temple of the Bona Dea. He raised the Colossus, using the architect Decrianus, and while keeping it upright had it moved from where the Temple of Rome is now even though it was so heavy he had to provide as many as 24 elephants. And after he had had Nero's features erased (it had been previously dedicated to him), Hadrian consecrated the statue to the Sun …

Although he had no interest in inscriptions being placed on his public works, he named many cities Hadrianopolis, for example Carthage and part of Athens. He also called by this name an infinite number of aqueducts.
Aelius Spartianus, *Hadrian*, XIX.2, 9-13

Civic munificence and statues

Providing representations of the Emperor and his family was very important in a world of vast dimensions but with no universal media apart from language and coins. Cities were adorned with monumental inscriptions and statues of local worthies and benefactors. These decorated public places like the basilica and forum, porticoes, baths, and temples. Very few survive in their original places if they survive at all. The basilica at Herculaneum, buried by boiling mud from Vesuvius in 79, was adorned with statues of Marcus Nonius Balbus and members of his family. An inscription recorded his civic munificence.

Marcus Nonius Balbus, son of Marcus, proconsul, built the walls and gates of the basilica with his own money.
ILS 5527 (Herculaneum)

However, the most prominent records and images commemorated the imperial house. Titus' popularity before he became emperor in 79 seems to have stood him in good stead.

A military tribune in Britain and Germany, he earned great fame for his industry and no less for his modesty, as is evident from the great multitude of statues and busts of him as well as inscriptions in both provinces.
Suetonius, *Titus*, 4.1

On the death of Aelius in 138, his nominated successor, Hadrian made provision that the former be remembered before his own death later that year.

Indeed Hadrian ordered colossal statues of Aelius Verus built throughout the world, and also temples to be built in some cities.
Aelius Spartianus, *Aelius*, VII.1

Crooked landlords

These days, building legislation is supposed to guarantee against bad practices. Of course, it doesn't entirely succeed though things have improved. Rome had unending problems with tenements built too high, fires, collapses and dishonest landlords. The same problems were found elsewhere.

Most of Rome is propped up with planks to stop it falling down. The landlord stands in front of his crumbling establishment and announces, 'sleep well', even though he knows perfectly well it may not survive the night. I have to live where there are no fires or night alarms. Ucalegon in the apartment below is already screaming for water and carrying out his valuables but while smoke is already belching through your garret, you have no idea what is going on. If the alarm is raised on the ground floor, the last man to burn will be the man with nothing between him and the rain except for the tiles ....
Juvenal, *Satires*, III.193-202

Fire!

Out in Nicomedia a real fire took place causing havoc which was made far worse by the lack of a fire brigade, and the indifference of the population.

Pliny to Trajan

While I was engaged on my official business journey through a different part of this province, a huge fire broke out in Nicomedia. It consumed a number of private homes and also two public buildings: a hostel for senior citizens and a temple of Isis, despite the fact that they stood on opposite sides of the street. The reason it spread so far was partly thanks to the violent wind, and partly due to the laziness of the population who (I am told with certainty) stood stock-still watching this calamity. In any case, the city did not have a single fire appliance, bucket or one single tool for putting fires out. However, these will be prepared, according to the orders I have already issued.

Please decide, sir, if you think it would be appropriate to institute a guild of firemen, not more than 150-strong. I will ensure that only those who are right for the job will be admitted and also that privileges given them will not be put to any other use. As so few will be involved it will be easy to control them.
Pliny the Younger, *Letters*, X.33

Trajan to Pliny
You believe it would be the right thing to set up a guild of firemen in Nicomedia, based on those established in several other cities. But it must be borne in mind that this sort of organization has caused a great deal of political disruption in your province, especially the cities. Whatever we call them, and whatever they have been established for, nothing will stop them transforming themselves into political factions. A much safer plan would be to provide equipment which can be used for extinguishing fires, and to instruct property owners to use it, and if circumstances require, to summon assistance from the rest of the population.
Pliny the Younger, *Letters*, X.34

TRADE

More than anything else the cities and towns of the Roman Empire thrived on trade. The Mediterranean served as a great highway which allowed the passage of men and goods from places as diverse as North Africa to Gaul, from Syria to Spain, as well as acting as the final part of trade routes which stretched as far as India and China. Goods were also shipped out through the Aegean and up to the Black Sea, or west through the pillars of Hercules and out into the Atlantic and round Spain and Gaul past Britain to the Baltic. The result was a world in which Palestinian grain and Egyptian glass could be found in London, and British wool goods in the Eastern Empire.

Grain ships
Seneca recorded the arrival of ships at Puteoli by the bay of Naples.

We saw some ships (the ones called the mail packets) from Alexandria today, come into sight just like that. These are the ships usually sent in advance to announce the coming of the fleet following on behind. The sight is always greeted with great pleasure by Campanians. All Puteoli packed onto the dockside, every one of them picking out the Alexandrian ships from the great mass of other boats by the way the sails are set. They're the only ones permitted to keep the topsails spread. On the high seas, all ships use these sails because nothing else is as useful for speed as the topsail, the part from which the ship gets the greatest part of its motive force.
Seneca, *Letters*, 77.1ff

Under Claudius, the port at Ostia was substantially enlarged to allow more grain ships to come much closer to Rome.

Claudius was halted in the middle of the forum by a mob when a long and unbroken drought caused a grain shortage. He was subjected to so much abuse, and had so many pieces of bread thrown at him that he was barely able to escape into the palace through a side entrance. After this experience he did everything he could to bring grain into Rome, even during the winter. He guaranteed a profit to merchants by covering any losses himself from storms, and offered appropriate large cash sums to anyone who would build freight ships .... He built a harbour at Ostia by having breakwaters erected on either side and had a mole built in the deep water.
Suetonius, *Claudius* 19, 20

Improving trading communications

Transporting goods by road was cumbersome, dangerous, unreliable and expensive. Sometimes there was no choice but it was invariably cheaper to move freight ten or twenty times as far by water. Nicomedia (modern Izmit in north-western Turkey) lies some 18 miles north-west of Lake Sabanja which drains into the Black Sea. Pliny the Younger seems to have been involved in a scheme to connect it westwards to the Sea of Marmara, very close to Nicomedia itself. The meaning is not entirely clear but it seems that this would have enabled trade already coming from the Black Sea to have been shipped upriver to the lake, across it, and then down a canal which would come out close to the city. The canal was apparently never built.

Pliny to Trajan

When I consider how your exalted position is equalled by your magnanimous spirit, it seems that I should draw your attention to projects which are appropriate to your immortal name and glory, and which would be as useful as they are magnificent.

There is a substantial lake on the Nicomedia city limits. Across here marble, fruit, wood, and building timber are shipped easily and economically as far as the main road. From here great expense and a lot of trouble is involved in moving them on to the sea by cart. [Rectifying this] would mean a lot of work but there is no shortage of labour. For there are plenty of people in the rural areas and the city and it's certain that they would be only too happy to be involved in a project which everyone will benefit from.

All it needs is for you to send out an engineer or architect, if you consider it appropriate, to find out whether the lake is above or below sea level. The local engineers think that the lake is forty cubits above the sea. Examining the site myself I have discovered that one of the old kings of this region built a canal nearby, though I am uncertain whether its purpose was to drain the surrounding fields or to join the lake to the canal. As it was never finished I also do not know whether this was because it was abandoned on his death, or because the work looked as if it would never be finished. If the latter was the reason, it makes me all the more enthusiastic, for the sake of your greater glory (forgive me), to see you achieve what a king could only attempt.

Trajan to Pliny

It is possible that I might consider the prospect of joining your lake to the sea. But, first, a proper survey must be conducted to see how much water is in the lake and where its water comes from. Otherwise, being connected to the sea might lead to it being completely emptied. You may apply to Calpurnius Macer for an engineer and I will dispatch a man who knows about this type of work.

Pliny the Younger, *Letters*, X.41-2

Vested interests

One of the earliest accounts of pagan fears of Christianity comes from the Bible when Paul's teachings were perceived as a threat to the vested interests of Ephesus. Ostensibly a religious dispute, this is no more or less than an expression of rage by people whose livings depended on the immensely popular cult of the Temple of Artemis (Diana) just to the north-east of the city. There were many examples of popular local cults, which attracted pilgrims and tourists from across the Roman world and created livelihoods for locals who milked the cults for all they were worth.

A certain man named Demetrius, a silversmith, made silver shrines for Diana. This work brought considerable profit to the craftsmen whom he brought together with the workmen of similar occupation, and said, 'Men, you know that by this trade we have our wealth. Not only that, you see and hear, that not just at Ephesus, but almost all throughout Asia, this Paul has persuaded and turned away many people, saying, that they are not gods which are made with hands. So that not only this, our craft, is in danger of coming to nothing, but also that the temple of the great goddess Artemis should be despised, and her magnificence should be destroyed, whom all Asia, and the whole world worships.'

And when they heard these words, they were full of wrath, and cried out, saying, 'Great is Artemis of the Ephesians!' The whole city was filled with confusion; and, having caught Gaius and Aristarchus, Macedonians and travelling companions of Paul's, they rushed with one accord into the theatre. When Paul would have gone in to the people, the disciples persuaded him not to. Some of the associates of the governor of Asia, who were his friends, got word to him asking that he not risk himself by going into the theatre.

Some cried out one thing, and some another, because the assembly was in confusion. Most of them had no idea why they were there at all. Alexander was selected from the crowd, the Jews having picked him. He gestured to the crowd and would have made his case to the people. But when they realised he was a Jew, they shouted with one voice for two hours, 'Great is Artemis of the Ephesians!'

Once the town-clerk had calmed the people down, he said, 'You men of Ephesus, what man is there who does not know how it is that the city of Ephesus is a worshipper of the great goddess Artemis, and of the image which fell down from Jupiter? Seeing then that these things cannot be contradicted, you should be quiet and do nothing rashly. You have brought here these men who are neither robbers of churches nor blasphemers of your goddess. On which score, if Demetrius and the craftsmen who are with him have something against a man, the law is available and there are representatives. Let them bring a case against one another. But if you are asking anything about other matters, it will be settled in a lawful gathering, for we are in danger of being investigated for today's uproar as there is no reason with which we can explain this assembly.' When he had spoken like this, he dismissed them.

Acts of the Apostles, XIX.24-41 (based on the Authorised Version of the Bible)

MOMENTS IN CITY LIFE

Pompeii and other towns

Pompeii's destruction in 79 brought the city's existence to an end in an instant. One of the reasons we are so dependent on letters by people such as Seneca and Pliny the Younger is because we have little other evidence for general day-to-day life in Roman cities. But Pompeii is different. The ephemera of day-to-day life were left where they were and much has survived. The population of around 25,000 included people from all walks of life; their lives, interests, activities and prejudices were scrawled across the walls of shops, houses, and public buildings. Part of this was the dynamic of local politics in which various interests groups shrieked their allegiances and hurled insults at their opponents. The sources are from Pompeii recorded in Davis, William S. (1912-13), II, 260-5, unless otherwise indicated.

Gladiators
Twenty pairs of gladiators supplied by Quintus Monnius Rufus will fight at Nola on 1, 2 and 3 of May. There will also be a hunt.

Twenty pairs of gladiators supplied by Decimus Lucretius Satrius Valens, lifetime priest of Nero, the Emperor's son, and ten pairs of gladiators supplied by his son Decimus Lucretius Valens will fight at Pompeii on 8-12 April inclusive. There'll be a big hunt, and awnings. Aemilius Celer wrote this by moonlight.

Thirty pairs of gladiators and their substitutes, supplied by Gnaeus Alleius Nigidius Maius the quinquennial duumvir, will fight at Pompeii on 24, 25, and 26 November. There will also be a hunt. Hurrah for Maius the Quinquennial! Well done, Paris!

Elections
The election of Postumius Proculus of aedile is requested by the dyers.

Primus and his household are working for the election of Gnaeus Helvius Sabinus as aedile.

I beg you to make Lucius Caeserninus quinquennial duumvir of Nuceria. He is a good man.

The Isis worshippers, speaking as one, ask that Gnaeus Helvias Sabinus be elected aedile.

Tenancies

Available for let from 1st July next: shops with upstairs (fine upper rooms), and a house in Arnius Pollio block. Landlord: Gnaeus Alleius Nigidius Maius. Anyone interested in being a tenant can apply to Primus, his slave.

Available to let for five years from 13th August next up to the 13th of the sixth following August, the Baths of Venus, equipped for persons of quality, shops, rooms above the shops, and upstairs apartments in the property owned by Julia Felix, daughter of Spurius.

On the 18th June in the duumvirate of Lucius Veranius Hypsaeus and Lucius Albucius Justus, I, Privatus, slave of the colony of Pompeii, declared in writing that I had received from Lucius Caecilius Jucundus 1,675 sesterces, and previous to this day, on 6th June, I received 1000 sesterces as rent for the public pasture. This was done at Pompeii during the consulship of Gnaeus Fonteius and Gaius Vipstanus [59].

Theft and other suspect activities

A copper pot has been stolen from this shop. Anyone returning it will receive a reward of 65 sesterces. Anyone who gives up the thief will be rewarded.

At Nuceria, I won 8552 denarii at gambling; the game was fair!

I curse Tretia Maria, and her life and mind, and her memory, liver and lungs all mingled together. Thus she will not be able to speak about those secrets ....
RIB 7. Curse tablet from London.

Mysteries

Every day for the last 13, Austalis has been wandering around on his own.
RIB 2491.147. Graffito on a tile found in London.

Manufacturers

Inscriptions set out and engraved here for sacred buildings and public works!
Ireland (1983), 221. Inscription from Palermo, Sicily, in a bilingual Greek and Latin text.

Servandus (made this), at *Colonia Claudia Arae Agrippinensium* [Cologne].
RIB 2456.6 (on a figurine)

4 Decadence, cruelty and vice

Few people think of the Roman Empire without associating it with excess, licentious behaviour and appalling cruelty. In part this is due to the Roman historians themselves who lost no chance to condemn the memory of a bad emperor (and even the good ones) with tales of outrageous activities. Moral judgements were part of the ritual of documenting reigns. This is no better seen than with the reign of Claudius (41-54). Although historians like Suetonius acknowledged his achievements in other areas, it was the record of his susceptibility to powerful women and his capricious temper in Suetonius's biography, and Seneca's *Apocolocyntosis*, that proved the more durable legacy.

The image of decadent Rome is also partly due to the nineteenth-century's moralising attitudes to their own lives and everyone else's. We have inherited a picture of imperial Rome where debauched emperors deflowered anyone or anything that took their fancy while their promiscuous wives consorted with soldiers and slaves in equal measure. It is also true that the way in which the Romans recorded these acts illustrated that some of them had had a bellyful of their rulers' moral corruption. In the end the scandals are not really so very different from some of those that surround our own leaders and also the lives of many ordinary people.

Either way, life was freely abused and taken away. We can see that quite clearly in the circus activities and the attitude towards slaves. It is hardly surprising then that emperors and others were perfectly capable of handing out vicious punishments as amusements on a whim.

Perhaps one significant difference is that, generally speaking, the Romans were more open-minded about sex and violence. For them, these were just parts of normal life. They had, for instance, no concept of pornography and depicting copulation was as logical as depicting rural life and mythical scenes. Like most pre-modern peoples they had a more acute sense of the role reproduction and consorting plays in the cycle of life, and also accepted pain, cruelty and violent death. In an age when life was relatively cheap this is not so surprising. Even so, they seem to have been able to make the same moral judgements as we do about money and greed.

Money cannot make up for the excesses of a tyrant, and a bodyguard will never be enough to protect a ruler unless he has the goodwill of his people.

Herodian, *History of the Empire*, I.4.4, repeating a phrase found elsewhere, for example in Sallust, *The Jugurthine War*, X.4

THE GROWTH IN GREED AND OSTENTATION

Silver plate

In the eighteenth century, silver utensils became gradually cheaper in Britain as her wealth as a nation grew. To this day, nineteenth-century spoons and forks are still easy to come by, yet eighteenth-century silver becomes progressively harder to find as earlier dates are sought. Silver was of course a mark of wealth and success, and as people became more able to afford it as Britain's wealth and power grew, so they purchased more as a symbol of their status. The same seems to have happened in Rome, with Pliny the Elder observing that the Roman people seemed, strangely, to favour silver over gold and to have become ludicrously ostentatious and extravagant. Pliny was, however, following a familiar pattern in the imperial period. This was to look back to the later days of the Republic and spot the patterns leading to the loss of traditional virtues and values. We do the same, while simultaneously surrounding ourselves with more and more possessions.

Tastes in silver plate exhibit the most extraordinary variations thanks to the vagaries of people's preferences and no style of workmanship remaining fashionable for long. Furnian plate is sought after at one time, at another Clodian, and at another Gratian, because even the workshops are made to feel welcome at our tables. On another occasion, embossed plate and rough surfaces are in vogue, where the metal has been cut out along the lines painted on to mark out the decoration. Now we have even installed detachable shelves on our dressers to carry foodstuffs. Other pieces of silver plate are decorated with filigree so that as much silver as possible can be wasted by the file. The orator Calvus moans that saucepans are made of silver, but it was we who came up with the idea of decorating carriages with chased silver, and it was in our time that Poppaea, Nero's wife, had the idea of fitting her favourite mules with gold horseshoes ....

We know that Pompeius Paulinus, a Roman equestrian's son at Arles whose father's remote ancestors were skin-clad tribesmen, took 12,000lb of silver plate with him while he was serving with an army facing the very fiercest tribes. Now the fact is that for a long time women's beds have been covered all over with silver, and dining couches as well. It is recorded that Carvilius Pollio, a Roman equestrian, was the first to put silver on dining couches, but not to cover them all over or to reproduce the Delos style, but according to Carthaginian tastes. He also had beds made of gold in the Carthaginian style, soon afterwards silver beds were made in the Delos style. But Sulla's civil war expiated all these excesses.

For, a little before these deeds, silver platters were made which weighed 100lb. That there were more than 150 of them at Rome in this time is notorious, and also that many people were outlawed because of them, by the actions of those who were greedy for them. The chronicles, which attribute the civil war to such vices, are ashamed but our age is greater. Claudius' slave, Drusillanus (known by the name of Rotundus), treasurer of Nearer Spain, owned a silver dish which weighed 500lb (for which a special workshop had been built to make it) and eight companions, weighing 250lb each. How many of his fellow slaves carried them in, or dined off them? ….

Men have such a rage not only for masses of silver, but an almost more violent lust for objects of the finest workmanship. This is a long-established tradition, so that people of today need not bear the blame. Gaius Gracchus owned some dolphin figures which cost him 5000 sesterces per pound, while the orator Lucius Crassus had a pair of goblets chased by the artisan Mentor which cost him 100,000 sesterces, though I must admit he was too ashamed ever to use them. Conquering Asia brought luxury to Italy since Lucius Scipio had carried in his triumphal procession 1400lb of chased silver plate and gold vessels weighing 1500lb. This was in the 565th year since Rome was founded [189BC].

There was a much more devastating blow to our standards when we received Asia as a gift. Its bequest from King Attalus after his death was less to our advantage than Scipio's victory. On that day, any reservations about buying Attalus' effects in the Rome auctions vanished completely. The year was the 622nd since the founding of Rome [132BC] and in the space of 57 years our community had gone from admiring foreign riches to coveting them.

Pliny the Elder, *Natural History*, XXXIII.143-6, 147-9

The coming of the super-rich

Here, Pliny the Elder recounts the coming of the super-rich in the days of the late Republic. In fact the name *Dives* was even adopted, meaning 'Rich', and became part of family names.

Marcus Crassus, who belonged to the Rich family, had a saying that the only definition of a wealthy man was someone whose annual income could fund the maintenance of a legion. He owned land worth 2 million sesterces, and was second in riches only to Sulla. Not only that but he was dissatisfied without getting hold of all the Parthian gold as well. The truth is that he was the first man to get an enduring reputation for his wealth (and it's a pleasure to stigmatize such insatiable greed). But we now know since then many freedmen who were richer, three simultaneously not long before our own time during the reign of Claudius, being Callistus, Pallas, and Narcissus. We would have to leave these ones out if they were still in power. Gaius Caecilius Claudius Isidorus, in the consulship of Gaius Asinius Gallus and Gaius Marcius Censorinus [8BC], on the sixth day before the Kalends of February [27 January] declared in his will, that though he had suffered great losses by the civil wars, he was still able to leave behind him 4,116 slaves, 3,600 pairs of oxen, and 257,000 head of other kinds of cattle, besides 60 million sesterces in cash. He ordered 1.1 million sesterces to be spent on his funeral …. How insane it is to desire something in our lifetime which has either been accessible to slaves, or has even been beyond the greed of kings!

Pliny the Elder, *Natural History*, XXXIII.134-6, 137

We think we're badly off, living like paupers, if the bathroom walls aren't lit up with huge and expensive mirrors, if our marble from Alexandria isn't decorated with Numidian marble, if the whole surface hasn't been decorated with a veneer of elaborate patterns with all the variety of painted murals, unless the ceiling is obscured by glass, unless the pools we plunge our bodies (exhausted by hours in the sweat rooms) are lined with Thasian marble, once so rare it was hardly ever seen even in temples, and unless the water gushes from silver taps …. what about the baths owned by some ex-slaves? Take a look at their rows of statues, the clusters of functionless columns there only for decoration, all for the sake of spending cash. Look at the noisy torrents of water splashing down from one tier to the next. We've actually reached the stage of such fussiness that we moan if we have to walk on anything other than precious stones.
Seneca, *Letters*, 86.6

The pursuit of pleasure

Pliny made observations about life as it was. Others were more idealistic and turned their heads away from hedonistic indulgences. As tutor and adviser to Nero as well as living in the time of Tiberius and Caligula, Seneca was well able to form a judgement about the pursuit of virtue and pleasure. In a treatise on the pursuit of contentment he identified their respective haunts. His description of pleasure's transience is one that Oscar Wilde would have recognised — and ignored, as many of the early emperors did.

Virtue is a thing up high, illustrious and regal, invincible and impossible to wear down. Pleasure is a base thing, servile, idiotic and fleeting, whose home and haunt is brothel and drinking house. You will come across virtue in the temple, the form and the senate, standing before the city walls, dusty, stained, with calloused hands. You'll find pleasure more often loitering in the shadows, looking for the dark, near the baths and the sweat-rooms, places that fear the authorities, effete, lacking in energy, and stinking of wine and perfume, with a pasty complexion or painted and caked with make-up like a corpse. The greatest good lives forever, has no end and no limit, nor can it ever regret because a well-adjusted mind never changes, being neither consumed with self-disgust nor needing to change its course and that is always the best. But pleasure expires at its climax, quickly occupying the small space set aside for it. It soon tires and decays after its initial impact.
Seneca, *On the happy life*, VII.3-4

Sex appeal

Pliny the Elder was intrigued by how sex seems to give human beings no satisfaction at all, thus explaining the paradox that they indulge in it whenever possible.

Man is the only animal walking around on two legs. Man is the only animal for whom the first experience of sex is followed by disgust, no doubt serving as an omen for life which had a regrettable origin. All other animals mate at fixed periods during the year, but man, as was noted already, has sex at any time of day or night. All the others are satisfied by copulation, but for man this scarcely ever happens ….

93

Amongst human beings, men have thought up every perverse variation on sexual gratification, which are crimes against nature, but women have come up with abortion. Compared to wild animals, how much more culpable are we? Hesiod said that men have more libido in winter and women during the summer.
Pliny the Elder, *Natural History*, X.171-2

The benefits of frugality

Nearly a century before Horace had considered whether there was any great benefit to be had by living a life of frugality, and what the difference was between plain living and being stingy for the sake of it. The passage was expressed through the person of one of his neighbours, Ofellus.

Ofellus thinks that a stingy lifestyle differs from a frugal one because it's ridiculous to avoid one fault by simply adopting another. Avidienus, appropriately and inescapably known as 'Dog', eats five-year-old olives, wild cornels, and avoids drawing his wine until it has gone sour. As for his oil, you would be unable to bear its smell, but even when he is in his festive clothes and keeping a wedding or birthday feast, he scatters it on salad from a two-pound horn with his own hands, although he doesn't hold back with his vinegar. So which style would a wise man put into practice, and which of the two should he emulate? On one hand, as the saying goes, a wolf threatens, on the other a dog. He'll be considered decent if he is not offensively sordid, and is not considered despicable by being extreme at either type of conduct. Also, like old Albucius, he will not be cruel to his slaves, when he allocates them to their duties, nor like careless Naevius, will he offer his guests greasy water. That really is too much of a faux pas.

Learn now just what, and how substantial, the benefits are which frugal living brings.
Horaces, *Satires*, II.2.53-69

Everyday decadence

Whatever Horace's recommendations were, the poet Juvenal, writing around the early second century, had little doubt for the reason that decadence had become a part of everyday life.

You ask, 'but where do these monstrosities come from? What fountain do they flow from?' In the old days, the wives of Latium were kept chaste by their poverty. It was hard work and little sleep that kept vice from soiling their simple homes. Their hands were roughened and toughened by Tuscan fleeces, Hannibal approaching Rome, and husbands armed at the ready by the Colline tower.

We are now suffering the disasters of a long peace. Luxury, more fatal than any enemy, is on us now, wreaking revenge for a conquered world. From the day Roman poverty disappeared, we haven't been short of any crimes or lust … Disgusting money was the first to bring foreign habits amongst us. Riches have stripped the ages of their strength and them with revolting practices.

What decency does Venus see to when she is drunk? When she cannot distinguish head from tail, eats giant oysters at midnight, pours bubbling narcotics into her unmixed

Falerian wine, and swigs from perfume-flasks, while the ceiling spins dizzily around, the table dances, and every light is seen double!
Juvenal, *Satires*, VI.288-305

Effortless debauchery

The historian Herodian was given to including stock wise sayings in his history of the late second century and early third. They were usually apposite, not just to his own time, but all others.

Youthful passions can be easily distracted from acquiring moral standards and effortlessly glide into a life of decadence.
Herodian, *History of the Empire*, I.3.1

THE OUTRAGES OF TIBERIUS

Despite the various hand-wringing diatribes about Rome plunging headlong into decadence and indulgence it counted for little amongst certain members of the Roman establishment, mainly the emperors. They provided excellent copy for Roman historians who perceived the outrages of the court as fables and warnings from history, a role they have amply fulfilled ever since. Even Augustus himself was not able wholly to escape the charge of indulging in reprehensible behaviour. Suetonius recounted various charges, for example relating to over-indulgence in food and furniture, but pointed out for the most part Augustus led a blameless life and this more than made good most of the deficiencies.

These accusations or libels (whatever we call them) for abnormal vice, he was able easily to refute through his clean living at that time and afterwards. The accusation of his loathsome indulgence when he captured Alexandria could be rejected because, apart from one cup made of agate, he kept none of the furniture himself. Eventually he had all the day-to-day gold plate melted down. Augustus could not allay the charge that he was lustful and the story is that even in old age he liked to take the virginity of girls who were brought to him from everywhere, even by his wife.
Suetonius, *Augustus*, 71

The range of Tiberius' debaucheries

Tiberius succeeded Augustus in the year 14, and was the son of Livia, Augustus' wife, by her previous marriage. He had a powerful sense of duty but his manner alienated him. Part of this was his paranoid suspicion matched by an uncritical dependence and trust in Lucius Aelius Sejanus, prefect of the Praetorian Guard in Rome. Sejanus, however, planned to succeed Tiberius and spent his time encouraging Tiberius to exile members of his family. When Tiberius got wind of Sejanus' scheming, he denounced him in the Senate and brought him down. A purge followed but Tiberius proceeded to withdraw permanently from Rome to his retreat on Capri. There he did as he fancied.

Gnaeus Domitius and Camillus Scribonianus had entered on the consulship when the emperor, after crossing the channel which divides Capri from Sorrento, sailed along the Campanian coast, doubting if he should enter Rome, or, possibly, simulating the intention of going there, because he had resolved otherwise. He often landed at points in the neighbourhood and visited the gardens by the Tiber. But he went back again to the cliffs and to the solitude of the sea shores, in shame at the vices and profligacies into which he had plunged so uncontrollably that in the manner of a despot he debauched the children of free-born citizens. It wasn't just beauty and good looks which he felt as an incentive to his lust, but the modesty of childhood in some, and noble ancestry in others. Names never heard before were for the first time invented then, the *sellarii* from the abominations of the place, and *spintriae* from the numerous submissions to lust. Slaves were also set to work on seeking out and procuring, with rewards for the willing, and threats to the reluctant, and if there was resistance from a relative or a parent, they used violence and force, and actually indulged their own passions as if dealing with captives.

Tacitus, *Annals*, VI.1-2

How to deal with a generous fisherman

A few days after Tiberius arrived at Capri and was on his own, a fisherman appeared unexpectedly and offered him a huge mullet. Whereupon, in his panic that the man had climbed up to him over a rough and trackless rocky area from the back of the island, he had the wretched chap's face scrubbed with the fish. In the middle of his torture the man thanked his lucky stars that he had not given the emperor a huge crab he'd caught, so Tiberius had his face ripped up with the crab as well. He punished a member of the Praetorian Guard with execution for stealing a peacock from his plantations. When the litter in which he was making a trip was held up by brambles, he had the man who went ahead to clear a path, a centurion of the first cohort, stretched out on the ground and flogged half to death.

Suetonius, *Tiberius,* 60

A summary of cruelty

It's a long story to go through a detailed account of Tiberius' acts of cruelty. It'll be enough to mention the various types, as examples of his barbarity. Not a single day went by without an execution, not even those that were sacred and holy; because he executed some people even on New Year's day. Many were accused and condemned along with their children, and even by their children. The families of the victims were ordered not to mourn for them. Denouncers were voted special rewards and sometimes even the witnesses as well. Whatever an informer said was accepted without question.

Every crime was regarded as a capital offence, even uttering a few simple words. A poet was charged with having libelled Agamemnon in a tragedy, and a writer of history of having described Brutus and Cassius as the last of the Romans. The writers were put to death immediately and their works destroyed, although they had been read out in public to acclaim some years before Augustus himself. Some of those who were detained in prison were denied the consolation of reading and even the privilege of conversing and talking together.

Amongst those who were summoned to plead their causes some cut open their veins at home, confident they would be condemned anyway and wishing to avoid inconvenience and humiliation, while others swallowed poison in front of the Senate. But the wounds of the former were patched up and they were rushed half-dead, but still quivering, to jail. Everyone who was executed was thrown out upon the Stairs of Mourning and dragged to the Tiber with hooks, up to twenty being treated like this in a single day, including women and children.

Since ancient tradition made it a religious offence to strangle virgins, young girls were first raped by the executioner and then throttled. Those who wanted to die were obliged to live because Tiberius thought death so lenient a punishment that when he heard that one of the accused, called Carnulus, had foreseen his execution, he yelled out, 'Carnulus has given me the slip'. When he was touring the jails and one man begged for a quick execution, he answered, 'I am not your friend yet.' One former consul recorded this in his archives: at a large dinner-party, which the writer himself attended, one of the dwarfs standing by the table amongst the jesters suddenly asked Tiberius why Paconius, who was accused with treason, remained so long alive. The emperor at the time chided him for speaking so cheekily, but a few days later wrote to the Senate to decide as soon as possible about executing Paconius.

Suetonius, *Tiberius*, 61

Tourist spots

They still point out the scene of his executions on Capri. This was where Tiberius used to order that those condemned after long and choice tortures be flung headfirst into the sea before his eyes. Meanwhile a gang of naval troops waited below for the bodies and broke their bones with boat-hooks and oars, to wipe out any last trace of life. Among several different types of torture he came up with this one: he would trick men into filling themselves with copious draughts of wine. Then, suddenly tying up their private parts, would torment them simultaneously with torture from the strings and preventing them relieving themselves.

Suetonius, *Tiberius*, 62

A MONSTER

Few emperors gained a more frightful reputation than Gaius Caligula (37-41), a man whom Suetonius called a 'monster'. Caligula started off well, attending to government and reducing taxes. A bout of illness, and no doubt the circumstances he found himself in, led to power-crazed conduct which became the style for the rest of the reign and led, inevitably, to his own murder. Suetonius and others exulted in tales of this reign of terror.

Caligula and his sisters

Caligula and his sisters lived in habitual incest. At a large banquet he put each one of them under him, while his wife reclined above. Of his sisters, he is thought to have violated

Drusilla when he was still under age, and even to have been caught in bed with her by his grandmother Antonia, in whose home they were brought up together .... The rest of his sisters he did not love so much, nor think so highly of, but frequently prostituted them to his favourites, so that he was more prepared at the trial of Aemilius Lepidus to condemn them as adulteresses and was in the know about conspiracies against him. He not only made letters in their handwriting public, obtained by fraud and seduction, but also dedicated to Mars the Avenger, with an explanatory inscription, three swords devised to take his life.

Suetonius, *Caligula*, 24

Concern for the suffering

Once Caligula was passing a column of prisoners on the *Via Latina* when one of them, wearing a ragged old beard down his front, implored Caligula to have him put to death. 'So,' responded Caligula, 'you call that living do you, in that state?' That's the sort of answer to give to a person for whom death would be a blessed release. 'You're scared of dying? And you call that living, in that state?'

Seneca, *Letters*, 77.18

Torture over lunch

What Caligula did and said were equally cruel, even when he was taking it easy and given up to fun and feasting. While he was lunching or partying, capital examinations by torture were frequently conducted before him, and a soldier who was particularly good at chopping peoples' heads off, decapitated those who were brought from prison.

At Puteoli, at the dedication of the bridge that he built .... after inviting several to come to him from the shore, he suddenly had them all flung overboard; and when a few grabbed hold of the rudders of the ships, he pushed them off into the water with boathooks and oars. At a public banquet in Rome he handed a slave over instantly to the executioners for thieving a length of silver from the couches, with orders to cut his hands off and hang them round his neck on his chest. He also ordered that the slave then be led about around the guests, preceded by a notice board explaining the reason for his punishment.

When a gladiator from the gladiatorial school fought with him using wooden swords and fell deliberately, Caligula stabbed him with a real dagger and then raced around with a palm-branch, as victors do. Once when next to an altar he dressed up as a priest's assistant and a victim was brought along, he held his mallet up high and killed the man whose job was to kill the victim.

At one of his more lavish banquets he unexpectedly burst out laughing, and when the consuls reclining next to him, politely asked what the joke was, he answered, 'what do you think, except that one nod from me and you two could have your throats cut right here?'

Suetonius, *Caligula*, 32

Coveting other men's wives

Caligula seems to have been more or less indifferent about whom he had sexual relations with. Just about everyone took his fancy, but he was especially fond of forcing himself upon other men's wives.

Caligula had no respect for his own chastity or anyone else's. It is said he had debauched affairs with Marcus Lepidus, the pantomime performer Mnester, and certain hostages. Valerius Catullus, a young man from a consular family, proclaimed in public that he had slept with the emperor and worn himself out in bed with him. Leaving out any mention of his incest with his sisters and his notorious lust for the prostitute Pyrallis, there was hardly a single woman of rank whom he did not try his hand with. These women, as a rule, he invited to dinner along with their husbands. As they walked past the end of his couch, he would examine them with a critical and deliberate eye, as if he was buying slaves, even putting out his hand to lift up the face of any woman who looked down shyly.

Then, whenever he was in the mood he would leave the chamber, sending for the woman whom he liked best. He came back soon afterwards with evidence for what had taken place, and would openly praise or slate his partner, reeling off her charms or faults and commenting on her conduct. He personally sent divorce documents in the name of the absent husbands to a few, and had them entered in state records.

Caligula outdid experts from all ages in ingenious variations on reckless extravagance by inventing a new type of baths and unnatural forms of food and banquets. He would bathe in hot or cold perfumed oils, drink hugely-expensive pearls which had been dissolved in vinegar, and put in front loaves and meat made of gold in front of his guests, declaring that a man should live either in frugality or as an emperor. He even scattered large quantities of cash from the roof of the Basilica Julia amongst the people several days running. He also built galleys on the Liburnian model with ten banks of oars, sterns decorated with precious stones, multi-coloured sails, vast spacious baths, colonnades, and dining-halls, and even many different vines and fruit trees. This was so when he was on board he could lie at the dining table from an early hour, and coast along the shores of Campania to singing and chorusing.

Caligula built villas and country houses with a total disregard for the cost, caring about nothing unless it was to do what men said was impossible. So he built moles far out into deep and stormy seas, tunneled through rocks of hardest flint, built up flat ground as high as mountains and vice-versa. This was all done with incredible speed, since the penalty for a delay was death.

To cut a long story short, huge sums of money, including the 2.7 billion sesterces which Tiberius Caesar had accumulated, were squandered by Caligula in less time that it took a year to pass.

Suetonius, *Caligula*, 36-7

Making money in the oldest profession of all

Profligacy left Caligula with a cash-flow crisis. He scouted around for various ways of replenishing his reserves.

In order to leave no chance of plunder untried Caligula established a brothel in his palace, setting aside several rooms and furnishing them in a manner appropriate to the grandeur of the place, where married women and freeborn youths would stand on display. Then he sent his slave-prompters around the markets and basilicas, to invite men of all ages to have a good time, lending money on interest to those who came and having clerks publicly record their names, as contributors to imperial revenue. He didn't even refrain from making money out of gambling, and to increase his gains by lying and perjury. One time, having given up his seat to the player beside him and gone into the courtyard, he spotted two rich Roman knights on their way past. He ordered their arrest at once and their property confiscated and came back overjoyed, bragging that he had never played with better luck.

Suetonius, *Caligula*, 41

The would-be Midas

There is a process by making gold out of orpiment, mined in Syria for painters. It is found on the ground and looks like gold but is brittle and resembles selenite. Caligula, who was obsessed by gold, was interested in its potential. He ordered a huge quantity of orpiment to be melted down, and it definitely yielded some very good gold, but only a small amount. Consequently, even though the orpiment cost 4 denarii a pound [gold was worth 1500 denarii to the pound] Caligula lost money on a scheme which his own greed had encouraged him to start.

Pliny the Elder, *Natural History*, XXXIII.79

THE ACTOR AND AESTHETE

The last of the Julio-Claudians was Nero, descended from Augustus' sister Octavia. He was only 16 when he acceded in 54, and the first part of his reign was administered by his mother Agrippina the Younger (Caligula's sister), and his advisers Burrus and Seneca. The latter two helped arrange his mother's death and when Burrus died in 62 and Seneca retired, Nero was left to his own devices. Best described as a profligate aesthete with pretensions to acting, singing, athletics, artistic grandeur and divinity, he made the most of his absolute power and has gone down in history as the prime example of a dilettante and decadent ruler drunk with power.

The singing charioteer

Nero had long had a fancy for driving a four-horse chariot, and a no less degrading taste for singing to the harp, in a theatrical fashion, when he was at dinner. This he would remind people was a royal custom, and had been the practice of ancient chiefs; it was also celebrated in the praises of poets and was meant to show honour to the gods. Songs indeed, he said, were sacred to Apollo, and it was in the dress of a singer that that great and prophetic deity was seen in Roman temples as well as in Greek cities. He could no longer be restrained, when Seneca and Burrus thought it best to concede one point that he might not persist in both. A space was enclosed in the Vatican valley where he might manage his horses, without the spectacle being public. Soon he actually invited all the people of Rome, who extolled him in their praises, like a mob craving for amusements and which rejoices when a prince draws them the same way. However, the public exposure of his shame acted on him as an incentive instead of sickening him, as men expected.

Tacitus, *Annals*, XIV.14

Days of infamy

Not yet wishing to disgrace himself on a public stage, Nero instituted some games under the title of 'juvenile sports,' for which people of every class gave in their names. Neither rank nor age nor previous high promotion hindered any one from practising the art of a Greek or Latin actor and even stooping to gestures and songs unfit for a man. Noble ladies too actually played disgusting parts, and in the grove, with which Augustus had surrounded the lake for the naval fight, there were erected places for meeting and refreshment, and every incentive to excess was offered for sale. Money too was distributed, which the respectable had to spend under sheer compulsion and which the profligate gloried in squandering. Hence a rank growth of abominations and of all infamy.

Never did a filthier rabble add worse licentiousness to our long corrupted morals. Even, with virtuous training, purity is not easily upheld; far less amid rivalries in vice could modesty or propriety or any trace of good manners be preserved. Last of all, the emperor himself came on the stage, tuning his lute with elaborate care and trying his voice with his attendants. There were also present, to complete the show, a guard of soldiers with centurions and tribunes, and Burrus, who grieved and yet applauded. Then it was that Roman knights were first enrolled under the title of Augustani, men in their prime and remarkable for their strength, some, from a natural frivolity, others from the hope of promotion. Day and night they kept up a thunder of applause, and applied to the emperor's person and voice the epithets of deities. Thus they lived in fame and honour, as if on the strength of their merits.

Tacitus, *Annals*, XIV.15

A licence to vice

In Nero's fourth consulship, with Cossus Cornelius Lentulus the Younger for his colleague, a theatrical entertainment to be repeated every five years was established at Rome in imitation of the Greek festival. Like all novelties, it was variously canvassed. There were some who declared that even Pompey the Great was slated by the elders in his time for having set up a fixed and permanent theatre. 'In the old days,' they said, 'the games were usually exhibited with hastily erected tiers of benches and a temporary stage, and the people stood to witness them, that they might not, by having the chance of sitting down, spend a succession of entire days in idleness. Let the ancient character of these shows be retained, whenever the praetors exhibited them, and let no citizen be under the necessity of competing.'

'As it is, traditional morality, which has by degrees been forgotten, has been utterly subverted by the introduction of this lax tone. The result is that anything which suffers or produces corruption is to be seen at Rome. Degeneracy bred by foreign tastes is infecting the youth who devote themselves to athletic sports, lounging about and low intrigues. And all this encouraged by the emperor and Senate, who not only grant licence to vice, but have even driven Roman nobles into disgracing themselves on the stage, under the pretence of being orators and poets. What remains for them but to strip themselves naked, put on boxing-gloves, and practice such battles instead of the arms of legitimate warfare? Would justice be promoted, or would they serve on the knights' commissions for the honourable office of a judge, because they had listened with critical wisdom to effeminate strains of music and sweet voices? Night too is given up to infamy, so that virtue has not a moment left to her, but all the vilest of that promiscuous throng dared to do in the darkness anything they had lusted for in the day.'

Many people liked this licence, but they screened it under respectable names. 'Our ancestors,' they said, 'weren't averse to the attractions of shows on a scale suited to the wealth of their day, and so they introduced actors from the Etruscans and horse-races from Thurii....'

Tacitus, *Annals*, XIV.20

The blushing bride

Nero, to win credit for himself of enjoying nowhere as much as Rome, prepared banquets in the public places, and used the whole city, in effect, as his private house. Of these entertainments the most famous for their notorious profligacy were those furnished by Tigellinus, which I will describe as an example, so that I will not have to continually describe similar extravagances. He had a raft constructed on Agrippa's lake, put the guests on board and set it in motion by other vessels towing it. These vessels glittered with gold and ivory; the crews were arranged according to age and experience in vice. Birds and beasts had been procured from remote countries, and sea monsters from the ocean. On the lakeshore brothels crowded with noble ladies were set up, and on the opposite bank naked prostitutes making obscene gestures and movements could be seen.

As darkness approached, all the adjacent grove and surrounding buildings resounded with song, and shone brilliantly with lights. Nero, who despoiled himself with every legal or illegal indulgence, hadn't left out a single abomination which could heighten his depravity, until a few days afterwards he stooped to marry himself to one of that filthy herd, by name Pythagoras, with all the forms of regular wedlock. The bridal veil was put over the emperor; people saw the witnesses of the ceremony, the wedding dower, the couch and the nuptial torches; everything in a word was plainly visible which, even when a woman weds, darkness hides.

Tacitus, *Annals*, XV.37

The Great Fire of Rome

Nero had a wish, or more accurately, he had always been determined, to bring about the end of Rome. He declared Priam wonderfully happy in that he had seen Troy perish just as his power over her came to an end. Accordingly, Nero sent off various men on different routes pretending to be drunk, or involved in some kind of mischief, and at first had a few fires lit surreptitiously in different areas.

Naturally, the people were thrown into considerable confusion, neither being able to find the cause of the trouble nor to end it. In the meantime they met with many strange sights and sounds. They ran about as if distracted, some rushing this way, and others that way. While helping their neighbours, men discovered their own homes were ablaze. Others only found out that their property was on fire, by being told it was burned down. People would race from their houses into the alleys, hoping to help from outside, or would rush back into the houses from the streets apparently imagining they could do something from the inside.

The shouting and screaming of children, women, men, and the old merged in a ceaseless racket. What with the smoke and shouting no one could make out anything. All this time many who were carrying off their own property, and many more who were looting what belonged to others kept bumping into another and tripping over the goods. It was impossible to go anywhere but equally impossible to stay where you were. Men pushed and were pushed back, knocked others over, and were knocked over themselves. Many were suffocated or crushed. In brief, whatever misfortunes were possible in such a situation indeed occurred.

This situation lasted not one day, but several consecutive days and nights. Many houses were destroyed through a lack of firefighters and many were actually set ablaze in more than one place by people pretending to be rescuers. This was because soldiers (including the night watch), ever watchful for plunder, instead of putting the fires out, stoked them up.

While similar dramas were happening at many different locations, a sudden wind caught the fire and whipped it up over what remained. Consequently everyone stopped worrying about goods or homes, but all the survivors gazed on what appeared to be many islands and cities in flames from a safe place. No longer was there any grief for private loss, public lamentation swallowed up this as men reminded each other how once before most of Rome had been laid waste like this by the Gauls. While the population was in this state of high tension, and many driven demented mad by the disaster were leaping into the flames, Nero climbed up onto the roof of the palace. Here one could take in the whole fire in a panoramic view. He put on a professional harpist's outfit, and sang 'The Taking of Troy' (so he said), although to ordinary people, it seemed to be 'The Taking of Rome'.

The disaster Rome then suffered, was unparalleled except for the Gallic invasion [in 390BC]. The whole Palatine hill, the theatre of Taurus, and nearly two-thirds of the rest of the city were burned. An unknown number of people died. The population cursed Nero without a break, not speaking his name, but simply cursing 'those who started the fire'. This was made worse because they were disturbed by remembering the prophecy recited in the reign of Tiberius. It was to this effect, 'After three times three hundred rolling years, in civil strife Rome's Empire disappears'. When Nero, trying to lift their spirits, said these verses were nowhere to be discovered, they changed their tune and repeated another prophecy, said to be a genuine one by the Sibyl, 'When the Matricide reigns in Rome, then ends the race of Aeneas'.

And this is what actually happened, whether it was really revealed in advance by some divine force, or whether the people now for the first time gave it the form of a sacred utterance just adapted to the circumstances. For Nero was indeed the last of the Julian line, descended from Aeneas. Nero now started collecting huge sums of cash both from individuals and nations, sometimes using downright compulsion, with the great fire as his excuse, and sometimes extracting donations with so-called 'voluntary' offers. As for the Roman masses, they had the money for their food dole withdrawn.

Dio Cassius, *Roman History*, LXII.16-18

ANALYSING CRUELTY

It would be wrong to give the impression that the Romans to a man considered brutal behaviour to be the only option. Seneca wrote about anger and what led men to behave as they did.

It should now also be considered whether those who are routinely cruel and take pleasure in human bloodshed are enraged when they kill people who have done them no harm, nor even think that they have been … This is not rage, but brutality. For this does not cause harm just to repay an injury, but is even prepared to accept injury for the chance to cause harm, and the purpose of wanting to hit and mangle is not revenge but pleasure. Why does it happen? This anger comes from evil, and when anger from a temper, frequently and too-often lost, has no regard for mercy or any sense of humanity, it becomes cruelty. So, such men laugh and rejoice, enjoying great pleasure, and have an expression totally unlike anger, making ferociousness into a way of life.

When Hannibal saw a ditch filled with human blood, it is said that he shouted out, 'What a beautiful sight!' How much more beautiful he would have thought it if the blood had filled a river or lake. How extraordinary, Hannibal, that you born to bloodshed and used to killing from when you were a boy, find such a special pleasure in this sight? ….

Not long ago the governor of Asia, Volesus, decapitated 300 people on one day. As he swaggered about amongst the corpses, in the manner of someone who had committed an act of greatness worthy of admiration, he yelled out in Greek, 'what a kingly thing to do!' What would he have done if he *had* been a king? This wasn't anger, but an evil far worse and beyond saving.

Seneca, *On Anger*, II.5.3-5

Epitaph on the early emperors

Amongst others, Pliny the Elder looked back on the extravagances of the early emperors with amazement.

Julius Caesar, before he became dictator, was the first person serving as an aedile to use only silver equipment in the arena — that was during the funeral games organised in honour of his father. This was the first time that criminals obliged to fight wild beasts had had all their gear made of silver, something matched nowadays even by ordinary provincial towns. Gaius Antonius, and also Lucius Murena, held plays on a stage made of silver. The emperor Caligula brought 124,000lb of silver into the circus on a mobile scaffold. When he was celebrating the triumph when Britain was conquered, Caligula's successor Claudius advertised on notice boards that in amongst all the gold crowns was one given by Nearer Spain which weighed 7000lb, and another of 9000lb from Gaul. His successor, Nero, covered Pompey's theatre with gold just for the one day he was going to show it off to Tiridates, the king of Armenia. But how small that theatre was compared to Nero's Golden House which goes all over the city!

Pliny the Elder, *Natural History*, XXXIII.53-4

An explanation for Caligula and Nero

A breech birth is unnatural, being feet first, and this explains why those born this way are called Agrippa — having been born with difficulty. It is said that Marcus Agrippa was born like this and is practically the only instance of a successful person out of all those born in this manner. But it is thought he paid the price his unnatural birth promised. When he was a young man, lameness brought him misery. Throughout his life he was surrounded by fighting and death. All his offspring brought misery to the world, but most of all the two Agrippinas [the Elder: daughter of Agrippa; the Younger: granddaughter of Agrippa] who gave birth to the emperors Caligula and Nero, a pair of firebrands to the human race. Agrippina, Nero's mother, writes that he, who was an enemy to humanity for his whole life, was born with his feet first.
Pliny the Elder, *Natural History* VII.45

We've even seen people putting perfume on the soles of their feet, a gimmick Marcus Otho taught Nero. How on earth could anyone notice that? And what pleasure could that part of the body produce? Not only that, we've heard that someone who had no imperial connections ordered that his bathroom walls be showered with perfume, and that Caligula had perfume put in his bath. Afterwards, a slave belonging to Nero did the same thing, in order that it wouldn't be the prerogative only of an emperor.
Pliny the Elder, *Natural History*, XIII.22

FLAVIAN EXCESSES

The end of the Julio-Claudians by no means meant the end of debauchery. Vespasian's younger son Domitian paradoxically reigned longer than his vastly more popular father, and his brother Titus (who himself showed signs of turning into another Nero). He started off well, like so many who came before and after him, but soon slid into decadence, despite many positive achievements which included suppressing corruption amongst urban magistrates and provincial governors. But he earned the opprobrium of the senatorial class and his imperial successors through his unrestrained autocracy. Historians and other writers lined up to damn his memory the moment he was murdered.

The fly-swatter

When his reign began Domitian spent ages on his own every day doing nothing other than catching flies and stabbing them with a very sharp pen. As a result, when someone wanted to know if anyone was in a room with him, Vibius Crispus replied with wit, 'no-one, not even a fly'.
Suetonius, *Domitian*, 3

Excess lust

Domitian was excessively lustful. He referred to his continuous indulgence in sexual intercourse as bed-wrestling, as if it was a form of exercise. It was said that he shaved his mistresses with his own hand and went swimming with common sluts. Having continuously declined his niece (because he was involved in a liaison with Domitia), offered to him in marriage when she was still a virgin, he seduced her not long after she married someone else, and that took place when Titus [her father] was still living. Later, once she was fatherless and widowed, he regarded her with undisguised passion, and was even the cause of her death when he forced her to abort his child.

Suetonius, *Domitian*, 22

Dealing with adultery

Domitian's plan was to execute his wife Domitia for committing adultery. But after Ursus had persuaded him not to, he divorced her once he had murdered the actor Paris in the middle of the road because of her. When many people commemorated the spot with flowers and unguents, he gave orders for them to be killed as well. Following that he lived openly with his niece (Julia) as man and wife, and did not really try to pretend otherwise.

Many wealthy men and women were punished for adultery. Domitian had assaulted some of the women himself. Many people were executed or fined on charges of other crimes. In this way, one woman was sent for trial and executed for removing her clothes before a statue of Domitian.

Dio Cassius, *Roman History*, LXVII.12.1-2

BETTER TIMES

The soul of discretion

Trajan (98-117) was considered to be the second of the five 'good' emperors, whose reigns lasted from 96 to 180, and was the first to reign for a reasonable length of time. He is remembered best for his Parthian and Dacian wars. They won him, and many of his soldiers, glory, and led to the Empire reaching its greatest extent. Perhaps this was because, unlike most of his predecessors, he kept his indulgences quiet.

Trajan was not educated in the formal sense of the word with respect to speaking but he knew what it consisted of and could apply it. He possessed all qualities to a considerable level. Naturally I am quite aware that he adored boys and wine, but if these had led him to commit or tolerate any decadent or evil act he would have been censured. But as it was, he drank all the wine he wanted and stayed sober and no one was harmed by his relationships with boys.

Dio Cassius, *Roman History*, LXVIII.7.4

Hadrian's indulgence

Although he was noted for his strict views on military discipline and restraint, Hadrian had a weakness for a young man called Antinous. Disaster struck, and Hadrian never really recovered.

During a journey on the Nile he lost Antinous, his favourite, and for this youth he wept like a woman. Concerning this incident there are varying rumours; for some claim that he had devoted himself to death for Hadrian, and others — what both his beauty and Hadrian's sensuality suggest. But however this may be, the Greeks deified him at Hadrian's request, and declared that oracles were given through his agency, but these, it is commonly asserted, were composed by Hadrian himself.

Aelius Spartianus, *Hadrian*, XIV.5-7

Honest men

Not all Romans of course were villains, great or small, even if such people made better copy for the Roman historian and his modern counterpart. The Roman world also exhibited men and women of enormous dignity, honesty and integrity. Amongst all the emperors, Marcus Aurelius (161-80) was, and remains, a man of outstanding personal merit.

When it came to public expenditure, Marcus Aurelius was very careful. He outlawed libellous claims by dishonest informants, thereby labelling people who made false accusations as infamous. He refused to have anything to do with accusations which would increase the state coffers. He thought up many sensible ways to subsidise the poor. So that he could broaden the functions of the senate, he nominated senators to act as curators for many communities. In time of famine he donated city food stocks to Italian communities and he took measures to deal with the whole grain supply. He imposed restraints on all sorts of gladiatorial shows. He also reduced the cost of free theatrical shows, such that an actor could be paid five aurei but none should exceed ten. He also took care of the lanes and roads of the city with great diligence. The matter of the grain supply, he managed with great seriousness ....

He looked after the people no differently than is done under a free state. He was always very moderate in deterring men from committing evil deeds, encouraging them to do good, and rewarding generously. He forgave quickly, turning bad men into good and good men into better, and even put up with rudeness from some with forbearance.

Julius Capitolinus, *Marcus Aurelius*, XI.1-5, XII.1-2

THE RESTORATION OF DEBAUCHERY

In terms of outright decadence, the second century was not particularly notorious. Apart from the lunatic Commodus (180-92), none of the rulers really managed to match the worst examples of the first century. Men like Trajan, Antoninus Pius and Marcus Aurelius were long-lived and respected rulers of an age which Commodus brought to an end in a grotesque manner. The tragedy was that Marcus Aurelius had his own son. A system that had relied on adopting the best man around reverted to the dynastic succession that had reaped such an ill harvest in the first century.

A venal existence

Commodus was more interested in indulgence than ruling, and to begin with he handed power over to the commander of the Praetorian Guard, Perennis. Both, it seems (according to this account), had many shortcomings.

Perennis, being familiar with Commodus' personality, found out how to make himself more powerful. That was to encourage Commodus to give himself over to pleasure, while he took over all the responsibilities of government (an arrangement which Commodus was delighted to accept). So, under this system, Commodus led a venal existence amongst banquets and 300 mistresses. They were brought together for their beauty and chosen from Roman ladies of quality as well as sluts, and minions (300 of them too), whom he had indiscriminately press-ganged or bought from the rabble and nobility purely for their looks. At the same time, dressed as a sacrificial assistant, he killed the sacrificial victims. He fought in the arena with light sticks, but occasionally with sharpened swords while his bedroom servants played the part of gladiators.

Perennis had absolute power by now. He killed whoever he fancied killing, robbed loads of people, broke every law, and pocketed all the loot. For his own part, Commodus murdered his sister Lucilla after he had banished her to Capri. After violating his other sisters, so the story goes, he started an affair with one of his father's relatives and even called one of his mistresses after his mother. He threw his wife [Crispina], whom he apprehended committing adultery, out of his house, banished, and then had her executed. On his instructions his mistresses were violated in front of him and he couldn't even escape a reputation for having affairs with young men, soiling every part of his body in liaisons with either sex.

Aelius Lampridius, *Commodus*, 5

A love of cruelty

An expert in poor judgement, Commodus had Perennis killed in 185 and handed power to Cleander, a freedman who sold positions left, right and centre to make himself wealthier and also to pay for Commodus' high living. Nothing changed in the rule of a man who fancied himself as Hercules and who accordingly clubbed people for fun.

Commodus cherished the cult of Isis, even to the extent of shaving his head and carting a statue of Anubis about. He actually ordered the devotees of Bellona to slice off one of their arms out of his love of cruelty, and as for those of Isis, he made them beat their breasts with pine-cones, even to the point of death. He used to clout the heads of the Isis devotees with the face of the Anubis statue while he was carting it about ….

Pernicious also in fun he, for example, placed a starling on the head of a man whom he had seen had a few white hairs which looked like worms amongst the black. He made the man's head fester as a result of ceaseless pecking by the bird which thought, of course, that it was chasing worms. He slit open the belly of a fat person, so that his intestines poured out. He called other men 'one eye' or 'one foot' after he had plucked out one of their eyes or chopped off one of their feet….

He retained certain fellows amongst his staff named after men and women's private parts and he liked to kiss this lot. He also had in his entourage a man with a penis that was bigger than that of most animals, whom he named Onos [an ass]. He treated this chap with great affection, making him rich and promoting him to be a priest of Rustic Hercules.

It is said that, frequently, he mixed human faeces and the most costly foods and didn't hold back from tasting them.

Aelius Lampridius, *Commodus*, 9-11

ELAGABALUS

With the coming of the Severans at the end of the century a new era of decadence was heralded in. Amongst this new breed of rulers was Varius Avitus Bassianus, renamed Marcus Aurelius Antoninus and known to the world as Elagabalus due to his association with the sun-god Heliogabalus. His accession followed the defeat in 218 of a soldier-emperor called Macrinus who had ordered the murder of Caracalla in 217. Elagabalus was pushed into position by his grandmother, Julia Maesa, sister-in-law of Septimius Severus (193-211).

A new breed of pervert

Elagabalus quickly set a new tone, looking back to the old, but not so good, days. But in historical terms the account of Elagabalus' life belongs to a class to be read with some care. There are contradictions and obvious additions or interpolations in the account and it has long been recognised that the story was a compilation of anecdotes and more official and reliable information. So, while these tales make entertaining, if distasteful, reading, we should not take them entirely seriously. Either way it made no difference to Elagabalus who was murdered along with his mother in 222, their bodies being dragged through Rome and hurled into the Tiber.

Elagabalus devised certain new classes of vice, even exceeding the disgusting practices used by the perverts of the past, and he was very familiar with the practices of Tiberius, Caligula, and Nero.

Aelius Lampridius, *Elagabalus*, 33

A bad upbringing

He was completely controlled by his mother Julia Soemias to the extent that he conducted no official business without her say-so, although she lived like a tart and indulged in all sorts of lewdness in the palace. While we are on that, her affair with Caracalla was so notorious that Varius, or rather Elagabalus, was generally believed to be his son.

Aelius Lampridius, *Elagabalus*, 2

Unnatural lusts

After he had wintered in Nicomedia [Izmit], living in a disgusting way and indulging in unnatural vice with men, the troops soon started regretting the conspiracy they had organized against Macrinus to make this man emperor. They started thinking about his cousin Alexander who, when Macrinus was murdered, the Senate had hailed as emperor.

Who could put up with an emperor who took part in every type of unnatural lust, when not even an animal who behaved like that would be tolerated? Even in Rome all he did was send out agents to look for especially well-endowed men and bring them back to the palace so that he could enjoy their manhood.

What's more Elagabalus used to have the story of Paris acted out in his home. He would be Venus, and suddenly drop his clothing on the floor and fall naked to his knees, one hand on his breast, the other in front of his private parts, his bottom sticking out all the time and pushed back before his partner in depravity. Similarly, he would adopt on his face the expression with which Venus is normally painted, and he had his whole body shaved, declaring it to be the greatest pleasure in life to look fit and able to arouse lust in the greatest number of people....

Elagabalus even obliged some writers to record some unspeakable details of his profligacy which were intolerable to relate, considering that this was in a biography of him. He installed public baths in the imperial palace and simultaneously opened the bath of Plautinus to the people, so that in this way he might obtain a supply of unusually well-endowed men. He also took care to have the whole city and the docks searched for *onobeli*, as those were called who appeared especially randy.

Aelius Lampridius, *Elagabalus*, 5, 8

Violating the Vestal Virgins

Elagabalus took many he liked the look of from the theatre, the circus, and the arena and brought them to the palace. So great was his lust for Hierocles that he kissed him where it would be disgusting even to mention, declaring that he was celebrating the festival of Flora. He violated the purity of a Vestal Virgin, and by removing the sacred shrines he violated the religious rites of the Roman nation. He also wanted to put the eternal flame out.

In fact, he wanted not only to abolish Roman religious ceremonies but also those of the whole world, his one desire being that the god Elagabalus would be worshipped everywhere. He forced his way into Vesta's sanctuary, which only Vestal Virgins and the priests may enter, even though his body was stained by every moral flaw and he was in the company of others who had stained themselves.

He had a go at making off with the sacred shrine, but he grabbed only an earthenware version instead of the right one, which the Senior Vestal had shown in an attempt to trick him. When he found there was nothing inside, he flung it down and broke it. But the cult did not suffer from him, because several shrines had been made, so the story goes, just like the genuine article, so that no one would ever be able to steal it. Despite this, he nevertheless made off with the image he thought was the Palladium, and after covering it over with gold he put it in the temple of his god.

Aelius Lampridius, *Elagabalus*, 6

The sacrifice of high-born children

Elagabalus also sacrificed human victims, and to this end he gathered from all over Italy beautiful children of noble families, whose parents were alive, planning that the sorrow, if suffered by two parents, should be all the greater, I imagine. Finally, he kept near him every type of magician and had them carry out daily sacrifices, while he encouraged them on and thanking the gods because he found them to be well-disposed towards these men. All the time he would examine the children's body-parts and torture the victims in the custom of his own native practices.

He distributed gifts to the people, which they could scramble for, when he started his consulship. These were not mere pieces of silver and gold, indeed, or sweets or small animals, but fatted cattle, camels, asses and slaves. He declared that this was an imperial custom. He viciously attacked the memory of Macrinus and even more viciously Diadumenian [the son and putative heir of Macrinus] because the latter had been given the name Antoninus (Elagabalus called him a Pseudo-Antoninus) and because it was said that from a hopeless profligate he had turned into a very brave and honourable, dignified and austere, person.

Aelius Lampridius, *Elagabalus*, 8

Unsuitable appointments

Elagabalus appointed a dancer from the Roman stage to be prefect of the Praetorian Guard, a charioteer called Cordius to be prefect of the watch, and a barber called Claudius to be prefect of the corn-supply. To other prestige positions he promoted men who had nothing other than the size of their private parts to recommend them. To collect the five-percent inheritance tax he appointed a muleteer, and he appointed a messenger, cook, and locksmith. Whenever he visited the Praetorians' fort or the Senate he took his grandmother Julia Maesa along with him …. so that he might be more respected as a result of her status. On his own, he got none at all….

He preferred it if perverts were seated next to him at banquets, and took a special delight in touching them up or fondling them. Whenever he took a drink, one of them was normally chosen to pass him his goblet.

Aelius Lampridius, *Elagabalus*, 12

Sporting excesses

The story goes that he gave a naval display on the waterways at the amphitheatre, which had been filled with wine, and sprinkled a perfume made from wild grapes on people's clothing. He drove a chariot pulled by four elephants on the Vatican Hill, demolishing tombs in his way. He also harnessed four camels to a chariot at a private show in the amphitheatre. Another story is that priests from the Marsic region helped him collect serpents which he suddenly released before the sun rose, a time when the people usually gathered for the more popular games. He wore a tunic made of gold cloth, or a purple one, or a Persian type decorated with jewels. On those occasions he would say that his pleasures were weighing him down.

Aelius Lampridius, *Elagabalus*, 23

New women and lavish banquets

Elagabalus never had sexual intercourse with the same woman twice except for his wife. He established brothels in his home for his friends, his clients, and his slaves. He never spent less than 100,000 sesterces on a banquet (equivalent to 30lb of silver). Sometimes he even spent as much as 3 million, when the total cost had been worked out.

Aelius Lampridius, *Elagabalus*, 24

He enjoyed being a girl

He always bathed with the women at the public baths, and he even treated them himself with a hair-removing cream which he then put on his own beard and (though it's shameful to say this) in the same place and at the same time as the women were treated. He shaved his underlings' pubic areas, controlling the razor with his own hand — which he then used to shave his own beard. He scattered gold and silver dust around a portico and then complained that he was unable to scatter amber dust as well (he often did this when he walked to his horse or carriage, just as they do these days with sand).

Aelius Lampridius, *Elagabalus*, 31

Damage limitation

The death of Elagabalus in 222 was followed by the accession of his 13-year-old cousin Severus Alexander. He, too, was largely under the influence of his mother, in this case Julia Mamaea, sister to Elagabalus' mother. The reign started off promisingly with efforts made to wipe out the damage done in the previous four years. These measures indicate how corrupt the imperial system had become.

To begin with, statues of deities which the previous emperor had had removed from their locations, were restored to their original ancient shrines and temples. Undeserving people who had been promoted to positions of high status and power, or those who had been advanced because of their notorious criminal activity, had all their privileges removed and were ordered to go back to the jobs and positions they had had before. The complete body of civil affairs and administration was handed over to men who had the greatest reputation for legal skills and as rhetoricians. Military responsibilities were entrusted to those who had proved their reputations in war and in imposing discipline.

Herodian, *History of the Empire*, VI.1.3-4

WOMEN OF EASY VIRTUE

Sempronia

Lucius Sergius Catilina, of a Republican senatorial family, was an ambitious young man who thought nothing of using murder and other crimes to forge his career path, helped along his way with the support of Crassus. This was not particularly unusual during the 60sBC but in 64 and 63 he lost elections in his bid to become a consul, and was abandoned by Crassus. The defeats turned his mind and he embarked on a suicidal conspiracy to overthrow the state. He found support from unusual quarters, including aging prostitutes and the remarkable Sempronia.

The story is that around this time Catiline gained a number of supporters of all types. These included a number of women who, when younger, had enjoyed a lavish lifestyle funded by working as prostitutes. As they grew older, their incomes were reduced but they made no change in their lifestyles and fell headfirst into debt. Catiline considered that these women would be useful for stirring up trouble amongst city slaves and arranging arson attacks, and that either their husbands would be persuaded to join as well or they could be murdered.

One of these women was Sempronia who had usually acted like a man in her boldness and daring. This was despite the fact that Fortuna had treated her kindly, beginning with a good family and looks, and following that with a husband and children. She had studied Greek and Latin literature, and could play the lyre and dance though rather better than necessary for a woman of quality. She also had other abilities of the type which encourage decadence. She held honour and decency in lower esteem than anything else. She took no more care of her reputation than she did of her money. She was so lustful that she more often approached men than vice-versa. She had already broken numerous solemn promises, used perjury to default on debts and had been an accessory to murder. Her extravagant living plunged her into debt. But she had abilities which should not be looked down on: she could compose poetry, she was funny and her conversation was modest, gentle or vulgar as needed. Frankly, she was a woman of great wit and very charming.
Sallust, *The Catiline Conspiracy*, 24-5

A discreditable empress
The emperor Claudius (41-54) acceded as a figure of fun, but proved himself a capable administrator. However, his indulgence was his wife Messalina who humiliated him with her insatiable desire for sex.

Messalina, the wife of the emperor Claudius, believing this would be an authentic royal triumph, chose a certain woman who was the most notorious amongst prostitutes, for a contest in sex, and defeated her with a score of twenty-five partners in a match lasting a whole twenty-four hours.
Pliny the Elder, *Natural History*, X.172

PRIVATE AND PROVINCIAL DECADENCE

Brutalizing Britain
The attractions of vice and other decadent pastimes were not lost on the peoples of the Roman provinces. Even in Britain, little more than thirty years after the invasion in 43, being Roman started to suit a population being drawn into the net.

In order to make a scattered, barbaric, population used to peace and quiet through easy living Agricola provided private encouragement and public assistance to build temples, basilicas, and homes. He congratulated the hard workers and slated the lazy. In this way an honourable rivalry replaced force. He likewise provided Roman education for the chiefs' sons, and showed such a preference for the native abilities of the Britons over the professional skills of the Gauls that those who had only a short time before refuted the Latin tongue now aspired to be competent in it. Hence, too, a liking grew up for our style of dress, and the toga became fashionable. Little by little they were led to things which favour decadence: porticoes, baths, sumptuous banquets. In their ignorance, they called all this civilization, when it was in reality just part of their enslavement.

Tacitus, *Agricola*, 21

Private cruelty

Cruelty was not the preserve of the emperors. In an age when life was cheap, and a slave's life even cheaper, the death of a man could simply be a source of entertainment.

Vedius Pollio, Roman equestrian and one of the deified Augustus' inner circle of friends, discovered that the moray eel provided him with the opportunity of demonstrating his cruelty, when he threw condemned slaves into pools of moray eels. It was not that land animals were not good enough for this, but because no other beast made it possible to have the sight of a man being ripped to pieces in an instant. It is said that they are driven especially insane by tasting vinegar.

Pliny the Elder, *Natural History*, IX.77

Outdoing the Caesars

Even the lunacy of Caligula and Nero was outdone by the resources of one private citizen. It could be argued that Marcus Scaurus, when he was aedile, outdid anyone else in undermining morality, and whose promotion to a position of influence was an even worse crime than his stepfather Sulla's murder of so many people as a result of his death sentences.

When he was aedile, Scaurus erected the greatest building ever put up by the hand of man. It was not only greater than any temporary projects but designed to last for eternity. It was a theatre which had a stage with three storeys and 360 columns. This was in a city that beforehand had slated a distinguished man for his six columns of Hymettan marble. The bottom storey was built of marble, the middle one of glass, an example of extravagance that had not been heard of before or since, and the top one made out of wood covered with gold leaf. The columns in the bottom storey were nearly 38ft high each.

There were 3000 bronze statues placed between the columns. It could seat 80,000 even though Pompey's theatre, accommodating 40,000 is quite big enough these days despite the fact that Rome is much bigger and the population many times greater. The remainder of the theatre's equipment, which included costumes woven with gold thread, scenery and other fittings, came to so much that when superfluous everyday pieces were removed to Scaurus' villa at Tusculum, he lost 30 million sesterces when the house was sent on fire and burnt down by enraged servants.

Scaurus got one thing out of that fire — no one could match his madness in the future.

Pliny the Elder, *Natural History*, XXXVI.113-116

THE DEMON DRINK

The veneration of drunkenness

In antiquity alcohol was used to some extent as hallucinogenic drugs were in the 1960s. Certain individuals, such as the Augustan poet Sextius Propertius, venerated the way in which intoxication was believed to lay a path to higher levels of awareness.

Like Ariadne of Theseus who lay languidly on the lonely shores of Crete as the ship sailed away,
Or Andromeda, freed from the rocks at last, and first overcome by sleep
Or a bacchante, exhausted from dancing, lying on the grassy banks of the river Apidanus.
In this way, Cynthia with the breath of a sleeper, lay in bed with limp unconscious hands for a pillow.
When I came back late one night, unsteady with drink, my way lit by lads holding torches, I tried to make my way to the bed she rested so gently on, while I still had some control over my senses.
Fired up with double the effect, from either side, by the two extreme divinities Love and Intoxication, urging me to slide my arm under that sleeping girl to clutch her, kiss her lips and push home my advances, I lost my nerve to wake her that way, terrified of her scornful tongue.
Propertius, *Poems*, I.3

Bacchus and the pleasures of life

In one of his rural idylls Virgil, another far more famous Augustan poet, recorded how Bacchus, and his powers over the world of nature, were regarded as a fundamental symbol of fertility and beneficence. This romantic image of the vine and wine lay at the heart of Roman spiritual veneration of the pleasures of life.

Look, here are four altars we build; and I for you
Two beakers yearly of fresh milk afoam,
And of rich olive-oil two bowls, will set;
And of the wine-god's bounty above all,
If cold, before the hearth, or in the shade
At harvest-time, to glad the festal hour,
From flasks of Ariusian grapes will pour
Sweet nectar. Therewithal at my behest
Shall Lyctian Aegon and Damoetas sing,
And Alphesiboeus emulate in dance
The dancing Satyrs. This, your service due,
Shall you lack never, both when we pay the Nymphs
Our yearly vows, and when with lustral rites
The fields we hallow. Long as the wild boar
Shall love the mountain-heights, and fish the streams,
While bees on thyme and crickets feed on dew,

Your name, your praise, thine honour, shall endure.
Even as to Bacchus and to Ceres, so
To you the herdsman his yearly vows shall make;
And thou thereof, like them, will bind them to their vows.
Virgil, *Eclogues* V.67-80. Trans. John Dryden

The effects of wine

Despite the veneration felt for wine and its effect, more thoughtful Romans were perfectly well aware that it could cause men to behave in the most appalling way.

When the power of wine has entered a man and its heat dispersed, coursing through the veins, why is it that the limbs become heavy, why are his legs shackled, staggering, his speech slurred, his brain befuddled, his eyes watery, why do noise, belches and provocations burst forth and all the other related things follow? I say, why should this be, unless it is that impetuous violence of wine is accustomed to disorientate the spirit while it is still in the body? But if anything has the potential to be confused and impeded then that shows that if a substance only a little more effective found its way in, that thing would die and lose its chance of a future.
Lucretius, *On the Nature of Things* III.476-487

Wine as a poison

One of the powers that wine has is to heat the internal organs of the body when it is drunk, and of cooling the external parts when it is poured over them. It would not be inappropriate to mention here what that famous philosopher Androcydes wrote to Alexander the Great when he was trying to discourage his intemperance: 'O King, when you are just about to start consuming wine, remember that you are drinking the blood of the earth. Hemlock is a poison to humans, and wine poisons hemlock'. If Alexander had listened to this advice, he would certainly not have murdered his friends in his drunken rampages. So, in fact, it is quite reasonable to say that there is nothing more useful for invigorating a body, and nothing so destructive to our pleasures when moderation has been forgotten.
Pliny the Elder, *Natural History*, XIV.58

Payback time

Even in the best conditions, drunkards never see sun come up and consequently shorten their lives. That's why there are pale faces, sagging cheeks, inflamed eyes and shaking hands that spill full cups. This is the reason for the speedy payback in the form of horrific nightmares and for insatiable lust and joy in overdoing it. The breath reeks of the wine-jar the following day and everything is forgotten, the memory is dead. That's what people refer to as 'taking life as it comes' but while some men lose the past behind them this lot loses tomorrow as well!

Tergilla criticises Cicero for the fact that his son used to knock off one and half gallons at a time, and that when he was drunk he flung a wine goblet at Marcus Agrippa. In fact, those are the usual signs of being drunk. But doubtless Cicero junior wanted to outdo the

reputation of his father's murderer, Mark Antony, in this area because Antony had earlier done everything to be champion at this game by publishing an autobiography of his own boozing. But by having the front to brandish his claim in that book, he shows clearly (in my opinion) the range of troubles he imposed on the world thanks to his drinking.
Pliny the Elder, *Natural History*, XIV.147-8

THE CHRISTIAN VIEWPOINT

For early Christians, the Roman indulgence in lust and intoxication was part and parcel of the same package of decadent behaviour. Writers like Tacitus looked down on decadence and perversity in the imperial court, and regretted the decline. For Christians the behaviour was a mark of how the old order needed replacing with a more censorious and intolerant regime. Christian writers exhorted people to give up temptation, using Venus as a symbol of lust and Bacchus (sometimes called Liber) as a symbol of drunkenness.

Lust and drunkenness go hand in hand

However, Venus and Liber are close friends. Sworn together the two devils of lust and intoxication are close friends. So, the house of Venus is also the house of Liber. Appropriately enough, stage performances which as well as being dedicated to Liber (called the Dionysia by the Greeks) were also introduced by him. As is obvious, theatrical arts are patronised by Venus and Liber. Those aspects which are characteristic of, and peculiar to, the theatre — the wanton mannerisms and posture, are dedicated to Venus and Liber, both decadent deities, the first due to sexual depravity, the second to dressing up like women. Everything else performed with singing and tunes belongs to Apollo, the Muses, Minerva and Mercury. Oh Christian, you will despise the works whose authors you cannot help loathing.
Tertullian, *On Spectacles*, X.6-9

The sensual impact of food

Some of the Christian commentators seem to have been more obsessed with sex and lust than the society they were so quick to criticise. Saint Jerome was especially preoccupied with the subject. While he was not actively discouraging his female acolytes from any sort of physical relationship he kept an eagle eye on other sources of temptation and decadence which apparently even included food.

I am not condemning food which God created to be enjoyed without giving thanks, but I do insist that for youths and young women some types of food provoke sensual behaviour. Neither the fires of Mount Etna, the island of Vulcan, or Mount Vesuvius and Mount Olympus, boil with as much raging heat as do the bones of the young when they are filled with drink and inflamed with banqueting. Many men can quash greed under their feet, and discard it as easily as if it was a purse. Compulsory silence is as good a remedy to a libellous mouth. A man's appearance and style of dress can be changed in one hour. All the other sins lie outside us, and what is outside us can be easily discarded. Lustful desires on their own, given to men by God in order to have children, if they go outside their boundaries turn into a sin, and thanks to the laws of nature rages to force its way to lustful intercourse. You must fight with yourself daily, seeing that you were born in sexual desire, not to live a life of sexual desire. This is what the apostle said in a different way, 'All the sins that a man commits are outside his body, but he who fornicates, commits a sin against his own body.

Jerome, *Letters*, 54.9, written in the year 394

The carnality of heretics

Although the Christian writers, theologians and apologists could barely contain their revulsion at pagan habits, when it came to other Christian sects, they really let rip with their pens. In the fourth century, once Christianity was legitimised, the stage was set for the Christian establishment to fragment in public amongst its various groups. What began as theological disagreement over a single word or phrase could degenerate into open tribal warfare conducted in the streets or by the pen. The abuse would not have disgraced a drunken tavern. Here St Augustine indulges in a nauseating bout of breathtaking smugness, having spotted what he regarded as decadent behaviour in a rival establishment.

I gave a short sermon with the intention of giving thanks to God because we heard coming from the heretic church the row from the usual feast they were celebrating (at the exact time we were thus engaged, they were still nursing their cups), I commented that the day's beauty seemed more so when compared with the night and that the colour white gives more pleasure when it is set against black. In this way, perhaps our spiritual get-together would have been a less gratifying experience without being set against the gluttonous carnality from elsewhere.

Augustine, *Letters* 29.11, written in the year 395

A LIFE WORTH LIVING

A tombstone from Rome shows that whatever the problems with the paths to vice and ruin one man at least was going to take them all with him. He seems to have died happy, regardless of where his soul ended up.

To the Spirits of the Departed, Tiberius Claudius Secundus. He has everything here with him. Baths, wine and sex destroy our bodies. But only baths, wine and sex make life worth living! Good health to you and yours. He made this himself for his wife Merope Caesonia, his family and his descendants.

ILS 8157 (Rome)

5 Corruption, swindles and double-dealing

In a world which stretched as far as the Black Sea in the east and the Atlantic Ocean in the west, it was almost impossible for the Roman state to control its officers and enforce the law everywhere. In practice the Empire ran on a system of compliance, resembling aspects of the modern United States. Each province, like the American states, retained some of its own local laws while at the same time forming part of the Empire. Every province had to swear allegiance to the emperor and that meant also being subject to the laws and edicts of the emperor.

This was no democracy, and corruption was rife throughout the system, requiring constant vigilance. Throughout the provinces ordinary people were subjected to the consequences of dirty deals done in the forums of Rome and in their own provincial assemblies. The local worthies parcelled up the local economy for themselves, creamed off percentages and lined their own pouches. At the bottom, ordinary provincials ducked and dived as well.

MONEY

The root of all evil

In an essay exploring the causes of anger, Seneca analysed money as the ultimate source of misery and confrontation. The passage is depressingly cynical but there are many people who have won money in our own time who have found everything he said to be true.

A wise man will never stop being angry once he starts. Everywhere is packed with crime and vice. Too many misdemeanours are committed for there to be any possible means of stopping them. Men flounder in a huge competition of wickedness. Everyday there is more desire to do wrong, and less fear of doing so. Any regard for doing the right and more just thing is banished, lust throws itself wherever it wants, and crimes are no longer kept secret. They stride about before our very eyes, and evil has become so conspicuous, and achieved so much power over everyone that innocence is not rare — it no longer exists at all. Is it only the odd man or a few who break the law? Everywhere, people rise up to erase any difference between right and wrong, as if they had been whistled up to do so….

The outcry is almost all about money. That's what wears the courts out, puts father against son, contrives poison, arms the legions and robbers. Money is stained with our blood. Thanks to money, the nights are scarred by quarrelling husbands and wives, crowds mass before the magistrates' benches, kings rant, ransack and topple nations that were built out of the labour of aeons, just so they can hunt for gold and silver in the ruins.

You might say it's a pleasure to find a sack of cash in the corner. But that is what men will scream for until the eyeballs pop out of their heads. For the sake of things like this the law-courts echo to the sound of lawsuits and jurors are called in from far away to decide which man's greed is the most justified.
Seneca, *On Anger*, II.9 and III.33

Money as the basis of status
Horace considers how money was the foundation of Roman status and whether the benefits it conferred were worth the trouble. The reference to the Arch of Janus in Rome is an allusion to the Roman bankers who worked nearby.

Silver is not so valuable as gold, gold is less valuable than virtue. 'Oh, citizens, citizens, money is the first thing to seek; virtue after riches. That's the rule proclaimed by the Arch of Janus from top to bottom. That's the lesson sung by old and young alike, 'with writing tablet and satchel slung over the left arm.' You have good sense and morals, eloquence and honour, but there with six or seven thousand short of the 400,000 [needed to be an Equestrian], you'll just be one of the crowd. But boys having fun shout out, 'you can become a ruler, if you keep as a straight as a rule'. Let this be our bronzen wall, to have no guilt in out hearts, no misdemeanour to make us go white.

Pray, tell me which is the better course, the Roscian Law [which dictated seating positions in the theatre according to wealth] or the children's ditty which offers a kingdom to whose who do right, a ditty once uttered by the manly Curii and Camilli? Does the man who tells you to 'make money, money, by the right way if possible, if not, any way so long as it's money' just so you can site closer to the front to see the miserable plays of Pupius, give you good advice? Or the man who's always there, encouraging you to stand on your own two feet in defiance of scornful Fortune?
Horace, *Letters*, I.1.52-69

Petty greed
Pliny the Younger recounts a dinner party where the host looked after himself and not his guests.

To Junius Avitus
Repeating in detail, of no consequence anyway, how I came to be dining with someone, in spite of his not being a close friend, would take too long. His frugality, which he described as 'elegant', looked to me to be simultaneously sumptuous and cheap. For the best dishes were given to him and a chosen few, along with some cheap cuts to everyone else. The wine had even been poured into tiny little containers in three classes. This was not so the guests could choose but so that they could not refuse what they were offered.

In the way he classifies his friends one sort was for him and us, one for his less-important friends, and the last for all our freedmen ….

The reason I am telling you this is to make sure that a young man like you, with such a promising future, does not fall into the trap of cheapskate extravagance which can be found in some houses …. You should bear in mind that nothing deserves to be avoided more than this novel combination of indulgence and meanness. These vices are quite bad enough individually, and they are worse when combined.

Pliny the Younger, *Letters*, II.6.1-2, 6

Easy money

Here Petronius provides a satirical description of how to make money in business through the mouth of his character, the freedman Trimalchio.

I developed a love for business. I won't hold you up for a moment. I built five ships, obtained a cargo of wine (which was worth its weight in gold at the time) and sent the lot to Rome. You might think I was conned. All five were wrecked, and that's the truth — it's no fantasy. Neptune drank 30 million sesterces-worth in one day. Did I give up? Oh no, the loss had no more effect on me than if it hadn't happened. So, I built more, bigger, and better ships so that no one would be able to say I lacked courage. There's something rather safe about a large ship, you know. I obtained another cargo of wine, bacon, beans, perfumes, and slaves. Fortunata did a noble thing then. She sold all her jewellery and clothes, putting the 100 gold coins into my hands. Those coins were responsible for my fortune. I cleaned up a cool 10 million on the trip. Immediately I bought all the estates which had belonged to my patron. I built a house and bought slaves and cattle. Everything I touched grew like wildfire. When I ended up with more money than the nation I packed it in. I gave up active work and from then on I financed freedmen.

Petronius, *Satyricon*, 76

CORRUPTION

The ways of the world

Here Gaius Sallustius Crispus describes his own youthful foray into politics. Born in 86BC, he was forging his political career in the 50s, the time of Julius Caesar and the dictators, just as the Roman Republic was gradually coming to an end. Accusations of corruption tainted his career and he was expelled once from the Senate for immoral behaviour. Here he describes his own plunge into the dark side and it helps explain how, when he retired, he was extremely wealthy.

Just like many other young men, my own first instinct was to commit myself completely to politics. Many obstacles confronted me. No-one took any notice of self-control, integrity or virtue.

Dishonest behaviour, bribery, and a quick profit were everywhere. Although everything I saw going on was new to me — and I looked down on them with disdain —

ambition led me astray and, having all the weakness of youth, could not resist. Regardless of my efforts to dissociate myself from the corruption that was everywhere, my own greed to get on meant that I was hated and slandered as much as my rivals.
Sallust, *The Catiline Conspiracy*, 5

The path to power
The lawyer and politician Cicero wrote a treatise on duty. He analysed the cause of greed and corruption, no better illustrated in the political machinations of the late Republic in his own time. He recorded the views of Crassus, a cynical politician, who became a member of the ruling Triumvirate.

Men seek wealth, first to pay for life's necessities, then for enjoyable pleasures. However, amongst those for whom ambition is foremost, the passion for riches has a view to power and the means to award favours. For example, Marcus Crassus said not long ago that there was no amount of wealth sufficient for the man who wished to be premier citizen in the nation, unless he could finance an army with the income.
Cicero, *On Duties*, I.8.25

The fireman
Plutarch provides us with an explanation of how Crassus realised his financial ambitions.

Crassus spotted how fire and the collapse of buildings due to their closeness to one another, and their size, were frequent daily events in Rome. Consequently he bought slaves educated as builders and architects. Then, once he had more than 500, he purchased houses on fire, or near a fire. The house-owners, terrified and bewildered in the heat of the moment, would sell up for a knock down price. In this way, most of Rome ended up belonging to Crassus. Despite the fact that he owned so many workers himself, he built no houses for himself apart from the one he lived in. He had a saying that men who liked building had no need of enemies. They would bring ruin on themselves.
Plutarch, *Crassus* 2.

Every man's soul has its price
In Italy, at Pompeii, the election slogans daubed on the walls of private houses and shops testify to the manoeuvring of local politicians and their supporters. It is plain from some of them what these would-be public servants had offered in exchange for election.

I request that you elect to the post of aedile, Gaius Julius Polybius. He gets hold of good bread.
CIL iv.429

The legacy of corruption
The decadence of the first century AD (described in Chapter 4) also resulted in

corrupting the Senate, forced to stand by while hideous crimes were committed in the name of the state. In the early second century Pliny the Younger looked back on the effect on his peers, unable to look up to the previous generation for an example.

What lessons could be learned in those days, what was there to be gained by learning, when the Senate was obliged to twiddle its thumbs or perpetrate some disgusting crime, and was kept in session for a laugh or was humiliated when it could never see serious legislation through, but often with a tragic outcome? When we became senators we participated in this evil, carrying on participating and enduring them for years, until our spirits were worn down, broken and wrecked with permanent damage. Consequently it has only been a short time (the shorter, the better it seems), since we started to want to know what we could do and put our learning into effect.
Pliny the Younger, *Letters*, VIII.14.8-10

IMPERIAL ADVANCEMENTS

Brotherly love
Thanks to his munificence, Titus (79-81) was greatly esteemed by the Roman mob. He also generally managed to avoid putting people to death. Scandal surrounded his early death, little more than two years after the death of his father. It seems his jealous brother Domitian was keen to succeed.

It is said that while Titus was still breathing and might even have got better, Domitian put him in a box packed with snow in order to send him on his way more quickly, fabricating a claim that Titus' illness might need treating with cold. Anyway, he rode to Rome before his brother was dead and entered the praetorian camp where he received the imperial title and authority, once he had given the soldiers all that his brother had given them.
Dio Cassius, *Roman History*, LXVI.26.2

Septimius Severus rids himself of a rival
In the year 193 Septimius Severus was governor of Upper Pannonia. He viewed the events surrounding the death of the lunatic Commodus (180-92) with interest, and initially declared his loyalty to Pertinax. When Pertinax was murdered and the Praetorians sold the Empire to the short-lived Didius Julianus (see Chapter 2), Severus allowed himself to be declared emperor. He had first to rid himself of two rivals: Pescennius Niger, governor in Syria, and Clodius Albinus, governor in Britain. With skilled duplicity Severus made friends with the latter, enabling him to defeat Niger unmolested, recognising that the governor of Britain had a ready-made means to seize power.

Severus, who by nature was cautious and suspicious, had been becoming wary of the garrison in Britain, a large and powerful army of first-class fighters. Albinus, the governor and a senator of patrician birth, was their leader. He had been brought up with a silver

spoon in his mouth and a comfortable living inherited from his ancestors. Severus was keen to hoodwink Albinus into supporting him, because there was a danger that relying on his wealth and family history, his personal reputation in Rome, and the strength of his forces, might provide him with an incentive to go to war to become emperor. Under such circumstances he might make a try for the purple and seize Rome, which was close to him, while Severus was engaged in the East. Severus won Albinus (who was stupid and vain) over by feigning to give him an honour. He was completely fooled this time by the promises Severus put in letters to him. Severus declared Albinus to be Caesar, thus pre-empting Albinus' ambitions by giving him a share of power …. Albinus happily accepted the position since he was only too happy to get what he wanted without having to go to war over it. Severus permitted coins in Albinus' name to be issued, and by allowing statues to be put up he provided public recognition of the favour he had bestowed.
Herodian, *History of the Empire*, II.15.1-3

Having fallen for the ruse, Clodius Albinus was left with a false sense of security. Severus, having defeated and killed Niger, turned to the west and defeated Albinus at Lyons in 197. Albinus committed suicide and Severus dealt viciously with Albinus' memory.

Albinus' head was sent off to Rome with instructions that it should be displayed in public at the top of a pole. This was so that the Roman people would be able to see his level of rage and how angry he was with Albinus' friends. Then he set things to rights in Britain and split the governorship of that province into two separate commands … All of Albinus' friends, regardless of whether they had joined his cause of their own free will or been coerced to, were executed and their property seized.
Herodian, *History of the Empire*, III.8.1-2

PROVINCIAL CORRUPTION AND EXPLOITATION

From the reign of Augustus to Trajan about 40 trials are recorded which involved corrupt provincial administration, or roughly one every three to four years. As these largely come only from the extant texts of Tacitus and Pliny the Younger it follows that there must have been more, perhaps many more. Even so, this was considered to represent an improvement over the days of the Republic when Roman administration had been 'discredited by the infighting amongst men of power, and the greed of administrators' (Tacitus, *Annals*, I.2), and helped popularise rule by an emperor. One of the most notorious Republican governors was Verres.

Verres: the greedy and lecherous pig
The case against Gaius Verres was heard in Rome in 70BC, following representations made by Sicily. Cicero was responsible for the prosecution on charges of extortion. Despite attempts by Verres and his associates to infect the court with corrupt officials the case proceeded. Before its conclusion, however, Verres exiled himself and was then

subjected to being made an outlaw together with punitive fines. He was executed in 43BC, as indeed was Cicero. This excerpt from Cicero's speech gives an indication of the cynical way a Roman governor might exploit a province. But, at least there was recourse to law.

The treasury was sacked by Verres and he ransacked Asia and Pamphylia ... During the time that Verres was governor of Sicily, the inhabitants had no resort to the law, nor decrees of the Roman senate, nor universal human rights. Sicilians now only hang on to whatever this extremely greedy and lecherous pig overlooked or what was left over once he had had his fill. During a period of three years not one case was heard without him intervening. No one's inheritance from his father or grandfather was so secure that it would not be seized from him in the courts if Verres demanded. A new, immoral, law meant countless quantities of cash were taken off farmers. Our most faithful allies were treated as if they were slaves, and Roman citizens were tortured and put to death as if they were slaves. Bribes secured the acquittal in the courts of the guiltiest men and simultaneously honest, conscientious men were prosecuted and tried *in absentia*, found guilty and exiled.
Cicero, *Prosecution of Verres*, I.1, 4-5

The ravages of Cilicia
In the year 51BC Cicero became governor of the province of Cilicia (western Turkey) for the one-year term normal for governorships of senatorial provinces. He landed at Ephesus on 22 July. As he made his way inland he found a wealthy province ravaged by taxation and its consequences, not least of which was the sale of taxes (the sale of anticipated revenues to moneylenders for instant cash to pay sums demanded).

On 31 July I made my eagerly anticipated entry into this desperate province which has been ruined forever (I am not exaggerating). I stayed for three days each in Laodicea, Apamea and Synnada. All I have heard about is the inability to pay the poll taxes which have been levied, the sales of taxes everywhere, grumbling and complaining from the communities, and horrifying excesses more appropriate to a wild beast than a human being. To be blunt, they are all completely fed up with their lives. But there is some consolation to these communities that I have spared no expense, and nor has anyone on my staff, legates, quaestor and all.
Cicero, *Letters to Atticus*, V.16 (dated 15 August 51BC)

Britain: ripping off the Trinovantes and Iceni
Britain in the year 60 was a new province, barely a generation old. Heavily-garrisoned and half-conquered the land was rife for the carpet-baggers. First in the queue to clean up were the veteran soldiers of the XX legion. Installed in the new colony at Colchester the idea was that they should present to the natives a good example of Roman life. They did anything but that and instead spent their time ripping off the newly-conquered tribes. Part of the reason, undoubtedly, was that Britain was regarded as so barbaric and so inferior that any abuse was permissible. Indeed, part of the glory of

conquering Britain had been the defeat of somewhere so exotically remote and untamed. Oppressing the island peoples was thus all part of the psychological achievement.

The story begins with Prasutagus, king of the Iceni. The tribal territory spread across eastern Britain, covering the modern counties of Norfolk and Suffolk. Prasutagus had been allowed to remain king by the Romans for his lifetime. He knew what would happen when he died and tried to make provision for the hand-over. Thanks to the historian Tacitus we have a graphic account of the consequences, with additional details supplied by Dio Cassius. The crisis not only cost many men and women on both sides their lives, but also nearly cost Rome her new province.

Prasutagus, king of the Iceni, famous for his long period of prosperity, had made Nero his heir together with his two daughters. He believed that this symbol of deference would protect his household and his kingdom from wrong. But the opposite occurred. His kingdom was ransacked by centurions, and his household by slaves, as if they were spoils of war. To begin with, his wife Boudica was flogged and his daughters raped. The Iceni chiefs had their family estates taken from them and the king's relatives were enslaved, as if the nation had been given to Rome as a gift.

Having now been reduced to the state of a province, the Iceni were stimulated by these insults and the prospect of worse to follow to go to war. They also incited to rebellion the Trinovantes and other tribes, not yet crushed by slavery, who had made a secret arrangement to recover their freedom. Hatred was focused most intensely on the veteran soldiers. These new settlers at Colchester had thrown people out of their houses and evicted them from their farms, and called them prisoners and slaves. The soldiers had encouraged the veterans to act beyond the law, because they lived the same way and wanted the same licence.

Tacitus, *Annals*, XIV.31 (part)

The confiscation of money awarded by Claudius to the most important Britons provided an excuse for going to war. This money was supposed to be repaid, Catus Decianus the procurator of the island, insisted. That was one cause of the rebellion. Seneca had lent 40 million sesterces to the islanders who did not want it [the meaning of the text here is uncertain], hoping for a high rate of interest, but subsequently called it all in at once and used tough tactics to get it back. This provided another motive to revolt. But Buduica [sic], who they considered a suitable leader and who was in control of the whole war, was the person who was mainly responsible in working up the natives and encouraging them to fight the Romans. She was a British woman of royal birth who was more intelligent than women usually are.

Dio Cassius, *Roman History*, LXII.2.1-2

The temple built for the cult of the deified Claudius [in Colchester] could be seen from everywhere as if it was the citadel of perpetual tyranny. Men chose to act as priests there had to pour away their fortunes into it on the pretext that it was for religious purposes. The colony looked as if it would be easy to destroy because it had no fortifications, a precaution our commanders had overlooked by spending time on what would be pleasant rather than useful.

In the meantime, for no apparent reason the statue of Victory at Colchester fell down, facing away from the enemy as if it was running away from them. Women, frenzied with excitement, foretold imminent destruction. It was said that ravings in an incoherent language had been heard in the senate-house, that shrieking had resonated in the theatre, and that an image of the ruined town had been seen in the Thames estuary. Even the sea itself had looked like blood and when the tide went out things that looked like human bodies were to be seen, interpreted by the Britons as promising and by the veterans as worrying.

Since Suetonius, the governor, was far away, the townsfolk begged for assistance from the procurator, Catus Decianus. He did no more than send a maximum of 200 men, lacking proper arms while in Colchester there was only a small garrison. Relying on the temple for protection, and handicapped by secret supporters of the revolt who frustrated their plans, the Romans had not built a ditch or a rampart. Not only that they had not evacuated the old men and women so that only the young men would be left to face the enemy.

Thus, as if it was in middle of peace, they were surrounded by a huge multitude of barbarians. Everything was ransacked or burned in the attack. The temple, where the soldiers had gathered, was stormed after a siege lasting two days. As Petillius Cerealis, commander of the IX legion, came to the rescue he was routed by the victorious enemy and his infantry wiped out. Cerealis escaped with some of his cavalry into their fort and was saved by its defences. Terrified by this disaster, and the rage of the province which his greed had provoked into war, the procurator Catus crossed into Gaul.

Conversely, Suetonius, with admirable self-possession marched right through the middle of the enemy to London which, despite not being honoured with the status of a colony, was a very busy place thanks mainly to its throng of traders and communication routes. When he got there he doubted its suitability as a headquarters. Considering his minimal force, and remembering how Petillius' rash actions had been punished, he elected to save the province by sacrificing a town. The tears and laments of the population, begging for his help, did not put him off giving the orders to depart and to take anyone who would go with them. Those who could not move thanks to their sex, old age, or a love of the place, were left to the enemy.

Verulamium suffered the same disaster because the barbarians, who took great pleasure in plunder and cared about nothing else, ignored the forts with their garrisons of troops and attacked whatever looked as if it would offer most to those in search of spoil and which was not easily defended.

It seems that about 70,000 citizens and allies fell in these places which I have described. The enemy was not concerned about taking prisoners and selling them, or any of the normal commerce of war, but on killing, on the gibbet, by fire and crucifixion as if they were men who would soon pay the penalty and wanted their vengeance now.

Suetonius already had the XIV legion, a detachment of the XX and auxiliaries from nearby, when he prepared to stop playing for time and fight a battle. He picked a spot approached by a narrow gap, cut off at the rear by a forest having first made sure there was no trace of the enemy anywhere except to his front where there was a plain with no cover and thus no chance of ambushes. He maintained his legions in tight formation surrounded by the light-armed troops and with the cavalry densely packed on the wings.

On the other hand, the hordes of infantry and cavalry in the army of the Britons were moving all over the place excitedly. This was the largest there had ever been, and such was their confidence that they had brought their wives, riding in carts placed around the edge of the plain, to witness the victory [fictitious speeches by Boudica and Suetonius follow in Tacitus' account].

Suetonius was confident of victory when he gave the signal for battle to commence, so great had been the enthusiasm which followed his speech and so quickly had the veterans, with their long experience in the army, prepared to hurl their spears.

To begin with, the legionaries held their position, clinging to the narrow gap for its natural security. Once the approaching enemy had allowed them to exhaust their spears by aiming confidently, they all sprang forward in a wedge formation. The auxiliaries burst forward in the same way while the cavalry, wielding lances, broke through any sections which resisted strongly. The remainder took to their heels but their escape was thwarted by the cordon of carts. Our soldiers did not even spare the women, and pack animals, run through with spears, added to the pile of corpses.

A great glory, which matched our victories in former time, was won that day. It is said that little fewer than 80,000 Britons fell that day while only about 400 of our soldiers were lost and a similar number wounded. Boudica committed suicide with poison. So did Poenius Postumus, camp prefect of the II legion, when he heard about the success of the men of the XIV and XX. He felt that he had cheated his legion of its chance for glory and going against all military precedent by contradicting the commander's orders, by throwing himself on his sword.

Now the whole garrison was brought together and kept mobilized to conclude the war. Nero strengthened the forces by sending 2000 legionaries from Germany: eight auxiliary cohorts and 1000 cavalry. When they arrived, the soldiers of the IX were brought back up to strength with legionaries. Auxiliary infantry and cavalry were installed in new winter camps. Any tribes whose loyalties were still undecided or were still hostile were harried by fire and sword. But nothing distressed the enemy as much as famine. They had neglected to sow corn because people of all ages had joined in the war and had regarded our supplies as theirs.

But the more high-spirited tribes were only slowly reconciled to peace. This was because Julius Classicianus, installed as successor to Catus, was at odds with Suetonius and let his personal feelings interfere with the public interest. He put it about that everyone should wait for a new governor who, lacking an enemy's anger and a conqueror's pride, would be considerate to those who surrendered. At the same time he sent an official letter to Rome saying that no-one should expect an end to the fighting unless Suetonius was replaced, blaming the governor's disasters on his perverseness, and his successes to good luck.

Tacitus, *Annals*, XIV.31 (part)-38

Britain: Agricola's reforms

Despite the efforts of Classicianus (whose tombstone survives to this day in the British Museum in London), the Romans were still playing dirty tricks nearly twenty years later. In 77-8, Gnaeus Julius Agricola was sent to Britain as the new governor. Tacitus wrote the story of his life but, as Agricola's son-in-law, it is heavily biased. Nevertheless, the account provides a good example of how local officials worked the system. Here the Britons were supposed to pay tribute but the Romans found a way of selling them the goods (at a profit of course) to pay the tribute with, and also forcing them to trudge miles across country to do it.

Agricola equalized the burden of grain and tribute demands to make them less onerous. He abolished the various profit-making scams which were harder to bear than the tribute. The Britons had been forced to indulge in a farce of turning up at locked granaries and buying grain in order to hand it straight back. In this way they disposed of their obligations, but at a price. Routes off the beaten track and remote places were announced, so that tribes wintering nearby had to deliver the tribute in remote and faraway places. In the end, something that was straightforward for all was made profitable for a handful.
Tacitus, *Agricola*, 19

North Africa: extortion and oppression

Britain was not the only province to suffer corrupt officials. The North Africans brought a case in Rome against their ex-governor.

The province of Africa brought a charge against their former governor, Marius Priscus, who pleaded guilty and asked that a commission calculate what compensation should be provided. Cornelius Tacitus and myself received instructions to speak for the provincials. We considered it our duty to advise the Senate that a commission was inadequate for dealing with crimes on this scale. These involved Priscus being bribed to sentence innocent people to punishments and even execution.

Catius Fronto, acting for the defence, delivered a plea that the charge be reduced to the matter of compensating extorted monies. As he is very experienced in the art of provoking sympathy, the sails of his speech were blown along by his pathos. A very unpleasant row and outcry all-round followed, with one side insisting that law restricted the Senate's judicial powers and the other saying the opposite and that Priscus should be punished in a manner reflecting his guilt.
Pliny the Younger, *Letters*, II.11.2-5.

In the end, Priscus was exiled from Rome and Italy and had to pay back the bribe of 700,000 sesterces. But his powerful friends and lawyers had saved him from receiving his just deserts. He escaped being sentenced for what he had done to innocent people, and hung on to his position and estates. In North Africa in the late second century one procurator was in league with leaseholders to intimidate and beat tenants. The local tenants, ever mindful of the need for humility, wrote to the emperor Commodus for his help.

From Lurius Lucullus on behalf of tenants on the estate to the Emperor.

That you may learn of the collusion which your procurator has been operating, uncontrolled, with our enemy Allius Maximus and also almost all the main lessees, to the dereliction of rights and the detriment of your revenue. Consequently, for years whenever we filed petitions with him, pleading and pointing out your divine edict, he has avoided investigating anything. Also, he has given way to the tricks of Allius Maximus, chief lessee, who is so popular with him, to the extent that he has sent troops into the Buritanian estate and ordered some of us to be arrested and tortured. Others have been chained up, and some (including Roman citizens) beaten with sticks and clubs.

All we had done to deserve this was that, confronted with injury, tangible and oppressive to a degree only matching the level of our unimportance we had resorted to sending off a letter of complaint, begging for your imperial help.... We utterly wretched men, are driven again now to beg for your divine providence. Thus we ask you, most sacred emperor, to come to our assistance ....

CIL viii.10570 and 14464, Dated to 180-3

In reply, Commodus instructed his procurators to make sure that nothing was illegally forced out of any of the tenants. However, the officials who erected the inscription took care to amend the edict in their favour. The words in italics were added by them, and show just how hard it was to wipe out law-breaking and exploitation in an Empire ruled from so far away.

Taking account of tradition and my order, procurators will ensure that nothing *more than three blocks of two days' work per man* is illegally imposed on you in violation of normal practice ....

The far-reaching consequences of exploiting Africa

In the reign of Maximinus I (235-8), a rebellion blew up in North Africa. The cause was straightforward enough. This time it was a procurator who thought exploitation would further his own career. Not only did he earn his own death but the rebellion occasioned a year of blood and chaos in which five emperors, including their nominated successors, died.

The rebellion was caused by a severe procurator in the Carthage region, who customarily imposed utterly vicious sentences on, and requisitions from, the people. This was in the hope that Maximinus would make a favourable note of his name because the emperor chose men who were known to follow his own policies. Even where treasury officials were honest men, and this was very rare, they copied the others with reluctance because of the dangers confronting them and because they knew about the emperor's greed.

Amongst the Libyan procurator's generally oppressive carryings-on was the way he tried to extort cash quickly from young men from well-to-do noble families of Carthage. He imposed fines on them in the courts and seized their ancestral family property. Humiliated and angered by this treatment they promised to pay up the money but asked the deadline to be delayed by three days. All those who had been subjected to this action, or thought they might be in the future, formed a conspiracy. Their rural supporters [i.e. their tenants] were told by them to enter the city at night, armed with clubs and axes. The rural people collected in the city, obeying their landlords, concealing their weapons for an improvised war under the garments they had on. As Libya has a substantial population with many people working on the land, a very large mob had collected.

Soon after sunrise, the youths turned up and instructed their large crowd of tenants and so on to follow on behind as if they were part of the gathering. But they added that the men should keep the weapons they had brought hidden for the moment and strictly avoid any soldier or ordinary person who might set about them in revenge for the action they were soon to take. The young men themselves approached the procurator with daggers hidden in their clothes, making out that they were going to talk about paying their fines. Suddenly they rushed him, when he was relaxed, and stabbed him to death. Then, as his guards drew their swords in an attempt to avenge his murder, the countryside workers routed them as they waved their clubs and axes in defence of their masters.

Once they had done this, the wealthy young men were faced with a quandary. Their solution to possible capture and defeat was to visit the home of the governor, the aged Marcus Antonius Gordianus Sempronianus and declare him emperor. Gordian accepted, and the Senate in Rome approved. But only a 21-day reign followed before his son, Gordian II, was killed in battle by one of Maximinus' supporters, Capellianus, governor of Numidia, and Gordian I committed suicide on hearing the news. Meanwhile the Senate elected Balbinus and Pupienus to rule and Maximinus was killed by his own soldiers. Balbinus and Pupienus lasted three months before being killed by the Praetorian Guard. Gordian I's grandson was made emperor as Gordian III and a relatively stable six years followed before he too was murdered.

Herodian, *History of the Empire*, VII.4.2-4

Insider trading

One of the weaknesses of relying on local officials to operate imperial policy was that those officials got wind of changes in the law before anyone else. Not only could imperial pronouncements be altered, but there was always a chance to capitalise on devaluation of coinage.

Coinage was a fundamental part of the Roman system of exchange, and value was directly linked to intrinsic value. In other words, the value of a gold or silver coin was dictated by the amount of precious metal in it. In an unsophisticated economy, it was seen as simple enough to make the money go further by putting more base metal into the coins, or devaluing it. Not only that, but local currencies circulated in the cities of the Eastern Empire and there was a profit to be made in the exchange. The city governments were on the case and here we see the measures adopted by one such body to curb corruption, and the measures taken by a man of substance to cash in.

The council and the people have decreed: if anyone, free or slave, other than the lessee or banker, is apprehended buying or exchanging currency in any way, that person shall be summoned to face the banker on the evidence brought to the council by any citizen who wishes to do so.

Once convicted before the judge and council, where the accused committed the crime without profit, the banker and informant who gained the conviction will have the right to get the money back, with the former retaining the guaranteed right of legal execution against the defendant.

If he profited, a convicted freeman will pay a 500 *denarii* fine to the sacred treasury of our most divine imperial lords, 250 *denarii* to the town council, and 100 *denarii* to the informer who obtained the conviction. The money found to be involved shall go to the banker. A convicted slave shall be handed over to the judges before the council by his master, given 50 lashes, imprisoned, and sentenced to remain thus for six months. However, if the master wishes the slave not to be treated in this way, the fines stated above will be payable to the treasury, the city and the informer who obtained the conviction.
Edict of Mylasa in Caria (Asia Minor). *OGIS* 515, dated to 209-11

Privileged information

Nearly a century later, coinage was subjected to continual change as the Empire struggled to find ways to pays its vast numbers of soldiers and officials. Dionysius, probably one of those officials, wrote to Apio, who was likely to have worked for him as a bailiff. Dionysius had information that could make him a killing and others go bust.

Dionysius to Apio, Hail.
The divine fortune of our rulers has instructed that coinage struck in Italy shall be reduced to half the value of a *nummus* [a standard unit of coinage]. Hurry and spend all the Italian cash you can and buy any goods for me at the price you find being charged.

I'll point out from the start that if you play any tricks I'll be sure to catch you out. I pray that you live long in good health, brother.
Rylands Papyrus 607, about 300

RELIGIOUS CORRUPTION

Crooked priests

The cult of Claudius at Colchester (see above) involved corruption and exploitation. This was not the only case of crooked cults and clerics. In the year 313 the emperor Constantine I legitimised Christianity. He packed his court and government institutions with new men, some of whom spotted the chance to line their nests by destroying the old temples. In the year 360 Julian the Apostate became emperor. A committed pagan, and one of many who believed Christianity to be fatally stricken by infighting, he decided to clean up government.

Julian turned to the palace officials and sacked anyone in that category, or who could be included …. admittedly, most of those wretches indulged in a full portfolio of vices, to the extent that their corrupt desires infected the whole Empire. Many people were damaged, more through the example they set than their license in misdemeanours.

Some, grown wealthy by robbing temple property and smelling out a profit wherever one was to be had, leaped from total poverty to colossal riches in a single jump. They had no sense of a limit to bribery, theft, and prodigality, being entirely used to taking goods off other people.

In this way decadence, perjury, and spurning a good name grew. Insane pride destroyed their honour through their disgraceful profiteering. At the same time outright greed and the bottomless depths of banquets grew out of control.

Eventually, victories in battle were replaced by dining triumphs. Extravagant use of silk and other fabrics became more common, and concern with culinary skills grew. Ostentatious locations for extravagantly appointed houses were enthusiastically sought. Ammianus Marcellinus XXII.4

A less than Christian bishop

Not long after Julian's reforms, Georgius, bishop of Alexandria, found himself suffering the wrath of the local mob, thanks to his personal style of spiritual leadership (sadly, it was not unique). The crowd had already executed Artemius, duke of Egypt, after he had been accused of all sorts of oppression and corruption. This was an age when certain Christian leaders, who were often new men elevated way beyond their abilities, abused their status and indulged in corruption and oppressing traditional cults. The origins lay in the reign of Constantine I (307-37) who legitimised Christianity under the Edict of Milan. In order to gather around him a loyal body of administrators, he favoured the promotion of people who had no family or personal associations with traditional paths to power. This resulted in the displacement of old families and the introduction of individuals who could provoke extremely hostile responses from reactionary sectors of the population. A sure way to do so was to line one's own pockets and expend energy on destroying paganism.

The Alexandrians .... turned their wrath on Bishop Georgius who had frequently made them suffer his venomous jaws, as you might put it. The tale is that he was born in a fullers works in the Cilician town of Epiphania and did extremely well out of ruining many others. Afterwards he was ordained bishop of Alexandria, a move neither to his advantage or that of the district. The city is often the setting for riots and rebellion originating in nothing more than impulse and which have no basis. To these lunatics, Georgius was potent provocation once he was appointed after he had filled the ears of the emperor Constantius with names of people he said were rebelling against his authority. Forgetting his position, which warranted justice and reason, he descended to the lethal methods of the informant. Amongst other things, it's alleged that he also informed Constantius of this: because all the buildings standing on city land had been put up by its founder, Alexander, at state expense then it was only right they be used to raise money for the treasury.

He added another crime to these wicked acts, which not long afterwards sent him plummeting to his doom. While he was coming back from the emperor's court and passing the beautiful Temple of the Genius where there was the customary large gathering, he looked right at the temple and announced, 'how long will this shrine remain standing?' When they heard this, many were shocked as if a bold of lightning had struck, and started fomenting secret schemes to destroy Georgius in whatever way, fearful that he might even try to get that building knocked down.

When the happy news arrived that Artemius had been killed the people were inspired by this unexpected pleasure, gnashing their teeth and shrieking horrible oaths, went for Georgius and grabbed him, doing all sorts of horrible things to him and treading on him. After that they dragged him around all spread out and executed him.

With Georgius, both the superintendent of the mint Draconius, and the honorary count Diodorus, were pulled around with ropes lashed to their legs and killed. Draconius, because he had knocked a pagan altar over just set up in the mint, which he was responsible for. Diodorus, because while overseeing the building of a church, he had, without good reason, shorn the curls of some lads because he thought it was a custom belonging to some pagan cult.

Ammianus Marcellinus, XXII.11.3-9, concerning the year 363

CORRUPTION AMONGST THE LOWER ORDERS

Unpaid debts

In northern Britain at the end of the first century, Octavius was pressing for payment.

Octavius to Candidus, his brother, Hail

I will settle the 100lb of sinew from Marinus. From when you wrote about this affair he has made no mention to me. Several times I have written to you that I have purchased 5000 *modii* of grain ears, for which I need money. Unless you send me some, no less than 500 [*denarii?*], the outcome will be the loss of what I paid as a deposit, about 300 [*denarii*], leading to ruin and embarrassment. Thus, I ask you, send me some money as soon as possible.

Tab. Vindol. II.343. From Vindolanda, c. 90-105

Rings

In Pliny the Elder's view, finger rings had come to represent not just an ostentatious symbol of wealth, but also as a medium for corrupt practices, while also having to be used as a security device against light-fingered slaves and house guests. In the end though, the rings used for security were easily stolen themselves.

At first it was customary to wear rings on one finger only, the one next to the little finger. This we can see was the case on the statues of Numa and Servius Tullius. Later on, habits changed and rings were placed on the finger next to the thumb (even on statues of the gods). Most recently, the fashion has been to put them on the little finger as well.

It is said that amongst the Gauls and Britons the middle finger is used. But nowadays amongst we Romans that is the only finger left out because all the other fingers are loaded with rings, with smaller rings even being specially adapted for the smaller finger joints. Some people jam several rings on the little finger alone, while others use this for just one ring, the one used for sealing up their signet ring, which is kept carefully under lock and key as a great rarity, much too valuable for the indignity of day-to-day use. It is brought out of its box as if it was a sanctuary.

In this way, the wearing of one ring on the little finger is no more than brandishing the fact that the owner has far more valuable possessions locked away at home. Some people show off their rings while others consider it much too hard work to wear more than one at a time. Some people, who are particularly anxious about the safety of their gems, fill the circle of gold tinsel with a lighter material, thinking that will help protect it in a fall.

The habit is followed by others of keeping poison hidden beneath the intaglios on their rings, thus wearing them as instruments of suicide. Demosthenes, the greatest of Greek orators, did this for example. In any case, how many crimes associated with money, were actually executed by rings [used for seals on forged and faked documents]? Happy and genuinely innocent were the times when no seals were used for anything. Today, even our food and drink has to be protected from theft with the use of rings. This is thanks of course to those armies of slaves, and crowds of foreigners, who come into our homes, in such quantities that we have to employ someone to tell us what their names are. Surely it was different in our ancestors' times, when no-one had more than one slave who belonged to his master's family, called Marcipor [the boy of Marcus] or Lucipor [the boy of Lucius] or whatever, and ate with him together. This was when there was no need to take precautions by keeping an eye on the staff. But now we not only buy trinkets that are bound to be stolen, but we buy the hands that do the stealing as well. Far from the signet ring being sufficient to keep the actual keys sealed away, the ring is often swiped from the owner's hand while he is in a deep sleep, or on his deathbed.

Pliny the Elder, *Natural History*, XXXIII.6.24-7

Redress

In theory, there was plenty of recourse to justice where disputes arose. In practice, men of power like Marius Priscus (see above) got off and the ability of the Roman state to enforce reforms, laws or any other provisions to limit corruption was, frankly, limited. Only where honest individuals held positions of power was there any real chance of maintaining standards. Not surprisingly, ordinary people had no real chance of pursuing their grievances through official channels. They often turned to the gods. Their pleas highlight the day-to-day inconveniences of casual theft and dishonesty.

May the person who stole Vilbia from me be turned as liquid as water....
Bath 4. Undated lead curse tablet from Bath (Britain).

Docilianus, son of Brucerus to the most holy goddess Sulis.
I curse the person who has made off with my hooded cloak, male or female, slave or free, that .... the goddess Sulis bring death upon .... and prevent him from sleeping, having children, now and in the future, until he delivers my hooded cloak up to the temple of the goddess' divinity.
Bath 10. As previous.

6 Villas, relaxation and rural bliss

The Romans indulged in a permanent fantasy of a bucolic and idyllic Italian past. Despite the fact that the Empire only functioned as an institution through the medium of its army, cities, and communications, there was an ever-present sense that living in and off the countryside was the only means to find inner peace. Literary descriptions of rustic topics were favoured by the poets and other writers, for whom this rural foundation to Roman life was a patriotic symbol of Roman austerity, restraint and hard work. These qualities were seen as the explanation for Rome's power and success but of course it was the latter which presented the Romans with their greatest challenges so far, in the form of luxury, excess, indulgence, and decadence.

As the Romans became more and more dependent on the advantages of urban life and a cosmopolitan economy so they agonised over what they had lost, just as we do. As a Roman read the *Georgics* of Virgil to dream of a past paradise, so we sit down to watch television dramatisations of Jane Austen novels filmed in soft focus on eighteenth- and nineteenth-century country estates. These films generally ignore the practical realities for most people at the time, including the workers in the factories of the Industrial Revolution.

Of course, living in the countryside is, was, and always has been extremely hard. But in the ancient world the contrast between town and country, thanks to the lack of machinery, was perhaps not quite so acute as it has become. This was especially true for the wealthy in any province. The labour-intensive nature of the pre-modern age means that for those who could afford armies of staff and slaves, and this includes most of the men who chose to write about their country houses, life in a Roman villa could be extremely pleasant. For this reason above all, the letters of the younger Pliny provide us with an exceptional resource for appreciating villa life. Several of his letters are quoted here, and with good reason. For the same reason, the wealthy landowners in the England and the north American eastern seaboard of the seventeenth and eighteenth centuries found in descriptions of villa life a model for themselves.

At the very least a villa offered a blissful escape from public life and the stinking racket that was Rome, even if for Juvenal country life was for bumpkins. Nowadays we call these places weekend cottages, an escape from city business, pressure, pollution and noise. The affluent Roman's desire to escape the city seems to have been for exactly the same reasons. The well-to-do seem invariably to have ended up investing time and money in rural retreats. These were usually substantial establishments, and they could in exceptional cases resemble villages or small towns even if their owners still indulged in the vanity they were 'roughing' it, perhaps in the manner that Queen Victoria's children were allowed to run small 'farms' on the royal estates in the nineteenth century. Where archaeology has played a role, it has often been possible to find evidence for urban contraction and decay in the provincial cities of the north-west during the third and fourth centuries. Simultaneously the development of grandiose villas in prime land seems to have taken place. Unfortunately it is almost impossible to trace any one family's growth to wealth or land ownership but it is possible that the great families in a province found it expedient to control affairs through their local cities from a distance in their rural retreats. Certainly there is apparently a correlation between the decline in urban investment and the explosion in rural aggrandisement.

ESCAPING TO THE COUNTRY

A new estate

Roman villa owners in all provinces and at all times had in mind the habits of families and men in Italy early in the imperial age. Our main accounts of villa life belong to the first centuries BC and AD. Here, Horace luxuriates as he surveys the scene of his new estate.

This is just what I had been praying for: a modest-sized plot of land, where there might be a garden, and not far from the house a spring with a ceaseless flow of water, and above these a small piece of woodland. The gods have given me all this but more of it and even better. I am happy. Mercury, I ask nothing more from you except that you ensure these blessings last the rest of my life. So long as I have not grown richer from doing evil, nor become poorer through excess or neglect, or offer such stupid incantations as these, 'If only this or that could be added on that corner, which spoils the shape of my little farm! If only a lucky spade-thrust would reveal a jar of cash to me, just like the man who once found buried treasure and went on to buy and farm the same land which he used to be paid to work on, made rich by Hercules' favour'. So long as what I have makes me comfortable and happy, then this is how I pray to you, 'make my animals grow fat, and as you have been, remain my guardian angel!'

Now that I have escaped from Rome to my castle in the hills, what better subject to devote my satires and prosaic muse to? In this place there is no jockeying for position to destroy me, no heavy south wind, no sickly autumn which Libitina, goddess of funerals, does so well out of ....

As soon as I reach the Esquiline Hill, a hundred worries of others race through my mind and all around me, 'Roscius implores you to meet him at the Wall of Libo [in the Forum] before the second hour of daylight'. 'Horace, the clerks ask you to make sure you come back today to attend to some new and important business of wide popular concern.'

'Get Maecenas to put his seal on these documents.' If you only agree to try, he will insist that if you will, you can.

In the middle of such trivial concerns, alas, I waste the whole day, praying all the time, 'oh, country home, when will I see you, when will I be able, with ancient books and with sleep and time to relax, gorge myself on forgetting life's cares! When will I be served beans, Pythagoras' soul-mates [Pythagoras had promoted vegetarianism on the grounds that animals had souls too], which have been well-greased with fatty bacon!'
Horace, *Satires* II.6.1-19, 32-9, 59-64

Torquatus, if you can lie at my table on couches made by Archias [a maker of simple furniture] and do not recoil from a supper of herbs only, from a plain platter, I will expect you at my house when the sun goes down. You'll down wine bottled in the second consulship of Taurus [26BC] between the marshes of Minturnae near Petrinum and Sinuessa. If you have anything better, then order it sent here, or otherwise do as you are told. My fireside has long been lit for you, and the furniture tidied. Say goodbye to your aspirations and the struggle for money and defending Moschus. Tomorrow is Augustus Caesar's birthday which gives a good excuse for lying in. We'll be able to stretch out the night, without any comeback, enjoying relaxed conversation.
Horace, *Letters*, I.5.1-11

A beloved rural inheritance

Writings like those of Horace helped impregnate the sense that a rural retreat from town was more than a convenience. It was a spiritual retreat and the credential of a person of quality. Generations indulged in literary rehearsals of the qualities of their country homes. They almost all read alike in their basic essence. Here, Ausonius, a Gallo-Roman of the fourth century, writes about his country estate around 400 years after Horace. It is perfectly obvious that he felt much the same way.

Hail to my little hereditary family estate, land of my ancestors, which my great-grandfather, grandfather and father looked after so carefully, which the last of those left me when he died too soon, even though he had reached a venerable age. I had not wanted to be able to be your owner this early. Indeed it is the way of things when a son follows his father but where there is mutual love, it is more pleasant for both to run the place together. Now all the work and trouble has fallen on me. In the past I only had pleasure while my father did all the work.

It's only a tiny estate, I admit, but there never was a property which seemed small to people whose souls are matched, no, it's more than that: people whose souls are one and the same …. I have 200 acres under the plough, 100 acres are planted with vines, and half this amount is pasture. My woodland comes to more than double all that put together, and I have exactly the right number of cultivators. There is a spring near my house and a small well, in addition to the pure clean river which carries me in my boat on its tides away from home and back again. Invariably I have two-years worth of food in store because the man with inadequate supplies is a short distance from starvation.

My estate is neither too close to the town nor too far which means I avoid its crowds

while still enjoying its conveniences. So, whenever I have had enough of one place I go from one to the other, and enjoy town and country in turns.
Ausonius, III.1.1-10, 17-32

CITY SICKNESS

Driven from the city
Here Seneca regales a friend with a tale of how illness drove him to get out of town, only to find that the only thing wrong was that he had been in town in the first place.

I have escaped to my place at Nomentum — escaped from what? Can you guess? Rome? No, a fever, and just as it was breaking down my resistance as well my doctor being certain that it had started with a disturbed and erratic pulse, knocked out of its normal rhythm. So I immediately ordered my carriage to be brought out, and although my Paulina tried to make me stay, I insisted on driving off....

I imagine you're keen to find out whether this decision of mine to leave did anything for my health? As it happens, as soon as I had left behind that crushing air in Rome and that stink of smoky cooking hearths which belch out, along with all the ashes, all the poisonous fumes they've stored inside whenever they're fired up, than I noticed an immediate improvement in my condition. You can just imagine how invigorated I felt when I reached my vineyards. I ploughed into my dinner — you might as well be talking about cattle sent out into spring pastures! So, now I am quite restored. All that listlessness, physical upset and unsettled mind, didn't last. I am getting stuck into some solid work.
Seneca, *Letters*, 104.1, 5-6

Could there be an image of more chaos than Rome? But even there (if you want) you're free to follow a peaceful life. But if I was given a free choice of posting, I'd escape a long way from Rome's environs, let alone a sight of the city itself.
Seneca, *Letters*, 28.8

It's all in the mind
Elsewhere, Seneca conceded that rural bliss wasn't a guarantee of peace of mind.

I've seen for myself people who are totally depressed in cheerful and very pleasant country villas, and others in totally secluded places who looked run off their feet. Consequently, there is no reason to feel you could be enjoying more peace of mind than you would if you were in Campania. While we're on that, why aren't you anyway? Beam your mind over here!
Seneca, *Letters*, 55.8

INVESTING IN THE RIGHT VILLA

Building the villa

Cato's work on agriculture belongs to the pre-imperial age and outside the scope of most of this book. But his treatise was a standard handbook, used by any Roman who needed to know how to run a villa estate. This helps explain its survival. Here he advises on picking the right spot. An aesthetic and comfortable villa was essential to the estate working properly.

The landowner should spend a lot of time thinking about building .... Build when you get to the age of 36, if the plantations are sorted out. Make sure that the villa house and the farm buildings all go up at the same pace. It's a good idea for the master to have a sound barn and storage facilities, and a large number of oil and wine vats, so that products can be stockpiled while waiting for the price to rise. This will be advantageous to his wealth, self-esteem and reputation ....

Build a villa you can afford. If you are building on what is largely a good farm, then putting the villa house in a good place, where your country living will be comfortable, means you will want to go there and often. The farm will therefore become more productive, less will go wrong and more money will come in. Forethought is better than being wise after the event. Act the good neighbour and don't let your staff commit crimes. Popularity in the area will mean your produce sells better, bringing in contractors for jobs is easier, and extra labour can be found. If you are building then the neighbours will help you with the work, muscle and materials. If you do suffer misfortune (perish the thought) they'll help you out.

Cato, *On Agriculture*, 3, 4

The advantages of Italy

What useful produce exists which not only doesn't grow in Italy, but which doesn't grow in the most perfect way there? What spelt can be compared to that grown in Campania? What wheat to that grown in Apulia, wine to that grown Falernia, what oil to the Venafran? Is it not the case that Italy has so many trees it looks like an orchard. Is 'vine-clad' Phrygia (as Homer called it) any more 'clad' with vines than this country? Or Argos, which the same poet calls 'corn-rich', any more 'rich' in corn than here? Where does a *iugerum* produce 10 to 15 *cullei* of wine as some areas in Italy do.

Varro, *On Agriculture*, I.2.6-7

Home improvements

In this letter Cicero comments on the various villa estates belonging to his brother Quintus. This was the year in which Quintus was serving with Caesar in Britain and Gaul, and thus too involved to be able to see to his affairs personally. Cicero found himself dealing with an indolent builder.

Cicero to his brother Quintus

I was at Arcanum on September 10th [54BC] .... On your Manilian estate I came across Diphilus even more behind than he usually is despite the fact that he had nothing outstanding except the baths, an ambulatory, and an aviary. I was very pleased with the villa because the colonnade pavement gives it the sort of dignity that can't be matched; I've only appreciated this since the whole colonnade has been visible and the columns polished. I will make sure the stucco work is done properly because everything hinges on that. As far as I could see the pavement was being put down properly. I gave orders that some arched roofs, which I didn't like, were changed.

With respect to the spot where I am told your written instructions specify the antechamber should be built, i.e. in the colonnade, I preferred it before. There doesn't seem to be enough room for an antechamber. It isn't usual for one to be built at all, except in those houses with bigger atriums, and nor would it have been possible to build apartments and bedrooms of that type into it. The elegant curve of its ceiling alone will make it a fine summer-room in its present form. But if you don't agree, write to me as soon as you can.

I moved the bathroom stove into the opposite corner of the apodyterium because it was placed in such a way that the vent pipe (out of which flames pop) was right beneath the bedrooms. There was one roomy bedroom and another up high for the winter. I was very pleased with these because they were spacious and located in exactly the right place: one by the ambulatory and the other by the baths. Diphilus had installed columns which were neither vertical nor facing one another so, naturally, he will have to take them down. One day he will find out how to use a plumb-line and tape. All things considered, I hope Diphilus' work will be done in a few months. Caesius, who was with me then, is supervising carefully ....

On September 13th I was at Laterium .... I thoroughly approved of Nicephorus, your bailiff; and, I asked him whether he had received any instructions from you about that little house being built at Laterium which we spoke about. In reply, he said that although he had agreed to do the work for sixteen sesterces, you had afterwards added a lot to the job but without any more money; so, he had abandoned the project.

I can certainly assure you that the additions you decided on, and are making, are very pleasing to me. Nevertheless, the villa as it is seems to me to have a kind of 'philosophical' mood to it which reproves the madness of other villas. But it'll be delightful once all the extra work is done. I much admired your landscape gardener. By covering everything with ivy from the foundations to the gaps between the columns in the colonnade, he has made it look to me as if the Greek statues are working as landscape gardeners and advertising the ivy. Now the apodyterium is the coolest and mossiest there is.

Cicero, *Letters to his Friends*, III.1.1-2, 5

Land as capital

This letter from Pliny the Younger is significant for emphasizing the great importance of land as the principal form of capital. Clearly, Pliny does not need the land but it is important to put his money into land, so here he speculates on the wisdom of buying up the neighbouring, but run-down, estate.

To Calvisius Rufus

As usual, I need your advice on a property matter. The estate next door, which runs into mine, is up for sale. There are many good reasons why I should buy it, and just as many just as important why I should not. The main recommendation is the convenience of having the two estates joined, and next the practicality and amenity of visiting both for the price of one journey. Both estates could be run by the same bailiff and almost by the same managers. Only one villa would need to be maintained and furnished while the other was just kept in good repair.

In this assessment I am including furniture, housekeepers, landscape-gardeners, workmen, and even hunting equipment, as it makes a lot of difference whether you keep these altogether into one place or split up into several. On the other hand, I fear it might be foolish to expose so large an estate to the same weather and risks of other accidents. Having property in different places might be a better insurance against hazards of fortune. Quite apart from that, it's very pleasant to experience a change of air and setting, and to travel between one's properties.

But the main factor to take into account is this. The land is rich, fertile, and well irrigated. It's made up of meadow, vineyards, and woodland producing enough timber to maintain a modest, but steady, income. This productiveness is being ruined by poor agricultural methods. The last owner frequently requisitioned and sold the tenants' possessions to make good their arrears, only to compromise their potential for the future so that their debts just piled up again. These tenants will have to be re-established with slaves bought by me, at top prices, because they will need to be good ones. I don't keep chain-gang slaves myself and they are not used on the estate.

All that remains is to tell you the price: three million sesterces. It was once five million but a combination of hard times and few tenants (and thus reduced income), has lowered its value. You probably want to know whether I can raise the money needed. My estate is admittedly almost all held in land but I have some cash invested and I can easily borrow whatever I need from my mother-in-law, whose capital is as freely available to me as my own. So, don't worry about that if you can deal with the other points which I would be very grateful for your full consideration of, seeing as no-one can match your experience and wisdom in important money matters. Farewell.

Pliny the Younger, *Letters*, III.19

Buying and selling land

For all the villas that are now known from aerial photographs (visible as crop-marks) or which have been excavated, little or nothing survives to tell us about land ownership and buying or selling in any one case. While deeds and records must have existed in vast quantities they have simply decayed. One exception is a wooden writing tablet from London. It records a lawsuit concerning a plot of woodland in Kent and it appears that one Lucius Julius Bellicus has brought a case to be heard in London concerning its ownership. Sadly of course, we do not know where the land was but it shows how laws governing tenure in the countryside were administered from the towns. On one hand that reflects the administration of the Roman world, and on the other how landowners needed to divide their business between town and country.

During the second consulship of the Emperor Trajan Hadrian Caesar Augustus, and that of Gnaeus Fuscus Salinator on the eve of the Ides of March [14 March 118]. Coming to the matter presented, the wood *Verlucionium*, more or less seven and half acres in area, which is in the canton of the Cantiaci in the settlement of Dibussu.... up to the boundaries of the heirs of .... and the heirs of the estate of Caesennius Vitalis and the boundary road, Lucius Julius Bellicus stated that he bought it from Titus Valerius Silvinus for forty *denarii*, as stated in the bill of sale. Lucius Julius Bellicus attested that....

RIB 2504.29, wooden writing tablet from London. Latin analyzed and read by R.S.O. Tomlin

Spoilt for choice

It scarcely seems possible that Pliny the Younger could have had time to enjoy all his property. Here he admits to owning several houses by Lake Como, and taking particular pleasure in two of them. He is delighted to discover that a friend is engaged in building improvements, thereby making Pliny feel justified in his own indulgences.

To Voconius Romanus

You write to say you are building. It's very good to find a defence, because I am already doing the same and now it seems sensible thanks to you. Our situations are similar as well. You're building on the coast and I am building on the shores of Lake Como. I have a number of villas on the lakeshore, but there are two I am especially fond of and which therefore keep me busiest. One stands on rocks overlooking the water, as at Baiae, and the other is at the water's edge. So, I call one Tragedy because it looks as if it is on an actor's boots, and the other Comedy because it's down low.

Each has its own individual appeal, and the contrast between the two makes them all the more appealing to the occupant. The first has a panoramic view across the lake and the second provides a much closer one. Tragedy's height means it looks over two bays and has a straight drive looking down on the shore while the latter is built around the curve of just one bay and follows it round on a wide terrace. The high villa is untouched by water and the fishermen can be seen down below while the water breaks at the low one and you may fish there yourself, throwing the line from your room (almost from your bed!), as if you were on a boat.

It's these features which are making me improve both of these delightful places. But I don't need to justify myself to you, someone who I know is doing the same himself. Farewell.

Pliny the Younger, *Letters*, IX.7

Mocking the country retreat

Juvenal, who was happy to paint a colourful picture of the chaos that was Rome, was also disparaging about retreating to the countryside.

If you can manage to tear yourself away from the circus events, then the annual rent for a gloomy garret in Rome would buy you a first-class house at Sora, Fabrateria or Frusino. There you'll have a small garden, a shallow well from which water can be drawn with ease without use of a rope in order to water your produce. Make your home there, with garden tools for companions, nurturing a neat garden good enough for a hundred vegetarians to dine off. It really is quite an achievement, however remote a place you're in, to be able to own a single lizard!

Juvenal, *Satires* III.223-231

MY PLACE IN THE COUNTRY

A description of my villa

This letter by Pliny the Younger is the most famous of all villa descriptions. It is frequently quoted and there need be no further justification for its inclusion here. What is interesting is how Pliny places a great deal of emphasis on the aesthetic location and the opportunity to find peace and quiet. Yet it is quite plain that this was a busy house, because he makes allusions to quarters for his staff and also the level of self-sufficiency which the estate offered. This was where he could get on with his own writing and find pleasure in reading his favourite authors. So precise is the description that it has been possible to make a visual reconstruction of this house and a model is on display at the Ashmolean Museum in Oxford (see the Loeb edition, volume II, p. 554 for a plan).

Nonetheless, for all its solitude, Pliny's Laurentine villa was first and foremost a retreat from Rome which being only 15 miles (25km) away was easily reached on horseback. Laurentum lay on the coast, just a handful of miles south of Rome's bustling port at Ostia. So this was also a busy area and the coastline was extremely popular amongst the urban elite who chose it for their country houses.

Pliny the Younger to Clusinius Gallus

You express surprise that I am so fond of my Laurentine or, if you prefer, Laurens, place but you will stop being surprised when I familiarise you with the villa's beauty, its advantageous location and the panoramic view of the coast. It's only 17 [Roman] miles from Rome so that when my business in the city is done I can spend my evenings here after a good and satisfactory day at work.

There are two different routes to get here. If you come the Laurentum way, you need to turn off at the 14th milestone. If you come via Ostia, then turn off at the 11th. Both roads are sandy here and there, which makes them laborious and slower by carriage, but quick and easy on horseback. The landscape has much variety. The view is blocked off by woods in some places and in others it extends over wide open spaces where numerous flocks of sheep and cattle herds (driven down from the mountains by the extreme weather) are growing fat on the spring warmth and verdant pastures.

My villa is the right size for me but not costly to maintain. The front hall is plain, without being mean, through which you come to D-shaped colonnades which enclose a small and cheerful intermediate courtyard. This is an excellent place to escape to in bad weather, not only because it's protected by windows, but especially because a part of the roof sticks out over the colonnades to provide shelter. The middle of these colonnades leads through to a well-lit and pleasing inner hall. From there it leads into an elegant dining room which runs down to the seashore, so that when the wind blows from the south-west it is gently splashed by the waves which work themselves out at its base.

On every side of this dining room there are folding doors or windows of a similar size through which you have a view of three different seas, as it were, from the front and the two sides. From the back you can see through to the inner hall, the courtyards and the colonnades and from the entrance hall through to the distant woods and mountains.

To the left of this dining room, a bit farther back from the sea, is a large bedroom and beyond that another one, but smaller, which has one window facing the rising sun, and another the setting sun. This room also has a view of the sea, but from a safer distance. In the angle formed between this bedroom and the dining room is a corner where the sun's warmth is retained and concentrated. This forms the household's winter quarters and the gymnasium because it is sheltered from all the winds except the one which brings rain and it can still be used after the weather has broken.

Joining this angle is an apsidal room, with windows so arranged that the sun shines in all day. One wall is fitted with bookcases containing the works of authors I never grow tired of. Next to this is a bedroom opposite a corridor fitted with a raised floor fitted with pipes which take in hot steam and circulate it at a fixed temperature. The other rooms on this side of the villa are set aside for my slaves and freedmen but the majority of these are smart enough to put guests in.

There is a very refined bedroom on the other side of the dining room, and then another which can serve either as a large bedroom or medium-sized dining room and which benefits from bright sunlight reflecting off the sea. Behind this is another room with an antechamber. It's high enough to keep cool in summer but being protected from the wind it acts as a refuge in winter. Another pair of rooms like this are separated off by a single wall.

Next comes the bath suite's cold bath. This is large and roomy and has two curved baths built into opposite walls which are quite sufficient considering that the sea is so close. Next is the oil and massage room, the furnace chamber, the boiler-room, then two sanctuaries which are tasteful and very sumptuous. This leads to the hot swimming pool from which bathers survey the sea. Near this is the ball-court which the sun warms as it goes down. From here you go up to a tower which is a two-up, two-down, arrangement of rooms, as well as a dining room which has a panoramic view of the sea, the coast, and all the beautiful villas along the shore. At the other end is a second tower with a room lit by the sun as it rises and as it sets. Behind here there is a large wine-cellar and granary, and underneath a roomy dining room where the sea can only just be heard, even when it is rough. It looks out across the garden and the drive.

The drive is marked out with a box hedge, or rosemary where the box has gaps, because boxes grow very well if the buildings give it shelter but withers when exposed to the wind or sea spray, even from some distance. The inner part of the drive has a shady vine pergola where the path is so soft and forgiving that you can walk on it barefoot. The garden is mainly planted with mulberries and figs, which this soil favours as much as it repels everything else. Over here there is a dining room which despite being away from the sea has a garden view which is equally pleasant. Two rooms run round the back part of it, through the windows of which the villa entrance and a fine kitchen garden can be seen.

This is where the covered arcade starts, which is long enough for it to be confused with a public building. It has windows on both sides, but more on the side facing the sea because there is only one in alternate bays on the garden side. When the weather is clear and calm these are opened and when it is stormy, whichever side is on the leeward can be opened. In front is a terrace smelling of violets. It's warmed by sunlight reflected from the arcade. Although it captures the sun's rays, it keeps the north-east wind at bay so that it is as hot on this side as it is cool on the other. For the same reason it acts as a protection against the south-west wind, and consequently acts as wind-break, regardless of where they are blowing from. These are the benefits in winter. They are even greater in summer because during that season it casts shade across the terrace all morning and over the adjacent part of the drive and garden in the afternoon, casting more or less shade on this side or that as the suns get higher or lower. The arcade itself has least sun when it is at its zenith and because the windows allow the west wind in to stir the air, the atmosphere never gets heavy and stale.

There is a suite of chambers at the far end of the terrace, arcade and garden, which are my favourites, truly cherished: I put them there. There is a sun room here facing the terrace on one side, the sea on the other, and gets the sun from both sides. Moreover, there is a bedroom with folding doors to the covered arcade, with a sea-view from its window. Opposite the dividing wall is an elegant private room which can be opened out into the bedroom by folding back its glass doors and curtains. This room is big enough for a couch and two chairs, with the sea below it, neighbouring villas behind it and woods beyond it. You can see these views individually through its numerous windows, or look at them all at once.

There is another bedroom next to this one which, unless the windows are opened, neither the voices of the slaves, the gentle rumble of the sea, flashes of lightning or even daylight, can penetrate. This profound peace and seclusion are made possible by a corridor separating the wall's room from the garden and, thanks to this intervening space, all sound is insulated. Tacked on here is a little furnace room and by opening or shutting a little flap you can let heat out or keep it in as you need. Then there is an antechamber and bedroom extended out into the sun to catch its rays immediately as it rises and keep them until after noon, albeit at an angle. When I slink off to this range of rooms I enjoy a feeling that I have left the villa altogether, particularly during the Saturnalia festival when the joint jumps with the row of festive shouting with holiday steam letting-off. I am not preventing anyone having fun, and they are not affecting my work.

There is only one problem amongst all the pleasures and conveniences of this location: the lack of running water but there are wells (or rather springs) in the area because they lie close to the surface. In fact the quality of this coastline is altogether remarkable because, wherever you dig, you will with the first turn of the spade expose a spring of pure fresh water with no trace of salt, despite being so close to the sea. The woods close by supply all the firewood we need. Everything else we need comes from Ostia. In fact, the village just beyond the next house, can supply all the basic commodities a modest man would need. It has three public baths which is very handy if my friends turn up unannounced or are to be here too briefly for me to fire up my own.

The whole coast here is very pleasantly scattered with villas, either arranged in rows or on their own which look like lots of separate cities when one looks at them from the sea or the shore which a long period of calm softens [underfoot]. More often, rough weather hardens the shore. Of course, the sea has few fish of value, although it provides us excellent sole and prawns. Besides in truth, our villa provides abundant inland produce, primarily milk, for the herds come down here from the pastures whenever they want water and shade.

Now am I seen by you to have good reasons to stay and to live here, and to hold in great esteem this retreat? You are too much a city man if you don't covet it! And I wish you did, so that all the attractions of our place will have the benefit of your company to recommend it. Farewell.

Pliny the Younger, *Letters*, II.17

ESTATE MANAGEMENT

Working on the land

While the villa owner enjoyed his country retreat and indulging in his rural fantasy the reality for the armies of slaves, tenants and peasants, who farmed the land was a life of toil. Even the word *villa* found itself converted into a rural slang form reflecting the back-breaking labour of lugging the agricultural produce off the land into stores at the villa and out again when it was time for the market.

The *vilicus* is appointed in order to till the soil. The name comes from *villa*, being the place where the crops are hauled, *vehuntur*, and out of which they are hauled by the *vilicus* in order to be sold. This is the reason why the peasants even refer to a road as a *veha* due to the 'hauling', and they call the place they do the hauling to and fro, the *vella* and not the *villa* ....

Varro, *On Agriculture*, I.2.14

The right land

The more wholesome the land is, the more valuable it is because a profit is guaranteed. Conversely, bad luck on unwholesome land, regardless of how rich it is, prevents the farmer making a profit. This is because when one dices with death, it's not just profits that are uncertain but also the lives of the farmers. So, when agriculture is unwholesome, it becomes no more than a game of chance in which the owner's life and his property are the stakes.

But science can reduce the risk. Even though wholesomeness is beyond our control and is instead in nature's power, produced by the weather and the ground, it still depends on us to a large extent because with care we can lessen its worst effects.

Varro, *On Agriculture*, I.4.3-4

The right place

Naturally there was no point in building a farm in the back of beyond, however good the land was. Not only did proximity to towns and cities provide markets, but it was also advisable to be close enough to local tradesmen and other estates. Far from being a self-sufficient community, the average estate would work best as part of a tightly-knit local economy.

Farms which have suitable facilities close at hand to transport produce to market and a handy way of bringing back items needed on the farm are profitable for this very reason. Many people have amongst their property a few which lack things like wine, grain or something similar, and these have to be brought in. Equally, there are plenty with these goods where a surplus needs to be despatched. So, having large gardens near a city is profitable. Some examples are violets, roses and many other products, for which there is a big market in a city. At the same time there is no money to be made by growing these products on a remote farm where there is no market to which they can be transported.

Also, if there are towns or villages nearby, or even the well-appointed estates and villas of wealthy owners, where essential farm goods can be bought at sensible prices and where surpluses of goods like crops, poles, and reeds, can be sold, then the farm will be more profitable than if these things have to be brought from far away. It might even be the case that the profits will be greater than if you supplied yourself by growing them on your own estate. This is the reason why farmers in this situation like to have men in the vicinity that can be contracted on an annual basis to supply their services such as physicians, fullers, and other artisans. This they prefer to men of their own on the estate because the death of a single one can wipe out the profit of one farm.

On a very large estate, owners depend for these requirements on their own people. If the estate is too far from towns or villages they equip themselves with smiths and all the other artisans needed on site. This prevents the ordinary hands from abandoning their work and having a holiday by taking it easy on working days, instead of improving farm profits by getting on with their work.

Varro, *On Agriculture*, I.16.4-5

The right man

A villa owner was almost by definition liable to be absent for much of the year, not least because wintering in the country could be a thoroughly disagreeable experience. Villa estates thus depended on employing a manager or bailiff who lived on the estate all year round. Pliny the Younger found that finding the right man to manage his wife's grandfather's estate was among his family duties.

To Calpurnius Fabatus

The Villa Camillia, which you own in Campania, is suffering from age and becoming decayed. Nevertheless, the more valuable parts are either still intact or only damaged a little. I will see to it that it is thoroughly repaired. Though I pride myself on having many friends, I have almost no one who matches your requirements for the job. All my friends are townsfolk to their bones, but managing a villa estate needs a strong and healthy

countryman who won't find the work too hard or demeaning, nor the solitude depressing. You think very highly of Rufus because he was a good friend of your son's, but I can't imagine what use he'll be to us here even if I am confident he will do all he can. Farewell.
Pliny the Younger, *Letters*, VI.30

Estate emergencies

While he was serving as governor of Bithynia and Pontus, Pliny grew anxious about some of his farms in Italy. He wrote to the emperor to request a leave of absence. Like all landowners he was completely dependent on tenants working the land but it is particularly interesting that he felt it was his duty to consider lowering rents when poor harvests had reduced the yield.

Pliny to Trajan

The farms, which I own in this region, earn more than 400,000 sesterces, and I can't put off letting them, not least because new tenants need to be there to take care of the vine pruning which must be done soon. Quite apart from that, the run of poor harvests we have had means that I have to consider putting the rents down, and I can't work out what they should be unless I am actually there. So, Sir, if you can allow me to be away for thirty days …. I will be indebted to your generosity …. I need at least a month because the …. farms I am referring to are more than 150 miles away from Rome.
Pliny the Younger, *Letters*, X.8.5

PASSING THE TIME OF DAY

Summer days

Pliny the Younger's description of a summer day at his Tuscan villa is an idyll only broken by the entertaining image of his tenants droning on with their customary rural complaints. In every way Pliny creates the perfect image of the educated wealthy Roman gentleman at ease in the Italian countryside. Apart from writing he appears to do little or nothing else that could be described as work. He might very well be describing his life as an educated and wealthy man of the eighteenth century in Europe or America. And, of course, it was this Pliny's style of life that was self-consciously emulated by such people.

To Fuscus

So you want to know how I spend the day during the summer in my Tuscan villa? I get up when I feel like it, normally when the sun comes up, and often before that but never later. The shutters stay closed because the darkness and peace help me meditate. Freed from all those external distractions I am left to my own thoughts and my eyes don't make my mind wander. With nothing to see, my eyes are controlled by my imagination.

Anything I am working on can be sorted out, chosen, and corrected, in my head. What I get done depends on how well I can concentrate and remember. Then I call my secretary, open the shutters, and dictate to him what I have knocked into shape. Then I send him away, call him back, and send him away again. At the fourth or fifth hour after sunrise (I don't stick to an exact time) I take a walk on the terrace or portico where I carry on thinking about or dictating whatever is outstanding on the topic I am working on. Once that's done, I go for a drive where I carry on as before when I was in my study or walking. I find the change of scene revives me and helps me concentrate.

When I get home I have a rest and then a walk. Then I read out loud a Greek or Latin passage with proper enunciation. The reason is more for my digestion than for the good of my voice, though both are improved by the activity. Another walk follows before I am oiled, do my exercises, and have a bath. If I dine alone with my wife, or with a few friends, we have a reading during the meal. Once we have eaten we either listen to music or a comedy. When that's over I take a walk with members of the household, several of whom are well educated. So, the evenings pass with all sorts of conversations and even when the days are at their longest, they end very pleasantly.

Sometimes I change the routine. If I have spent longer than usual studying or walking then I go out on horseback, rather than in a carriage, after my afternoon nap so that I still get the exercise but save time. Some of the day is given over to friends visiting from nearby towns, which can be a welcome interruption when I am feeling tired. I do go hunting sometimes, but I always take my writing tablets so that if I don't catch anything I can still come home with something. Some of my time, though they would prefer more, is spent on my tenants, whose characteristic farmers' moans lighten up our literary activities and civilized urban pastimes. Farewell.

Pliny the Younger, *Letters*, IX.36

An imperial retreat

In the hills east of Rome at Tivoli, Hadrian built his own rural retreat and modelled it on the whole Roman Empire including the spiritual world. Today it is a remarkable series of ruins, the size of a small town. In antiquity it must have been truly exceptional.

He finished off his Tivoli villa as a marvel, so that he named parts of it after the most famous provinces and places. For instance, he called them Lyceum, Academia, Prytaneum, Canopus, Poecile, and Tempe. And, so that he left nothing out, he also built a representation of the Underworld.

Aelius Spartianus, *Hadrian*, XXVI.5

Aesthetic domestic diversions

Banal an observation though it may be, until the coming of modern electronic and cinematic entertainment people were left to their own devices or live amusements. Here an Egyptian homeowner is booking some castanet dancers to liven up six days at his house. The importance of the booking is evident from the pay, board, and transport which are on offer.

To Isidora the castanet-dancer from Artemisia, of the village of Philadelphia.
I want to book you, with two other castanet-dancers, to perform at my home for six days starting on the 24th of the month of Pauni, as reckoned by the old calendar. The pay is 36

drachmae daily between you, and for the whole six days four measures of barley and twenty pairs of loaves. We will safely guard any costumes or gold ornaments which you bring and we will make two donkeys available when you come down here, and the same when you go back.

The 16th day of the month Pauni in the 14th year of Lucius Septimius Severus Pius Pertinax and Marcus Aurelius Antoninus Pius, the Augusti, and Publius Septimius Geta Caesar Augustus.

SP.20, written in the year 206

TOWN AND COUNTRY IN LATE ANTIQUITY

Houseguests

For the wealthy being a houseguest, and in turn inviting guests, was all part of villa life. Being ostentatious and sharing the fruits of ostentation were statements and credentials of belonging to the upper classes. Even in the mid-fifth century, around 350 years after the death of Pliny the Younger, villa owners competed with one another to offer the most lavish hospitality and to secure the most prestigious guests. Here the wealthy Gallo-Roman Sidonius Apollinarius, then in his mid-thirties, describes a particularly enjoyable visit a few years before he became Bishop of Auvergne.

To Donidius

You ask why I am making you disappointed for taking so long to arrive when I left for Nimes a long time ago. In reply, I'll explain the reasons for taking so long to get back and I won't take long to say why I was delayed because the same things please us both. I have passed the most delightful time visiting two beautiful places and their hosts, Ferreolus and Apollinaris.

Their estates join one another and the houses are quite close, though the road between them is a little too far to walk without being far enough to make it worth getting the carriage out. The hills rising above the houses are covered with vineyards and groves of olives. You might take them for Nysa and Aracynthus, those heights which poets praise. One of the houses looks out over wide and flat land, and the other across woodland, but however different their settings are they are equal in charm.

But, that's enough about the situations when I have yet to tell you about all the things I enjoyed so much. To begin with, some sharp-eyed trackers were despatched to watch out the whole way along my return journey, and the staff of both households patrolled not only the roads but also watched all the short-cuts and lanes to make it impossible for us to escape this delightful ambush. Of course we fell into the trap as willing captives and our guards immediately made us swear to abandon any idea of continuing our journey for another week. So every day dawned with a good-humoured contest between the hosts to decide whose kitchen stove should be fired up for my breakfast. It was impossible to be fair by alternating, even though one is owned by my kin and the other by my family, because Ferreolus is a prefect which, along with his age, prestige, and his relationship with me, gave him the first call on inviting me.

I was hurried from one pleasure to another. No sooner had I entered either's vestibule when we saw competing pairs of players in the ballgame engaged in all the ducking and diving moves. Elsewhere the rattle of dice and shouts of gamers could be heard. In other places abundant numbers of books were to hand — you might have thought yourself in a scholar's library, or in the Athenaeum or amongst the shelves of a bookseller. They were arranged such that religious works were stored next to the ladies' chairs, and those distinguished for their Latin eloquence were by the men's seats. The latter were sorted by style rather than content, because it was once common to read books written by authors whose style was similar. So here we had Augustine, there Varro, here Horace, there Prudentius. Those of us interested in theology eagerly read Turranius Rufinus' translation of *Adamantius* by Origen. We exchanged views on the condemnation of Origen by some priests for being incompetent and dangerously controversial. But the translation of his works into Latin was so true to the original that you could not say that Apuleius had done a better job with Plato's *Phaedo*, or Cicero with Demosthenes' *Ctesiphon*.

While we were all indulging in whichever of these pastimes took our fancy, the cook's messenger would turn up to tell us that it was time for refreshment. He was watching the hours marked off on the water clock and, sure enough, the fifth hour was just passing to show he was bang on time. Lunch was quick but lavish nonetheless in the style of a senator's household where tradition dictates the provision of many courses on a few dishes. That some were roasted and others stewed made for variety. While we drank there were stories to amuse or inform us. In short, we were profusely entertained in a moral and elegant way. When we left the table at the Vorocingus estate we went back to our lodgings and belongings. When we left the table at Prusianum, Tonantius and the other cream of young nobility here were turned out of their beds to save us carrying our luggage around.

Once we had had an afternoon snooze, we took a ride to revive our appetites for supper. Both my hosts were in the process of having baths built and neither was in a usable state. So, I set the jolly crowd that was my own staff on the job, in those rare occasions when they sobered up between bouts of drinking from the frequently-replenished communal bowl, to dig a trench as fast as they could near the spring or the river. Into this a pile of red-hot stones was thrown. While the trench was warming up a cover was built over it using hazel twigs plaited into a dome. Then rough goats' hair cloth was thrown onto the roof to shut out the light and close up the gaps between the twigs, and in this way to keep the steam in which is made by pouring boiling water on the stones.

In these steam baths we spent hours chatting and joking while the whole time we were immersed in a cloud of steam which made us sweat in the healthiest way. When we had sweated to our satisfaction we bathed in hot water. This relaxed us and eased out digestive systems before we rounded it all off with a bracing soaking of cold water from the fountain, the well or the river. I need to explain that the river Vardo flows between the two properties. When melting snow makes it flood it turns yellow, but normally it has a red tint from the brown gravel and runs, transparent, smooth and pebbly, along its course but is no less prolific in its supply and range of fish.

I could have told you about the suppers we had (and they were sumptuous!) but it's the fact I'm running out of paper, not a sense of shame, that's stopping me. The story of these feasts would be a jolly good one over the page but I don't like to ruin a letter with a blotchy pen. In any case I am just about to leave and hope, with the grace of Christ, that we will meet up soon. I'll be able to tell you about my friends' dinners much better when we eat at my place or yours provided that I get a week's breathing space to restore me to my usual healthy appetite. There's nothing better than frugal living to repair a system disrupted by excess!

Farewell

Sidonius, *Letters*, II.9, written c. 461-7

My place at Avitacum

On a different occasion, Sidonius wrote to another friend, called Domitius, to lure him to his own villa at Avitacum. Quite apart from his desire to attract his friend, the letter reveals much about the colossal degree of wealth some people enjoyed in the provinces. And yet this was a time when the Empire was under severe threat. The possibility exists that he is indulging in a certain amount of literary exaggeration, but it seems improbable that what he described was not largely based on truth even though no trace of his home and those of his friends has ever been found. The passage here describes the physical comforts of the house which resembles that of Pliny the Younger, but he moves on to a ludicrously self-conscious description of the rural concert of sounds which is supposed to make the place a total pastoral retreat and experience.

Considering Sidonius' high status as a Christian leader, his use of allusion and reference to myth illustrates how Roman villa life was inextricably linked with pagan myth and allusion. Of course, this is a deliberate stylistic allegory but its aping of references from 500 years before shows how entrenched these concepts were and in Sidonius' own background reading. Here he picks on the myth of Philomela and Procne, who were changed into a nightingale and swallow respectively. His reference seems to come from Ovid's *Metamorphoses* (VI. 668), though a reference also occurs in Virgil's fourth *Georgic*. The raven, used for prophecies, appears in one of Horace's *Odes* (III.27), and Tityrus in Virgil's first *Eclogue*. Paradoxically, he is at pains to make it clear that his bath walls are not covered with lascivious representations of scandalous and smutty tales from myth.

Indeed, it pleases you, listen to what the country place you are invited to is like. We are at Avitacum. That's the name of the farm which, being my wife's, is more pleasing to me than the estate I inherited from my father. That's the harmonious family life I enjoy with God's help .... The mountain to the west is covered with soil but difficult to climb. From it smaller hills run off like shoots from a double stem. These hills fan out to leave an area big enough for a house about 2.5 acres between them. But before they do that the hillsides hold the valley in straight lines right up to the villa with its north- and south-facing fronts.

The baths, which cling to the base of cliff covered with trees, are on the south-west. When the small branches are chopped off along the line of the ridge, they fall almost straight into heaps at the furnace mouth. That's where the hot bath is, the same size as the oiling room next door, apart from the fact that it has an apse with a hot tub through which hot water winds and bubbles its way through the maze of lead pipes in the wall. It seems like genuine daylight in the hot room with so much enclosed light modest persons feel as though they are even more naked than they are.

Next door is the expanse of the cold room. It isn't cheeky to suggest that you might compare it with public baths. For a start the architect has designed it a peaked roof shaped like a cone. The corners where the four sides of this building connect are covered with curved tiles with rows of flat tiles between them. The bath itself has been perfectly designed and measured so that chairs can be fitted into the semi-circular bath for all the bathers, without servants tripping over each other. The architect has also installed a pair of windows opposite each other where the vault sits on the walls so that visitors looking up can see the skilfully-designed coffered ceiling.

Plain white polished concrete is quite good enough for the inside walls. There are no lascivious stories illustrated with the naked beauty of painted figures because while the story might glorify art, it disgraces the artist. There aren't any actors with silly faces and dressed up like stage clowns in multi-coloured costumes, and there aren't any athletes writhing about in their various positions. Let's face it, in real life the gymnasium superintendent uses his stick to break up any suspect couplings!

To be blunt: you won't find anything drawn on those areas which isn't in the best possible taste. A visitor will only stop to read a few lines of verse. They are all you need because while no one needs to read them again, they can be read once without boring anyone. If you want to know what sorts of marble I have, the truth is that there aren't various coloured blocks from hillsides such as Paros, Carystos, Proconnesos, Phrygia, Numidia, and Sparta, and nor are there any of those stones from the purple heights of Ethiopian crags set up to look like an imitation of sprinkled grain. So while I'm not enriched with the icy severity of rocks from abroad my buildings (you can call them huts or shacks if you want) still have a natural cool. But I want to tell you what I have, not what I haven't got.

There is an outside annex attached to the east side of this hall. It's a swimming pool or if you prefer its Greek name, an ablution pool, with a capacity of about 40,000 gallons. People emerging from the heat of the bath face a three-arched entranceway in the middle of the wall. The middle section is held up with columns, not pillars, of the type known as 'purples'. A stream has been 'directed down from the mountain's brow' [Virgil, *Georgics*, I.108] and channelled round the sides of the pool to pour in through six projecting pipes capped with lions' heads. Anyone entering unprepared will think they are looking at real teeth, wild eyes and authentic manes.

If the master of the house is surrounded here by his visitors or his household it's very difficult to carry on a conversation thanks to the roar of falling water, so people have to speak right into each other's ears. In that way a perfectly innocuous conversation, drowned out by the racket, takes on a ludicrous conspiratorial mood. Leaving here means passing the front of the ladies' dining room. Next to this is, with nothing more substantial than would be used to divide up barracks, the room for domestic stores and the weaving room.

There's a portico on the east side which looks over the lake, supported by coloured pillars rather than hateful monolithic columns. Next to the forecourt a stretch of covered passage, without any partitions, runs inwards. There isn't any view from here, which means I can call it a cryptoporticus even if it isn't really an underground passage. At its end though one bit is divided off to make a very cool room where the prattling female slaves and nurses lay out their feast, good enough for the gods. But they race off when I and my family go for a sleep.

The cryptoporticus leads to the winter dining-room where the vaulted fireplace is stained black with soot from the fire lit so often. But why should I tell you that, when the last thing on my mind right now is to tell you to sit down by the fire? Let me tell you what suits you and the date. Out of this dining room we go to what is either a small dining or living room which is entirely open to the lake and vice-versa. There's a semi-circular dining couch in here, and a brilliant sideboard [presumably from the silver displayed]. There's an easy flight of stairs up to where they sit from the portico. The flight is neither short nor narrow. If you aren't busy eating then you will be absorbed by the view while you're relaxing in here.

Now, if someone brings you a cold drink from that most famous of springs, you'll be able to see crystals and flakes of snowy mist in the cups when they are filled to the brim. Meanwhile the glossy polish of the cups themselves is dimmed by the film of condensation caused by sudden cold. Next there are the drinks themselves which are appropriate for the cups, chilled ladlefulls of them which intimidate the thirsty, saying nothing of you, a champion at being abstemious ….

When you've done with eating you will find a welcome in a sitting room. This is a proper summer room because it never gets baking hot, being open only to the north and letting in only daylight not sunshine ….

How delightful it is to experience the resonance of cicadas chirruping at midday, frogs croaking as the evening draws in, swans and geese honking in the first part of the night and cocks crowing at dawn. And also to hear the augur's bird, the raven, greet the red blaze of dawn with its triple cry, Philomela the nightingale singing in the bushes in the twilight and Procne the swallow whistling amongst the rafters. You might like to add to this ensemble the rural muse with his seven-holed flute which those budding Tityri of our mountains, not bothering to sleep, keep playing in an all-night musical contest amongst the jingling sheep whose bleats resonate across the fields while they graze.
Sidonius, *Letters* II.2.3-14

A gentleman's retreat
Just like Pliny the Younger four hundred years before, Sidonius and his friends regarded a country retreat as a place for books as well as agriculture. Producing literary works for private performance and circulation and, perhaps, eventual publication, was part of the ritual.

To Consentius
Near to the city [Narbonne], the river and the sea, your estate provides banquets for your visitors, and you have a feast of guests. To begin with, the house stands high, and its walls are arranged with skill to create architecture with a symmetry beyond question …. apart from having a full larder and large quantities of furniture, it is packed with copious stores of books, amongst which you put in as much work as you do in the fields, so that it's

difficult to work out whether your estate or brain has been better cultivated.

As I recall it was here you produced with diligent labour .... iambics that bowled along, ingenious elegiacs, and well-formed hendecasyllables [an 11-syllable line] .... Through these verses it was inevitable you would win increasing acceptance amongst those of your own time and increasing fame in later ages....

Sidonius, *Letters*, VIII.4.1-3

THE PATH TO RUIN

Wealth of course depends on how capital and income is managed. Sensible Romans like Pliny the Younger organized their affairs so that their various estates paid for substantial legacies, freedom for their slaves, and grants to their cities. Some were not so sensible. Catullus recorded the profligacy of one Mentula, whose entertainment costs wiped out the profits of his estate.

It wouldn't be wrong to describe Mentula as rich, thanks to his Firmum estate which has so many wonderful features: all sorts of fowling, fishing, pasture, corn-fields and game. All for nothing: the fun is outstripping the expenses. So, I concede that he's rich, as long as everything stops. Let's praise the advantages of the estate, provided that Mentula himself goes without.

Catullus, *Poems*, 114

7 Provincials, foreigners and barbarians

The Roman Empire at its height stretched from southern Egypt to northern Britain, and encompassed the entire Mediterranean basin, the Near East, Central and North-Western Europe together with North Africa. So it is not surprising that a variety of opinions circulated about the various peoples that made up this extraordinary domain. This is manifested in a very definite social hierarchy centring on the older areas of Italy, southern Gaul, Spain and Greece. These were the areas from which most of the leadership classes were drawn during the first two centuries AD. Trajan and Hadrian, for example, were both Spaniards.

This Mediterranean-based élite regarded the more remote regions with a mixture of disdain, disbelief, and occasional admiration. It was from the more distant frontier provinces that the auxiliary units of the army were drawn, and where the versions of Roman life were perceived as the most gauche and clumsy. Britain seems to have been at the bottom of the pecking order, regarded even by the Gauls as the bottom rung of Roman civilisation. Historians like Tacitus mocked the way in which such people aped Roman ways.

IMPOSITION AND ACCOMMODATION

Local laws and customs
It was as much force of circumstance as imagination that led Rome to allow provinces generally to function according to local laws and customs. With such a colossal amount of territory it was impossible to enforce Roman law and life with the soldiers and officials available. Rome instead depended on compliance. When Augustus became emperor two classes of province came to exist. The older provinces like Greece were senatorial. The senate chose their governors, though there was naturally an element of fiction about this in the sense that the emperor had effective supreme authority. The other provinces were technically all one province, the emperor's, and this imperial province was divided into further provinces governed by his personal delegates, called legates.

Augustus governed the subject territories in the Roman way, but allowed nations secured by treaty to be administered according to their own customs. He did not think it would be a good idea to increase the former, or acquire new lands to increase the latter. Augustus thought it better for the Romans to be content with what they possessed, and he expressed this view to the senate. Therefore he did not wage any wars, at least in the meantime, and even gave away some kingdoms.

Dio Cassius, *Roman History*, LIV.9.1

The 'barbarian'

It is also true that the Roman world believed it had something genuinely good to offer to the rest of the known world, and this also went hand-in-hand with a degree of religious tolerance which the world has scarcely exhibited since. The Romans were fascinated by more exotic places too, and there was no more peculiar place than Egypt which remained forever mysterious and locked within its own arcane traditions. In the end, their definition of civilisation was to be Roman. Being uncivilised meant not only being not Roman, but being a barbarian. Herodian summed them up in one easy sentence.

Barbarians are liable to be easily provoked, even for quite haphazard reasons.
Herodian, *History of the Empire*, I.3.5

EGYPT

Egypt was a special province, unlike any other. It was the emperor's private estate but it also retained many of its ancient customs and local administrative structures. Augustus exploited its role in the Battle of Actium as Antony and Cleopatra's power-base to present the struggle as being one against an exotic foreign enemy, rather than a conflict with Antony (which of course in reality it was). Egypt's sands have preserved vast quantities of papyri, recording an enormous amount of administrative detail. This is sometimes misleading because Egypt was subject to many special conditions, including for example the fact that an Egyptian required special permits to leave the province. This enhanced its sense of peculiarity to the Romans.

By the Roman period, Greek was the day-to-day language but ancient temples and gods were still revered. The Roman emperor was depicted as a pharaoh on the walls of temples like that of goddess Hathor at Dendarah near Thebes where Trajan's image is prominently displayed. Only the wording of the hieroglyphs distinguishes him from the pharaohs of old. Not surprisingly, the Romans viewed Egypt with amazement and like modern tourists they wandered its ruins and tombs transfixed. To this day, graffiti in the Valley of the Kings and elsewhere record their travels. Descriptions of Egypt helped fuel their curiosity.

Strabo on Egypt

Strabo, despite criticising Herodotus for presenting Egypt as a kind of light-entertainment 'Believe it or Not' show, could not resist providing examples of Egypt as an enigma.

The government and garrison of Egypt

At this time Egypt is a Roman province. It pays a great deal of tribute and is well-governed by wise men sent there in succession. The governor sent there like this has the rank of a pharaoh. Next after him in precedence is the administrator of justice, who serves as the chief judge in many cases. Another official is the *idologus* who is responsible for looking into property no one has laid claim to and which, by right, becomes the emperor's. These men are accompanied by the emperor's freedmen and stewards. Their responsibilities cover other affairs of varying importance.

Egypt has three legions stationed in it: one at Alexandria, the other two in the countryside. In addition there are also nine Roman cohorts based in the city, three in Syene on the borders with Ethiopia to guard that region, and three elsewhere in the province. Three wings of cavalry are based in appropriate places as well.

Amongst the Egyptian-born magistrates in the cities, the first is the 'Expounder of the Law' who is dressed in scarlet robes. He receives the traditional honours of the land and is responsible for providing the city with necessary services. The second is 'Writer of the Records', the third is the 'Chief Magistrate', and the fourth is 'Commander of the Night Watch'. These officers were in existence during the time of the Ptolemaic pharaohs but, thanks to the poor government by those pharaohs, corruption destroyed the wealth of Alexandria.

Polybius expressed his outrage at conditions when he was there. According to him, the Alexandrians were made up of three categories: first, the Egyptians and natives who were quick-witted but lousy citizens, and meddled destructively in civic business. The mercenaries were second, a large but undisciplined group because it was an old custom to maintain foreign troops who, thanks to their useless rulers were a good deal more accomplished at lording it than being obedient. The last were the 'Alexandrines' who were disorderly citizens for the same reasons. But they were less trouble than the mercenaries because, despite being of mixed race, their Greek origins meant they clung on to Hellenistic customs.

These were, if not even worse, the social conditions in Alexandria during the days of the last pharaohs. So far as they could, the Romans corrected (as I have said) many abuses and imposed an efficient administration by installing assistant governors, nomarchs, and ethnarchs who were responsible for all administrative details.

The landscape and Egypt's peoples

Herodotus and other writers trivialize their histories by bringing in fantastic tales, as if they were musical and singing intermissions. For example they claim that the sources of the Nile are near the innumerable islands, at Syene and Elephantine, and that here the river is so deep it cannot be measured. There are many islands dotted about the Nile, some of which get submerged completely, others only in parts, at the time of the inundation. Higher land is irrigated with screw pumps.

Egypt has been inclined to peace from the very beginning, thanks to having her own resources and because it was difficult for strangers to reach. On the north she was protected by a harbourless coast and the Egyptian Sea. On the east and west she was protected by the desert mountain ranges of Libya and Arabia respectively, as I have said elsewhere. The rest of the area to the south is populated by the Troglodytae, Blemmyes, Nubians, and Megabarzae Ethiopians above Syene. These are nomads who are neither warlike nor numerous but considered to be so in antiquity because, like common robbers, they often attacked defenceless people. The Ethiopians, who live out towards the south and Meroe, are also few in number and not organized into one body. They live in a long, winding area on the riverbank of the type described earlier. They are also unprepared for war or, indeed, any other activity.

Right now the province is in the same peaceful state, which proves three cohorts (and even these are not up to full strength) are enough to guard Upper Egypt. Whenever the Ethiopians have tried attacking them they have placed their own country at risk. Other military forces in Egypt are few in number and the Romans have never tried to recruit and organize them into one army. This is because the Egyptians, and other nations roundabout, are not inclined to war, in spite of their large numbers. The first governor of Egypt appointed by Augustus, Cornelius Gallus, attacked the city of Heiropolis which had revolted [in 28BC] and captured it with only a small force. He put down a rebellion very quickly amongst the Thebans, which started off as a protest about tribute. Later on, Petronius stood fast, with his soldiers around him, against a mob of vast numbers of Alexandrians who attacked him by throwing stones. He killed some of them and made the rest give up.

Flora and fauna

A mention of these remarkable products must be added to what has been said about Egypt. For example, there is the so-called Egyptian bean on which the *ciborium* [a kind of drinking cup] is based, and papyrus because it is only found here and in Egypt. The peach only grows here and in Ethiopia. This is a tall tree with large and sweet fruit. There is the sycamine, which produces a fruit called the sycomorus, or fig-mulberry because it looks like a fig but its flavour is considered disappointing. Also the corsium (root of the Egyptian lotus) grows in Egypt. It is a condiment like the pepper, but a little larger. The Nile has huge numbers and varieties of fish, which have a particular and indigenous character …. and shellfish, which make a sound like that of wailing.

Animals only found in Egypt are the *ichneumon* [a weasel-like animal which steals crocodile eggs], and the Egyptian asp which has characteristics asps in other places do not have. There are two types: the first is one span long, whose bite kills more quickly than that of the other. The second is nearly six feet long, or so Nicander, author of the Theriaca, says. Amongst the birds are the ibis and the Egyptian hawk which, like the cat, is tamer than those in other places. The *nycticorax* [night-raven] is a distinct variety in Egypt. Our version is as large as an eagle, but in Egypt it is the same size as a jay and makes a different sound. But the tamest animal is the ibis, which looks like a stork in shape and size. There are two types, distinguished by colour. One resembles a stork, the other is black all over. Every Alexandrian street is full of them. They are useful for some things, but in other ways nothing but trouble. They are handy because they get rid of all sorts of little animals and the offal chucked out by butchers and cooking shops. They cause trouble because they eat everything, they are dirty, and only with great difficulty can they be stopped from making clean things, and other things not given to them, dirty.

Products and customs

Herodotus says of the Egyptians that they are the only people to knead clay by hand, and the dough for making bread with their feet. Caces is a special variety of bread. It helps prevent fluxes [diarrhoea, haemorrhages etc]. The castor-oil bean, *kiki*, is a variety of fruit sowed in furrows. An oil is secreted from it which is used in lamps throughout almost the whole country, but only poor people and labourers of both sexes use it for anointing their bodies. The *coccina* are Egyptian textiles made of a plant, woven like those of rushes or palm trees. Barley beer is a drink made only by the Egyptians. Many tribes commonly use it but they all prepare it in a different way.

But of all their customs, this is the most admirable: they rear all the children that are born. Both males and females are circumcised, as amongst the Jews, who are of Egyptian origin, as I noted when I was writing about them.
Strabo, *Geography*, XVII.1.52-53, 2.4-5; XVIII.1.12-13

Egyptian men

More than 300 years after Strabo wrote, Egyptians were still regarded as another race, and one which it was almost impossible to understand. To Ammianus Marcellinus, Egypt was a nation of vagabonds who were likely to have been beaten so severely for their individual crimes that it would appear they were experiencing a flush of embarrassment while refusing to pay their taxes.

Now, Egyptian men are normally rather swarthy and dark-skinned, have miserable expressions, are slim and tough and irascible in all they do, and they are given to arguing and demanding things. And if anyone of them blushes while withholding tribute, [it is because] he is displaying numerous wheals [from punishments] on his body. So far no one has been able to find a torture harsh enough to force a hardened thief from that province to name himself against his will.
Ammianus Marcellinus XXII.16.23

A Roman tourist in Egypt in the year 19

Egypt's principal value to the Empire was its grain. The grain dole, *annona*, was a vital means of placating the Roman rabble. Emperors knew that any failure in the supply could spell political disasters in the form of riots. Claudius (41-54) would later be mobbed when droughts compromised the harvest and built a new port at Ostia to guarantee imports. This description of Germanicus' visit in 19 provides us with an insight into the special measures Augustus had instituted for the government of this most important of provinces.

Germanicus set out for Egypt in the year of the consulship of Marcus Silanus and Lucius Norbanus [AD19] to study its antiquities, though his expressed motive was concern for the province. He lowered the price of corn by opening the granaries, and adopted many measures, which pleased the people. He would go about without guards, wearing sandals and dressed in the Greek style, imitating Publius Scipio, who (the story goes) habitually did this in Sicily, even when the war with Carthage was still at its height. Tiberius spoke leniently of his disapproval of Germanicus' dress and manners, but then sharply censured him for going to Alexandria without the emperor's leave, against the regulations of Augustus. Augustus, among other secrets of imperial policy, had forbidden senators and Roman equestrians of the higher rank to enter Egypt except by permission. This kept Egypt isolated which reduced the potential threat of Italy being starved out by an enemy who, however weak itself and however powerful the opposition, might be able to achieve this by holding Egypt by securing its strategically-vital positions on land and sea.

But Germanicus, who remained unaware how much opprobrium his trip had earned, sailed up the Nile from his starting point at Canopus. This city was founded by the Spartans because Canopus, a ship's pilot of theirs, had been buried there when Menelaus, returning to Greece, had been driven off course onto the Libyan coast. From here he went to visit the next of the river-mouths, sacred to Hercules who, the locals claim, was born here and was the first of that name. Others born later who showed the same qualities were given the same name.

Next, Germanicus visited the enormous ruins of ancient Thebes. On the towering masonry Egyptian inscriptions, with a complete record of the city's former greatness, still remained. One of the old priests, ordered to act as interpreter for his country's ancient language, told how once the city held 700,000 men of military age and how, with such an army, King Rhamses had conquered Libya, Ethiopia, Media, Persia, Bactria, and Scythia, and also controlled lands inhabited by the Syrians, Armenians, and their neighbours, the Cappadocians, from the Bithynian to the Lycian sea. The tribute imposed on these countries could also be read, the weight of silver and gold, the quantity of weapons and horses, the gifts of ivory and of perfumes to the temples, with the amount of grain and supplies supplied by each country. These revenues were as magnificent as is now levied by the might of Parthia or by the power of Rome.

Tacitus, *Annals*, II.59-61 [the order of Tacitus at this point is disputed]

Germanicus hears the Memnon sing

These statues of the Eighteenth-Dynasty pharaoh Amenophis III (c. 1391-1353BC) remain in position today. The temple in front of which they were erected, Amenophis III's funerary temple, had long since been demolished even in Germanicus' time. One of the figures had a natural flaw causing internal movement when the sun rose and heated it, which made a noise. It was a great sight for a tourist but an earthquake in the late second century AD caused it to fall down. With typical Roman pragmatism the fallen figure was sawed into manageable blocks and re-erected in the form it is today. But, sadly, the repair work unintentionally destroyed its internal flaw and it has been silent ever since.

Other wonders also attracted Germanicus' attention. Chief amongst these were: the stone colossus of Memnon which, when the sun's rays strike it, emits the sound of a human voice; the pyramids, raised to the heights of mountains by the wealth of kings trying to outdo each other, amongst the wind-swept and almost impassable wastes of shifting sand; the lake hollowed out of the earth to catch the Nile's overflow; and elsewhere the river's narrow gorge and great depth which no measuring line of the explorer can penetrate.
Tacitus, *Annals*, II.61

Germanicus was not the only Roman to marvel at the Memnon. Camilius made an early morning trip to hear them.

At half-past the first hour I, Camilius, heard the Memnon sing!
Latin graffiti on the foot of one of the Colossi of Memnon, as read by the editor.

Daily life in Egypt

Some other examples of Egyptian papyri from the time of the Empire are given in Chapters 2, and 5. These texts of Roman date come from papyri found at Oxyrhynchus, a remote provincial town whose location just happens to have been in an environment where casual jottings, letters, contracts, and other manuscripts survive scattered in the remains as rubbish, mummy-case packing, and other deposits.

Dioscorides, local justice in the district of Oxyrhynchus.
The assault at arms by the youths will occur tomorrow, the 24th. They are required to do their absolute best by tradition and just as much by the distinguished nature of the festival. Spectators will attend both performances.

Chaereman invites you to dinner, at the table of the lord Serapis at the Serapeum, tomorrow (the 15th), at 9 o'clock.

Greeting, my beloved Serenia, from Petosiris.
Be sure, my dear, to come on the 20th for the birthday festival of the god, and let me know whether you are coming by boat or by donkey, so that we may send for you accordingly. Take care not to forget. I pray for your continued health.

To Flavius Thennyras, local magistrate of the district of Oxyrhynchus, from Aurelius Nilus, son of Didysus, of the illustrious and most illustrious city of Oxyrhynchos, an egg seller by trade.
    I hereby agree on the August, divine oath by our lord the Emperor and the Caesars to offer for sale in public my eggs in the market place, and to supply to the said city, every day without a break. I acknowledge that it is illegal for me in the future to sell secretly or in my house. If I am found out doing so, I shall be liable to be punished.

I married a woman from my own tribe . .. . a freeborn woman, of free parents, and have children by her. Now Tabes, daughter of Ammonios and her husband Laloi, and Psenesis

163

and Straton their sons, have committed an act that disgraces all the chiefs of the town, and shows their recklessness. They carried off my wife and children to their own house, calling them their slaves, although they were free, and my wife has brothers living who are free. When I remonstrated, they seized me and beat me shamefully.

On the fourth day of this month, Taorsenouphis, wife of Ammonios Phimon, an elder of the village of Bacchias although she had no case against me, came to my house, and made herself most unpleasant to me. As well as ripping my tunic and cloak, she made off with 16 drachmae that I had set aside, the proceeds from vegetables I had sold. And on the fifth day her husband, Ammonios Phimon, came to my house, pretending he was looking for my husband, and took my lamp and went up into the house. And he went off with a pair of silver armlets, weighing 40 drachmae, while my husband was away from home.
Davis, 1912-13

THE RAPACIOUS SARACENS

This group of people were nomads who lived in the southern reaches of Egypt on the borders of Nubia (modern Sudan), an area which had caused trouble during the reign of Probus (276-282; see *SHA Probus*, XVII.2). There is some resemblance to Tacitus' descriptions of the Germans (see below), suggesting a certain amount of ritual in the description of barbarians.

At this time the Saracens, a people who should be avoided as friends or enemies, roamed across the country. If they found anything, they ransacked it in an instant like rapacious hawks who, on spotting some prey from high up in the sky, swoop down and carry it off or, if unsuccessful, do not hang about. Although I remember talking about these people in my account of the reign of Marcus Aurelius, and once or twice afterwards, I will briefly list here some more details about them.

Amongst these people, who came originally from the cataracts of the Nile and the borders of Blemmyae, all the warriors are of equal status. They are half-naked, wear coloured cloaks which reach down to their waists, and overrun various countries assisted by their swift and active horses, and fast camels, just the same in peace or war. No one in their tribe ever uses a plough, cultivates a tree, or grows food by tilling the land. They wander forever over different and wide-ranging areas, and have no home or any legal system. They cannot tolerate any climate for long, and no place or country pleases them enough to stay there. Their lives are perpetually nomadic.

Their wives are hired, on a special agreement, for a fixed term. So that there is some semblance of marriage in the agreement, the wife-to-be offers her husband a spear and tent as dowry, with the right to leave him after an agreed date, if she wants. The enthusiasm with which men and women give themselves over to the pleasures of married life is unbelievable. But all their lives they continue to wander about so widely and so unceasingly that the woman is married in one place, has her children somewhere else, and brings them up far away from either location. She is given no chance of ever remaining

quiet. All of them live on venison, and are further nourished by an abundant milk supply, many different herbs, and whatever birds they can catch by fowling. Many of them have been seen by us to have no idea about how to use wine or corn.
Ammianus Marcellinus, *Roman History*, XIV.4.1ff

THE JEWS

The Roman Empire was ruled, to a large extent, by consent. This was expressed in ritual acceptances of Roman power and ways, though for the most part each province was allowed to continue with its own local customs. Part of the obligation was paying lip service to the emperor's power and divinity. Most provinces were happy to do this; being pagan, it was quite easy to see the emperor as yet another component of the vast pantheon of deities. For the Jews though this was impossible. In the early imperial period there had been some accommodation. Under Claudius the client kingdom once ruled by Herod was restored to his descendants but after his death Judaea was governed by imperial procurators. They found themselves dealing with political tension created by the opposition between Jews and those who were prepared to work with Rome. The Jewish rebellion in 66 started when the sacrifices performed in the Temple for the welfare of the emperor were ended. Tacitus provides a bottled account of the Jews in order to prepare his readers for the story of the destruction of Jerusalem by Vespasian (see Chapter 2). It provides an interesting account of Roman perceptions, though of course it also seeks to justify the violence.

Some say that the Jews were originally exiled from the island of Crete and settled in the remotest parts of Libya around the time that Jupiter's power drove Saturn from his throne. Support for this theory comes from their name. In Crete there is a famous mountain called Ida and, consequently, the people there were called the Idaei, later lengthened into the corrupt form Iudaei. Another theory is that during the reign of Isis, Egypt's overflowing population, under the leadership of Hierosolymus and Judas spilled over into the neighbouring countries. Others say that they were a people of Ethiopian origin driven by fear and loathing of their neighbours, during the reign of King Cepheus, to find a new homeland. It has also been said that they were a horde from Assyria with not enough land who took part of Egypt. They established their own cities in the Hebrew area and the border regions of Syria. Another version gives them a very distinguished origin, saying they were the Solymi, a people celebrated in Homer's works, who called the city which they founded Hierosolyma [Jerusalem], made out of their own name.

But most of the writers are agreed that a plague broke out in Egypt, which caused terrible disfigurement to the body, and that King Bocchoris, seeking a cure, consulted the oracle of Amun. He was told to cleanse his kingdom, and to send into foreign parts these people who the gods hated. A thorough search gathered the Jews together who were abandoned by themselves in the desert. They sat there, motionless, transfixed by grief until one of the exiles, called Moses, warned them that there would be no help from God or man, as they had been forsaken by both. They were to trust in themselves, taking for a leader sent from heaven, the first man to help them leave their current misery. They agreed and set out, in their complete ignorance, trusting in chance. Nothing caused them more distress than the lack of water, and they collapsed on the point of death across the plain. Then a herd of asses was spotted leaving their pasture to a rock shaded by a wood. Moses went after them and, using the clue of a patch of grass, found an abundant spring of water. This provided relief. After a continuous journey, which lasted six days, on the seventh they seized a country, expelling the inhabitants. Here they founded a city and a temple.

Wishing to guarantee his authority over the Jewish nation in the future, Moses gave them a form of worship, which is different to that practised by other peoples. Things we regard as sacred are nothing to them, while they permit things we forbid. In their shrine, they have consecrated an image of the animal which guided them out of their long and thirsty wanderings, and sacrifice a ram, apparently to deride Amun. They sacrifice the ox, because the Egyptians worship it as Apis. They abstain from pork, in commemoration of what they suffered when they were infected by a disease to which the pig is susceptible.

Their frequent fasts bear witness to the long periods of hunger in the old days. Jewish bread, made without yeast, is still made as a memorial to when they hastily picked up the corn [*Exodus*, XII.34]. We are told that they adopted the practice of resting on the seventh day because this was the day on which their toils ended. After a time, the prospect of an easy life beguiled them into giving up work on every seventh year. But others say this observance is in honour of Saturn, either being a primitive part of their faith handed down from the Idaei, who are said to have shared Saturn's flight; or, because of the fact that Saturn, out of the seven planets which rule men's fates, moves in the highest orbit and has the greatest power. Also, many of the celestial bodies move in paths and tracks which are measured in multiples of seven.

Regardless of where these practices came from, their antiquity is what keeps them going. All their other customs, which are simultaneously perverse and disgusting, get their strength from their depravity. The most degraded members of other races, renouncing their own traditional beliefs, kept sending tribute and other gifts to them, thus making the Jews wealthier. Also, the Jews show unswerving mutual loyalty and are always ready to show one another compassion, although they regard the rest of the human race with hatred and hostility. They eat and sleep separately. Despite being, as a nation, particularly liable to lust they do not have intercourse with foreign women though there is nothing illegal about what they do amongst themselves. They adopted circumcision as a mark of distinction from other men.

Converts to Judaism adopt the custom, and this is the first lesson they have drilled into them, of hating all gods, rejecting their own country and valuing their children, parents and kin at nothing. Even so, the Jews make provision for their numbers to increase. Amongst them, killing a newborn baby is a crime. They believe that the souls of anyone killed in battle, or executed, are immortal. This explains their passion for propagating their race and their indifference to death. They prefer burying their dead to cremation, which corresponds to the Egyptian custom and they have the same beliefs about the Underworld. Their beliefs in sacred things are quite different. The Egyptians worship many animals and images in monstrous form. The Jews believe in only one god, and then

only manifested as a concept. They call those who make figures of God in a human form out of perishable materials, profane. They believe their God to be supreme and eternal, incapable of being represented, or of decaying. Therefore they will not allow any images to be erected in their cities, and even more so in their temples. Such flattery is not paid to their rulers, and nor is it paid to our emperors. Some people have thought they worshipped Father Liber, conqueror of the East, because their priests used to chant to the music of flutes and cymbals, wore ivy garlands, and that a golden vine was found in the temple. However, their institutions do not correspond with the idea because Liber established a festive and happy cult, whereas the Jewish religion is tasteless and mean.
Tacitus, *Histories*, V.2-5.

GAUL

Julius Caesar on Gaul

This passage is extremely well known but it remains fundamentally important to the study of prehistory. This concise description is a window into a world where literacy was almost non-existent. Students of prehistoric societies have no choice but to speculate, inconclusively, about the communities that interest them. Caesar's account is not definitive or comprehensive and, of course, it was written by an outsider. But what he has to tell us would be unrecoverable by archaeology and it is invaluable for this reason and also what it tells us about how the Romans viewed such peoples. Gaul was divided amongst several different tribal groups whose identities were defined by customs and language, and their territories by geography. Rome would change all that by overlaying its own cultural veneer.

All Gaul is divided into three. One part is lived in by the Belgae, another by the Aquitani, and the third by a people we call Gauls but who call themselves Celts. Each has its own language, customs, and laws. The Gauls and Aquitani are separated by the river Garonne, and the rivers Marne and Seine separate the Gauls from the Belgae. Amongst these, the Belgae are the bravest, being the furthest from the civilization and refinement of the Roman province. Traders who bring in the sort of goods that encourage softness visit them the least. They are also the closest to the Germans across the Rhine, with whom they are constantly at war. This is the same reason why the Helvetii also outdo the other Gauls in valour, because they fight the Germans almost every day, either trying to keep them out of Gaul, or trying to conquer German territory.

The part which the Gauls live in starts at the river Rhone and is bounded by the Garonne, the ocean, and Belgae land. Where it faces the Sequani and Helvetii it is bounded by the Rhine and extends to the north. Belgae territory starts at the edge of Gaul, reaches the lower Rhine and extends to the north and east. Aquitania extends from the Garonne to the Pyrenees to that part of the ocean which is near Spain, and lies between the west and north.
Caesar, *Gallic War*, I.1

Considering the state of civilization amongst the Gauls, their funerals are magnificent and costly affairs. They throw everything into the pyre including living creatures which they believe they were fond of in life. Up until recently, their slaves and retainers, who were also thought to have been cherished by their lords, were cremated along with them at the end of the funeral ceremonies.

Caesar, *Gallic War*, VI.19

Gaulish Druids

Nothing intrigued and frustrated the Romans more than bizarre religious sects and hierarchies. In general the Roman world was entirely catholic in its approach to new cults and beliefs. But sometimes the Romans came up against an uncompromising force of religious power which would not accept integration. The Druids of Gaul and Britain were considered to be about as way-out as possible. Here Caesar describes their organisation to a fascinated Roman public. There are odd echoes of the authority of medieval monastic society in what Caesar says about their powers, and their segregation from the rest of society. One might consider this quote from the autobiography *'Tis*, by Frank McCourt, where he talks about the power the priests and nuns of his childhood wielded over the ordinary Irish population. For Latin here, read Celtic and the Druids, 'When you know Latin and forgive sins it makes you powerful and hard to talk to because you know the dark secrets of the world' (1999, 7).

The two orders of nobles are made up of the Druids, and the knights. Druids are involved with all sacred matters, and deal with public and private sacrifices and any theological questions. Many young men cluster about them in order to be educated and hold them in great esteem. Actually, it is the Druids who settle almost all disputes, whether public or private. They take decisions on crimes that have been committed, or murders, or arguments over boundaries and wills, and decide what the compensation or punishments will be. Anyone who does not abide by their decisions is excluded from attending sacrifices, the greatest penalty they can impose. People who are banned this way are considered to be impious and criminal. Everyone gets out of their way and fear their society and discussions, terrified they might be harmed by coming into contact with them. If Druids seek justice they are denied it, and they receive no honours.

One Druid presides over all the others, and has supreme authority over them. When he dies, if there is any one amongst them who is more esteemed than the others, he succeeds. But, if there are many of equal prestige, someone is elected by the Druids' votes. Occasionally they even fight over who will be in charge. Druids gather together on a fixed date in a sacred place in the lands of the Carnutes, considered to be the very centre of all Gaul. Here all people engaged in disputes assemble from all over the place and accept their decisions and orders. It is believed that their organization was developed in Britain and was exported to Gaul. Anyone who wants to find out more about the Druid system normally goes to Britain in order to study it.

Usually, the Druids have nothing to do with war and do not pay war taxes like everyone else. They are exempted from serving as soldiers and any other duties. With such an attractive prospect, plenty of young men need no bidding to be trained by them while others are sent by their families. It's said that in the Druid colleges they commit a great many verses to memory and consequently some people spend up to twenty years being trained. They think it is inappropriate to write these verses down, though they use Greek letters to record almost everything else, including public and private accounts. In my opinion they have two reasons for this: they want to stop the litany entering the public domain; and they want to stop those who learn the litany from depending on writing and ceasing to develop the art of memorizing. It is true that using writing as a memory aid helps students be less diligent and not so good at remembering things.

The main tenet of their beliefs, which they teach, is reincarnation: at death the soul passes to another body. They consider this to be the best means to inspiring bravery because any fear of death is thrown aside. As well as this they have frequent debates about stars and their movements, the size of the earth and universe, the natural way of things, and what sort of powers and strength the gods have. They also hand down their beliefs to the young men.

Caesar, *Gallic War*, VI.13–14

Admitting Gauls to the Senate

A century later after Caesar, Claudius started to fill vacancies in the Senate in Rome with men from Gaul. This was extremely important because it not only represented the expansion of the concept of membership of the imperial ruling class. As Claudius pointed out to the senators, places like Athens and Sparta had destroyed themselves by not admitting the peoples they had conquered, and that Italy's own growth had set a precedent. The term 'long-haired' Gaul was how the Romans described the parts of Gaul (Aquitania, Belgica, and Lugdunensis) conquered in the first century BC and now ruled as imperial provinces. This distinguished it from Gallia Narbonensis (the south) which had been fully Roman for generations and which was ruled as a senatorial province. The text here is from Tacitus. It differs in detail and order from a contemporary inscription, found at Lyons, which records the same speech (*ILS* 212) and is a useful example of how the Roman rhetorical style involved embellishments and changes for the purposes of style and effect.

In the consulship of Aulus Vitellius and Lucius Vipstanus [AD48] the matter of filling up the Senate was being discussed. The leading citizens of 'long-haired' Gaul, as it is known, who had long possessed Roman citizenship and federal privileges, were seeking the privilege of holding public offices at Rome. The debate involved many different points of view, and was conducted before the imperial council by partisans adhering to diametrically opposed views.

One of the opinions asserted was that, 'Italy is not so weak that it cannot provide its own capital with a senate. Originally a senate made up of men born in Rome was enough for peoples who shared their blood, and there was no shame in the old Roman republic. Even today, examples of virtue and glory, which the Roman character exhibited under the old system, are cited. Isn't it enough that Venetian and Insubrian Gauls have already stormed their way into the senate, unless armies of foreigners were brought in to make the city look as it had been seized? What sort of future careers would be left to the remains of the nobility or the poor senator from Latium? Their prospects would be submerged by wealthy men whose forefathers, commanding hostile tribes, had assaulted our armies in battle and laid siege to the deified Julius at Alesia! But those happened a short time ago. What would happen if they remembered the men who came down to seize the spoils, sacred to Heaven, from the Capitol and Roman citadel? By all means let the Gauls enjoy the title of 'citizen', but don't let them degrade the senate's insignia, the glory of office.'

This argument and others like it cut no ice with Claudius who expressed his objections on the spot. Then, when he had convened the senate, he told them this: 'I am encouraged by my ancestors, the oldest of whom, called Clausus, was a Sabine and who was made a citizen and the head of a patrician family all at the same time, to stick to the same policy in my government by bringing into the city all conspicuous merit, regardless of where it is found. I am quite well aware that the Julii came to us from Alba, the Coruncanii from Camerium, the Porcii from Tusculum, and, leaving antiquity to one side, men were admitted to the senate from Etruria, Lucania, and across all of Italy. In the end, Italy was extended up to the Alps, which has brought whole nations and peoples, as well as individuals, into the Roman world.

The time of peace at home, and victory abroad, came when lands beyond the Po were admitted to citizenship. To these, colonies of veteran troops were added throughout the world and through them the exhausted Empire found new strength. Do we regret that the Balbi came here from Spain or other, just as distinguished, families came from Gallia Narbonensis? Their descendants are still here and their love for Rome is equal to ours.

'What else was it that ruined Athens and Sparta than the fact that in spite of their military power they looked down on the foreigners they had conquered as aliens? Our own founder Romulus was so wise that he fought and naturalized a whole people in a single day on more than one occasion. Some of our kings were foreigners. Likewise making the sons of freedmen into magistrates is not the novelty it is widely held to be, being routine in the old commonwealth.'

'It'll be said "But we fought with the Senones". Well, so did the Volscians and Aequians. "The Gauls captured Rome!" Well, the Tuscans also took hostages from us, and we fell under the Samnite yoke. Overall, if you look at all our wars none was shorter than the one we fought against the Gauls and since then there has been an unbroken and loyal peace. Now that customs, culture, and marriage have merged them with us, let them bring into our midst their gold and riches instead of keeping them to themselves.

'Senators, everything which we revere for its antiquity was once a novelty. Plebeian magistrates came after the patricians, Latin magistrates followed the plebeian, then magistrates from other Italian peoples. Our new scheme will also become established and what we justify today through precedents will, one day, be a precedent itself.'

A senatorial decree followed Claudius' speech, and the Aedui were the first to be allowed to becomes senators at Rome. This compliment was paid to their ancient treaty, and to the fact that they are the only Gaulish people called 'brothers of the Roman people'. Tacitus, *Annals*, XI.23-25

BRITAIN

Julius Caesar on Britain

Julius Caesar invaded Britain in 55 and 54BC. His purpose seems to have been for reconnaissance, to suppress support for his opponents in Gaul and, perhaps, for the sheer excitement and glamour of it. He provides the first detailed description of this remote, unknown land, which matched Egypt's exotic mysteries with its own strange mysteries. Like Egypt, Britain remained a perpetual source of fascination with tales of its strange tribes who lived in virtual darkness in marshes and forests. This image persisted long after most of southern Britain had been settled as a Roman province for centuries.

The inland part of Britain is inhabited by people whom tradition says were born in the island itself. The coastal area is lived in by people who crossed over from the Belgae region in order to plunder and make war. Almost all of these are named after the nations from where they originated and, having made their wars, stayed on and began to cultivate the land. The population is incalculable, and their buildings very numerous for the most part, just like the Gauls, and the number of cattle is very great. Tin is produced in the midland area, and iron in the coastal areas, but the quantity is small. They use imported brass. As in Gaul there is timber of every type except for beech and fire. They consider it illegal to eat hare, cocks, and geese. However, they breed them for entertainment and pleasure. The climate is more temperate than in Gaul, the cold being less severe.

The island is triangular in shape, with one of its sides facing Gaul. One angle on this side, which is in Kent (to where almost all ships from Gaul go), faces the east, and lower the south. This side is about 500 miles long. Another side faces Spain and the west, towards Ireland which is considered to be about half the size of Britain but the sea passage is the same length as between Britain and Gaul. In the middle of this crossing is an island which is called *Mona* [Isle of Man]. As well as this, many smaller islands are supposed to lie close to land, including some about which it has been written that night lasts for thirty days at the time of the winter solstice. In our enquiry about that, we found out nothing except that with accurate water measurements, we discovered the nights to be shorter than they were on the continent. The length of this side, according to the natives, is 700 miles. The third side faces north and faces no other land, but an angle of that side mainly faces towards Germany. This side is regarded as being 800 miles long. Consequently the circumference of the whole island is about 2000 miles.

The most civilized of all these nations is that in Kent, which is an entirely coastal area, and nor does this nation differ much from the Gallic way of life. Most of the island people do not sow corn but live on meat and milk, and wear skins. Indeed, all the Britons dye themselves with woad, which creates a bluish colour and thus a more terrifying appearance in battle. They wear their hair long and shave every part of their bodies except the head and upper lip. Groups of ten to twelve men maintain wives together in common, especially brothers with brothers, and fathers with sons. But if these wives have children, they are regarded as belonging to the union they were joined in when they were virgins.
Caesar, *Gallic War*, V.12-14

Cicero's brother in Britain

When Caesar invaded Britain and 55 and 54BC half the appeal was the publicity gained by being the first Roman to explore this exotic wilderness. Cicero was itching to hear the details from his brother Quintus, accompanying Caesar on the campaign. To the Romans, the prospect of hearing about Britain was as exciting as the tales of North America were to sixteenth- and seventeenth-century Europe.

Cicero to his brother Quintus, August 54BC

Oh, your delightful letter to me about Britain! I was terrified by the Ocean, and I was terrified by the coast of the island. For my part I'm not being disparaging about what's left of your expedition but it's more promising than it is frightening and I'm getting restless in anticipation rather than fear. But I can see that you are going to have some terrific things to write about. What places, what natural features of objects and places, what customs and habits, what tribes, and what battles you'll have to write about, then finally you have the general himself! *his brother Quintus*

Cicero, *Letters to his friends*, II.16.4

Even barbarians appreciate rational thought

Nevertheless, elsewhere Cicero argued that even the Britons would be able to appreciate that a mechanism designed to reproduce the movement of heavenly bodies (an 'orrery') was the work of rational thought, and that therefore the universe must too have been created by rational thought.

Let's imagine a traveller took to Britain or Scythia the orrery which was recently built by our friend Posidonius. Every time it goes round it reproduces the same movements of the sun, moon and five planets which occur in the sky in a twenty-four hour period. Isn't it the case that not one of the natives would doubt the orrery had been made by a rational being?

Cicero, *On the Nature of the Gods*, II.88

The obscure origins of the Britons

This account of Britain was written by Tacitus. He had never been there. Nevertheless, he was able to draw on the personal contacts of those who had visited it, as well as use official records. His analysis of the origins of some of the British tribes is very interesting because, while there is no proper statistical evidence based on human remains to support what he says, he was probably basing his words on tradition and the evidence seen by his contacts. This means there is probably a kernel of truth, though how much or how little cannot be assessed. The recovery of a fourth-century female skeleton in a coffin in London in the late 1990s led to claims that she was of Spanish origin, based on restorations of her face, and that thus she might have belonged to an emigrant family. Here we can see that it is no less probable that her family had come from Wales.

As is normal for barbarians, little is known about who the original inhabitants of Britain were and whether they were indigenous or foreign. They have a variety of physical characteristics. This makes it possible to draw some conclusions. Red hair and large limbs of the Caledonians obviously mean they have a Germanic origin. The dark skins of the Silures, their normally curly hair, and the fact that Spain is directly across the sea from them, are evidence that long ago Iberians crossed over and colonized these areas. The peoples closest to Gaul are also similar to them, thanks either to the permanent effects of their ancestry or because the climate in countries which are so close causes them to share physical attributes. But, a general survey makes me think that the Gauls established themselves in an island which was near them. Gaulish religious beliefs are reflected in British superstition. The language has few differences and they exhibit the same bravado in facing danger and, when it is imminent, they exhibit the same fear when they duck away from it. But the Britons have more spirit because they are not a people made soft and lazy by a long peace. In fact, we believe that the Gauls were once famous for their warmongering but, after a time, laziness followed the easy life and along with their freedom they said goodbye to their courage. The same thing has happened to the long-conquered tribes of Britain while the remainder are as the Gauls once were.

Tacitus, *Agricola*, 11

The Britons as fighters

Tacitus' next comments illustrate the paradox of Roman attitudes. On one hand they were determined to defeat recalcitrant tribes; on the other, they maintained an abiding respect for those who stood their ground and defended their homelands with verve and vigour.

Their strong point is their infantry, though some of the tribes fight from the chariot. The aristocrats are charioteers, their followers fight in defence. Once they were ruled by kings but are now split up into factions and groups led by chieftains. That they never act in unison is the greatest weapon we have against the more powerful of them. It is very rare for two or three to join forces to fend off a common enemy. So, as long as they fight independently, they are all conquered.

The sky is constantly obscured by cloud and rain, but extreme cold is unknown. Days are longer than in our part of the world. Nights are clear and in the most remote regions of Britain they are short so that only a brief interval separates dusk and dawn. It is said that, if there are no clouds, the sun's brilliance can be seen throughout the night, without setting or rising and only passing across the sky. What this means is that the low shadow cast by the flat extremities of the surface of the earth does not raise the darkness to any height, such that it cannot reach the sky and stars.

Apart from the olive and vine, and other plants which prefer warmer climes, the soil will produce all ordinary produce, even in abundant quantities. It does ripen slowly but it grows quickly. The cause is the same: the excessive moisture content of the soil and air. Britain produces gold, silver, and other metals, making conquest worth the effort. In addition, the sea produces pearls which are dusky with a bluish hue. Some say that their pearl fishers are not very skilled, because while in the Red Sea pearls are ripped, living and breathing, from the rocks, in Britain they are collected from where they are washed up. I would find it easier to believe that it is the natural quality which is lacking in the pearls, rather than our greed.

So long as there is no oppression, the Britons put up with conscription, taxes, and other imperial impositions with good humour. They have no time for oppression. Their subjection has brought obedience but not slavery.

Tacitus, *Agricola*, 12, 13 (part).

Definition of a Briton

There are very few extant personal comments by Romans on the Britons. The first one here comes from Vindolanda on the northern frontier. It is ambiguous in meaning because either it is referring to British tribes fighting the Romans, or British troops fighting as auxiliaries for the Romans. The writer seems to think little of their fighting methods, being frustrated by how mounted Britons did not use swords, and how the infantry never settled in one place or position to throw spears. The passage may be implying they did the opposite instead.

The Britons have no protection from armour. The many cavalry make no use of swords and nor do the wretched Britons settle down in order to hurl spears.

Tab. Vindol. II.164, c. 90-105

The poet Juvenal seems to have had direct personal experience as a young man of leading an auxiliary unit in Britain, probably in the late 70s. Apart from noting the oysters of Richborough (III.140), and the short nights (II.160) he also referred to,

IV, 140

The terrifying tribesmen of Britain and Germany.

Juvenal, *Satires*, XV.124

Very much later, the poet Ausonius fired off insults at a critic of his, one Silvius Bonus. He found ammunition in the fact that there was an amusing contradiction in the idea that one could be both British and 'good' (from *Bonus*).

That Silvius Bonus who has criticized my poetry, has all the more fully earned my lines of verse, as being at once 'good' and a Briton.

This Silvius is the 'Good'. 'Who is Silvius?' 'He is a Briton.' 'Either this Silvius is no Briton or he is really Silvius the Bad!'

Ausonius, XIX.107, 108

Even in the final years that Britain remained a Roman possession she was still perceived and presented to the rest of the world as remote and wild. Here a poetic personification of the province 'gives thanks' to Stilicho, a Vandal general then serving as 'Master of Soldiers' to the youthful emperor Honorius (393-423), who seems to have been responsible for leading a campaign against barbarians in the island.

Next to speak was Britannia, dressed in the skin of a Caledonian monster, with tattooed cheeks, with cloak of deeper blue than the heaving ocean, she sweeps to her feet. 'Stilicho also helped me when I was at the mercy of bordering tribes, when the Scots provoked the whole of Ireland against me and threatening oars beat the sea into foam. Thanks to the concern he showed, I had no reason to be frightened of the Scottish arms, shake with fear at the thought of the Picts, or keep watch along the beaches for the Saxons who might come regardless of where the wind was blowing from.'

Claudian, *On Stilicho's Consulship*, II.247-255

THE GERMANS

The German frontier was an almost perpetual source of trouble for the Romans. It represented the furthest and longest frontier in barbarian territory, requiring a vast permanent garrison strung out along the Rhine and other linking sectors of land-based frontiers.

Caesar on the Germans

The Germans .... have no Druids to control religious ceremonies, nor are they enthusiastic about sacrifices. They count as gods only things they can see and which help them: the sun, moon, and fire. They know nothing about others, not even by repute. They spend their whole lives on their own demarcated plot of land or estate. Magistrates and chiefs make an annual allocation of land to the tribes and groups which have gathered together as seems appropriate, and they force the tenants to move on somewhere else after a year. They say that there are several reasons for this: the worry that by remaining associated with one place, farming might prove more attractive than fighting; that individuals might want large estates, such that the more powerful might throw lesser individuals off their plots; that they might build better homes to avoid experiencing the greater extremes of hot and cold; and that an enthusiasm for money might cause the growth of factions and disputes. Their intention is to keep ordinary people happy by knowing that each man can see his wealth is the same as the most powerful.

German nations have the highest esteem for devastating their borders so that they have as wide a belt of desolation as possible around them. They regard it as the absolute proof of power when neighbours have to give up their land and nobody would dare to settle nearby. At the same time they think this will enhance their security because they have removed any risk of a surprise incursion. When a nation wages war, or defends itself, commanders are chosen to organise the fighting and they have powers over life and death. During times of peace there is no supreme overall commander but rulers of districts and regions administer justice amongst their peoples and settle disputes. There is no disgrace in robbery committed outside the borders of each of these nations. As it happens these are regarded as good training for the young men and a way of discouraging laziness.

When any one of the tribal leaders has announced in public that he will be in supreme command, 'those who will follow shall now declare themselves', then those who agree with the cause and support the man concerned all stand up and promise they will help him. This earns popular acclaim. If any of those who promised does not then follow, he is considered to be a traitor or deserter. Thereafter no one trusts them.

Germans think it is wrong to attack a guest. Anyone who has come to them for any reason the Germans will protect from any trouble and will treat them as sacrosanct. Everyone's house is open to them and food is shared with them.

Caesar, *Gallic War*, VI.21-3

A fatal misjudgement

The disaster of the year 9, when Quintilius Varus and his force of three legions was wiped out by German tribes, has already been discussed in Chapter 2. This passage provides something of the background by showing how fatally Varus misjudged the provincials he had been sent to govern. This reflected the differing mind-sets and echoes exist here with governors sent out from European countries to govern colonies in scattered parts of the world during the nineteenth century.

Quintilius Varus was born of a famous rather than noble family. He was mild-mannered and quiet, inclined to physical and mental laziness and more accustomed to an easy life in the camp, rather than action on the battlefield. He certainly didn't have a problem with money. Syria, which he was governor of, provides the proof of that. He went in there a poor man, and came out of it a rich man, leaving it a poor province. When he was appointed commander of the army in Germany he thought that the only human things about the people there were their voices and limbs, and that men who could not be brought to heel with arms, might be civilized by law.

Having marched into Germany with this idea in mind, as if he was amongst a people who loved peace, he spent the summer settling disputes and sending cases before a court of law. But the Germans, though anyone who does not know them would find it hard to believe, are at the same time as being extremely savage, superbly crafty. Indeed they are a people nature has made to practice dishonesty. Consequently, they drummed up one fake dispute after another, sometimes suing each other over fabricated losses, and all the while thanking Roman fair-play for the outcome of these cases and for the fact that their own barbarity was being softened down by this new and unfamiliar method. This led Quintilius to be so negligent that he began to think he was a sort of city praetor meting out justice in the forum, and not a general commanding an army in the middle of Germany.

Velleius Paterculus, *Roman History*, II.117-18

Racial purity

The Germans themselves, I should regard as being indigenous and barely mixed with other peoples through either immigration or friendship. This was because in the old days would-be emigrants travelled to their destinations by sea and not by land. In addition to that, the tracts of ocean beyond Germany, on the other side of the world, are hardly ever visited by ships from our part of the world. In any case, quite apart from all the dangers of a terrifying and unknown sea, who would ever leave Asia, Africa or Italy, to look for

Germany? Its vicious climate and wild landscape means that unless it is your home, it is neither nice to live in or look at.

Tacitus, *Germany*, 2

Personally, I agree with people who believe the German tribes are free from any trace of intermarriage with other nations. They are a distinct and unmixed race of people, unlike anyone else. This explains how it is that their physical appearance is the same, as far as one can tell from their vast numbers. They all have fierce blue eyes, red hair, large frames, powerful but only for sudden spurts of energy and thus less able to tolerate hard labour. They cannot put up with heat or thirst at all, while their climate and soil have made them immune to cold and hunger.

Tacitus, *Germany*, 4

The German sense of wealth

Tacitus here describes the German measure of wealth. He shows how the tribes who lived on the edge of Empire were being romanized by their proximity, rather than through integration. They were learning to use coins made of gold and silver from the Empire, and recognizing the convenience of a constant and reliable means of exchange. They had also learned to distinguish the older silver coins of the Roman Republic which bore a distinctive chariot reverse, and which were made of purer silver, doubtless because the Romans had learned to distinguish those coins themselves.

Although their country varies in appearance, it is generally either bristling with forests or reeking marshes. The side nearest to Gaul has the heaviest rainfall, and it is windier towards Noricum and Pannonia. Germany is productive in grain but unkind to fruit trees. It has many flocks and herds, but most of the animals are small and even the cattle lack their usual beauty and noble features. The people take most pride in how many animals they have, and this is the only measurement of wealth they value. The gods have denied them gold in silver, whether to punish them or do them a favour I cannot say. But I cannot state for a fact that there are no gold or silver-bearing veins in Germany, because who has ever looked? Either way, the Germans have a surprising lack of interest in owning or using gold and silver. You can see silver vessels among them, presented to their representatives and leaders, used with the sort of disregard appropriate to pottery. Tribes who live in the border regions value gold and silver for its use in trade. They know about, and express preferences for, some of our coins. Tribes in the heart of Germany use the simpler, and ancient, practice of bartering for goods. They prefer the old, well-known, coins: those with notched edges and struck with the two-chariot motif. They like silver more than gold, not because they have any great attachment to it, but because a large number of silver coins is more useful to commerce in cheap everyday objects.

Tacitus, *Germany*, 5

The influence of families and women

It may be a surprise to learn that, amongst certain tribes, women retained a special authority and status. This was not 'equality' as we see it in terms of equal qualification to fulfil posts and occupations, but it was certainly an 'equality', if not superiority, in fulfilling their own special tasks for which they were venerated. Tacitus seems to find this peculiar and almost incomprehensible. Perhaps this is far from odd, considering how in his own world, women forfeited all their property to their husbands and usually had none of the power and status these German women enjoyed. However, when it came to adultery the supremacy of men became more than evident.

They choose the kings from noble families, the generals for their prowess. The power of kings is not infinite or unlimited. Generals control the people by example rather than orders, being admired for their energy, and standing conspicuously at the front of the army. Only the priests are allowed to do more than this: executions, imprisonment and even floggings. Even then, they are not imposed as punishments, or on orders from the generals, but as inspirations from the god they believe goes with them on campaign. Certain images and symbols are also taken by them from their sacred groves into battle. The greatest stimulus to their courage is the fact that their mounted units or wedge formations are made up of families and kinsmen rather than being formed randomly and by chance. Nearby also are the people who they are most fond of, so that they hear women shouting and babies crying. To each man these are the most important witnesses, and it is their praise he wants to earn more than any other. A man takes his wounds to his wife and mother, those who will not shy away from counting them or demanding to see them. These women provide the soldiers with food and encouragement.

According to tradition, armies in the process of losing or having lost battles have been rallied by the women. With endless praying, and baring their breasts, they bring home to the soldiers the imminence of imprisonment, something the men are much more frightened of seeing happen to their women. Consequently, tribal loyalty can be much more effectively guaranteed when, amongst others, hostages of unmarried noble women have been taken. The Germans even believe that women have an unaccountable sense of prophecy. They seek their opinions and do not insult what they hear. Under the deified Vespasian we saw Veleda regarded by many of them as a goddess for a long time, but in ancient times they also venerated Aurinia and many other women without seeking to flatter them or as if they were fabricating goddesses ….

The women wear the same clothes as the men apart from the fact that they often wear trailing clothes, decorated with purple stripes. The upper part of this outfit does not widen into sleeves, leaving their arms and shoulders exposed along with the adjacent parts of the chest.

However, the marriage bond is strict amongst the Germans and there is nothing about them you could praise more. They are about the only barbarians to be happy with one wife each. The few who don't subscribe to this are not indulging in passion, but are those eager for polygamy as a means to have noble birth. The dowry is not given by the wife to the husband, but vice-versa. Her parents and relations stand by to approve the gifts, not presents to satisfy female indulgences or to adorn her, but things like oxen, horse and bridle, shield and spear or sword. The husband takes the woman to share these gifts and she, in turn, brings some piece of equipment to the man. This is the essence of what ties them together ….

There is no circus of seduction, or dinner-party intrigues to corrupt them. Neither men nor women pass secret letters. There is very little adultery, given the size of the population. Punishment for adultery is swift, and the husband has control. With her hair cut short, and her clothes removed, she is sent packing from her home by her husband in front of his relations, chasing her with a whip through the settlement. Prostitutes are never forgiven. However rich, beautiful, or young she is, she will never find a husband.
Tacitus, *Germany*, 7-8, 17.3, 18.1-3, 19.1-2

The manner of war

Although it is usually the case that the Roman war machine (see Chapter 2) was, and is, presented to the world as a model of organization and discipline it is just as obvious from this description of the Germans that the qualities were not unique. In spite of their lack of weaponry they plainly exercised considerable control over their forces in battle, making skilful use of their spears and maintaining a fierce discipline with catastrophic consequences for cowards. It is thus scarcely surprising that the Roman army was able to make use of these troops amongst its auxiliary forces in later years.

They do not even have very much iron amongst them, something which is plain from the sort of weapons they use. Few of them use swords or long lances. They carry a spear, which they call *framea*, which has a short and narrow head but is so sharp and easily handled that it can be used, as needed, for fighting at close quarters or from a distance. The mounted troops are satisfied with shields and spears. The infantry also launch showers of missiles, each soldier, wearing nothing or no more than a light cloak, having several and throwing them great distances.

There is no cult of ostentation: only their shields are adorned with choice colours. Breastplates are few, and only the odd one or two at most have metal or leather helmets. The horses are only remarkable for their lack of beauty and speed, and they are not trained, as ours are, to run around in all directions. Instead, they ride them straight ahead or to the right, in such compact formation as they turn that no one is left behind. Overall, their main strength is their infantry, and therefore they fight as one body. Members of the infantry who can run particularly fast are picked out of the whole body of young warriors, being well-suited to cavalry actions, and placed at the front of the line. The number of these men is fixed: one hundred from each district, and 'The Hundred' is exactly what they are called by their own people. What was once just a number has become a title and a badge of honour.

The battle line is drawn up in wedge formation. Pulling back is considered a tactical rather than a cowardly move, so long as the offensive is restored. Even when the battle has been indecisive, they carry off their dead and wounded. Abandoning one's shield is the worst crime. A man disgraced by this cannot attend religious ceremonies, or attend the council, and many such survivors of war have completed their infamy with the noose.
Tacitus, *Germany*, 6

THE HARDY HUNS

In the fourth century, the Roman Empire was increasingly aware of remote barbarian peoples on the move from deep into Asia and the north. They were attracted by the Empire, and their boldness was increased by the political fragmentation and instability in the world of late antiquity. The Romans despised such peoples. The description of the Huns by Ammianus Marcellinus is an exercise in the definition of a barbarian. The Hun's world is fundamentally disordered, and he has no fixed abode or sense of beauty, style and elegance. Most of all he is ugly and dishonest. In the end Marcellinus is almost describing them as sub-human.

The Huns have hardly been touched on in the old records. Living beyond the Sea of Azov, beside the frozen Ocean their barbarity knows no bounds. From the earliest days of childhood, the faces of infants are deeply cut with steel and these puckered scars slow down the development of hair which comes at the appropriate age. Consequently they grow up without any beards but have no charm, just like eunuchs. All have taut, strong limbs and thick necks and are so misshapen and deformed in such a horrible way that you might mistake them for two-legged animals, or the crudely-carved images on posts used for the sides of bridges.

They might be exceptionally repulsive as men but are so hardy in their lifestyle that they have no use for fire or delicious food. Their diet is made up of roots from wild plants and semi-raw meat from any sort of animal. They warm the meat up a little by placing it between their thighs and the backs of horses. They never live in houses, which they avoid like the tombs which are placed away from everyday activities. It is impossible even to find huts roofed with reeds. They wander and roam through mountains and forests and from the cradle they learn to cope with frost, hunger and thirst. They never go into the homes of strangers, unless they are forced to by need, because they feel insecure under roofs.

The clothes they wear are made of linen or field-mice skins, and this costume does for them inside and out. Once a dreary-coloured tunic has gone over their necks, there it stays until it is tattered and has become shredded to pieces from constant wearing. They cover their heads with round hats, and goatskins on their hairy legs. Their shoes are not shaped on lasts, which inhibits them from walking properly. Consequently they are not very good at fighting infantry battles.

They are practically glued to their horses, which are strong but ugly beasts. Sometimes they ride them side-saddle to perform their ordinary duties. Huns stay on horseback day and night, buying, selling, eating, drinking, and by leaning forward over their horses' narrow necks they fall into a sleep deep enough to dream any manner of dreams. They also gather on horseback to debate when something important requires discussion.

No king has any control over them. Instead they are happy with the wild leadership of chieftains under whose command they fight their way through any obstruction. Sometimes they are provoked to battle and when they are, they go into the fray in a wedge formation with a hideous medley of ghastly noises. For the sake of speed and surprise they carry few arms, and without warning, suddenly break up into scattered groups to make the attack. They race about, with no organised ranks, committing indiscriminate slaughter.

They are never caught attacking fortifications or throwing weapons at enemy forts because the only thing they care about is speed. Consequently they easily become notorious as the fiercest warriors in the world.

They hurl their missiles from some way away and use sharpened bone tips, ingeniously fastened on, instead of arrowheads. Then they gallop over the land in between, ignoring any danger to themselves, and use their swords in hand-to-hand fighting. While their enemies are fending off sword-thrusts, they hurl strips of cloth plaited into lassos over them and by trapping their arms and legs prevent them from riding or walking.

Not one of them does any ploughing or even touches a plough because they are entirely nomadic, with no homes, laws or even a customary diet, roaming far and wide like fugitives and travelling with the carts they live in. In these carts, their wives weave the rough clothing, have sexual relations with their husbands and give birth to the children, which they raise to adolescence. Not one of them, if asked, can tell you where he comes from because he was conceived in one place, born somewhere else far away, and brought up in a third place even further away.

The Huns are completely untrustworthy and capricious in maintaining a truce, blown away by the slightest breeze of a new prospect, and are completely committed to total violence and mayhem. Like mindless animals, they have no idea of the difference between right and wrong. In negotiation they are ambiguous and dishonest, having no respect for religion or any other belief. Gold drives them wild with greed. They are so unpredictable and easily provoked, that they can fall out with friends several times on the same day, even when there is no reason to be annoyed, and make it up even though nobody has to reconcile them.

This race of wild men, without any encumbrances, and burning with an inhuman lust for stealing other people's property, forced a violent path through the rape and killing of neighbouring peoples ....
Ammianus Marcellinus, XXXI.2.1-11

8 Disasters, omens and phenomena

The Romans lived in a world which they little understood, in spite of their unprecedented ability to exploit the environment. Like other men before or since, their world of gods and demons began where knowledge and understanding ended. Although the reasoned writings of men like Pliny the Elder, Celsus, and Vitruvius played a significant part in the dawn of the early science in the sixteenth and seventeenth centuries, they were part of a world in which disasters were more usually explained by omens, and natural phenomena as acts of the gods. Nonetheless, they provide a useful record of what perplexed the Romans and what provoked them to fear or take joy in.

AT NATURE'S MERCY

Pot luck

Almost all the Roman historians provide references to earthquakes, comets, terrible storms and volcanic eruptions. While the results could be devastating and tragic perhaps they at least enjoyed a freedom from worrying about them in advance - there was, after all, nothing they could really do. And, however horrific a storm, there were no power lines to bring down, no telephone communications to wreck, and no real expectation that immediate help would come from anywhere except from local resources. But the Romans recognised that bad luck could strike anyone, regardless of who he was.

It is true that one man's vineyards are planted over a wide area than another's, that a candidate of a better family comes down to the Campus, another of better character and greater fame. He gets on, that has a great crowd of retainers. Nature draws lots for those of rank and lower orders with impartiality. It's pot-luck, with enough for everyone.
Horace, *Odes*, III.1.9-16

DEALING WITH WATER

Special water
Vitruvius' work on architecture is mainly concerned with the practicalities of selecting sites, and designing and erecting buildings. However, in his eighth book he considered water in all its forms, because of its nature as the 'primordial element'. Here he describes the phenomena of healing waters.

Every hot spring has healing properties because it has been boiled with foreign substances, and thus acquires a new and useful quality. For example, sulphur springs cure pains in the sinews, by warming up and burning out the corrupt humours in the body by their heat. Aluminous springs, used in the treatment of the limbs when enfeebled by paralysis or the stroke of any such malady, introduce warmth through the open pores, counteracting the chill by the opposite effect of their heat, and thus equably restoring the limbs to their former condition. Asphaltic springs, taken as purges, cure internal maladies.

There is also a kind of cold water containing natron, found for instance at Penne in the Vestine country, at Cutiliae, and at other similar places. It is taken as a purge and in passing through the bowels reduces scrofulous tumours.

Vitruvius, *On Architecture*, VIII.3.4-5, *trans.* Morris Hicky Morgan

Mighty rivers
The Rhine and Danube are the two largest rivers in the north. One borders Germany, the other Pannonia. In summer they are deep and broad enough to be navigable, but in winter the low temperatures cause them to freeze over such that horses can use them as if they were dry ground. Once flowing currents, these rivers become so firm and solid that they don't just support horses' hooves and men's feet. Anyone needing to draw water doesn't bring along jugs and bowls but axes and mattocks to hack the water out and carry it home in their hands, without a container, as if it was a block of stone.

Herodian, *History of the Empire*, VI.7.6-7

A river bursts its banks
Pliny to Macrinus

Are your heavens as rough and stormy as they are here? Here everything is gales and floods. The Tiber has deviated from its channel and, bursting its banks, has become deeply spread out. Although being drained by the ditch which the far-sighted emperor built, it is drowning the valleys and flowing into the fields, and wherever there is level ground only water is seen. Then its tributaries which it usually absorbs and bears down to the sea are being pushed back as it spreads out towards them, pushing them back to flood areas which it cannot reach itself. That most pleasant of rivers, the Anio, which the villas on its banks seem both to invite and constrain in its course, has almost entirely ripped up and carried away the woods which shade its banks. High land has been overthrown so that, in order to find a path through the mass of debris in its way, it has demolished houses, risen and spread all over the desolation which it has caused.

People who live on the high ground, placed beyond the flood's reach, have been the sad spectators of its awful consequences, seeing expensive furniture, cultivation equipment, ploughs, driverless oxen, herds of cattle, tree trunks, and timbers from neighbouring villas, all floating past in utter disarray. And nor have these high places, out of the flood's way, escaped the catastrophe. Continuous downpours and blustering storms, as ruinous as the river, have poured down on them and wrecked all the estate walls which marked out valuable property. In the same way it has damaged and even demolished some public buildings, whose collapse has maimed, crushed and buried large numbers of people, so that a terrible loss of life has been added to the destruction of property.

I am very worried that this widespread destruction should have reached as far as you. If it has not, I implore you to put my fears at rest immediately, and tell me in any case. Fearing disaster, or knowing it has happened, has pretty much the same effect apart from the fact that suffering is limited but apprehension is not. We can suffer no more than has happened, but our fears extend to every possibility. Farewell.

Pliny the Younger, *Letters*, VIII.17

A most unusual spring

Pliny to Licinius Sura

I have brought you from my homeland a little present of a query. It deserves to be considered by your great knowledge. A spring rises in a mountain, runs through the rocks, and is caught in a little dining-chamber cut out by hand. It's held there for a while before running down into Lake Como. This is its remarkable nature: it fills up with water and drains out three times a day, by exactly the same amount. You can see it quite clearly, and it is very pleasant to watch it. You relax nearby to eat, and also drink from the spring (because it is very cold) itself. Meanwhile, the water rises and falls regularly. If you put a ring or anything else on a dry part, the water gradually rises to cover it before it is revealed once more when it subsides. If you spend long enough watching, the sequence can be seen three times.

Is there a concealed airflow obstructing and then opening the spring, which first rushes in to stop the water and is then forced out by the water's resistance leaving it free? The same thing can be seen in bottles and other similar containers where there is no free and open passage, even when held upside down or at an angle. The air rushing out obstructs the passage and the contents are discharged in fits and starts with a repeated sound like gulping. Or perhaps this small quantity of water flows and recedes in the same way that the sea ebbs and flows? Or is it like those rivers which flow into the sea but meet contrary winds and the swell of the ocean and are forced back up their channels. Just like that then, is there something intermittently obstructing the spring in its progress? Or does the water come from a subterranean reservoir, and while it is accumulating the spring flows more slowly and in reduced quantity; once it has reached capacity it runs out fast and full once more? Or, finally, is there some sort of underground force of water which forces out water when the spring is dry, but holds it back when it is full.

Being so well qualified for the enquiry, you will look into what causes this wonderful phenomenon. I shall be satisfied if I have given you an adequate description of it. Farewell.

Pliny the Younger, *Letters*, IV.30

In the presence of a phantom
Pliny to Licinius Sura

Leisure offers the opportunity for me to learn, and you to teach. Therefore I should like to know very much if you believe that phantoms exist and have their own form and being, or whether they lack substance or reality and exist only in our fears. I myself am encouraged to believe in their existence largely because of what I have heard about the experience of Curtius Rufus.

While he was still an anonymous nobody, he was on the staff of the new governor of Africa. He was strolling up and down his portico one afternoon when a gigantic figure of a beautiful woman appeared in front of him. To set his fears at rest, she said she was the spirit of Africa, and that she had come to foretell his future: he would return to Rome and hold public office, and then come back to Africa as governor where he would die. And that is exactly what happened.

What's more, the story continues by saying that when he disembarked at Carthage the same woman met him on the shore. What is certain is that when he became ill, he considered his future in terms of what had already happened and his bad luck by his earlier good fortune and gave up any chance of surviving even though all those around him were sure he would live....

Pliny the Younger, *Letters*, VII.27

PORTENTS

In the Roman world, natural phenomena or mysterious events were often interpreted as omens, especially with hindsight. The tradition was well-established, and it was particularly attractive to historians who liked the impending sense of doom it created.

The betrayal of Gracchus

During the Second Punic War in 212BC against Carthaginian forces in Italy, Tiberius Sempronius Gracchus was ordered to bring his troops up to reinforce the main Roman column. His betrayal at the hands of Rome's Lucanian allies was later seen to have been foretold.

Something happened when Gracchus was offering sacrifices before he started his march. It was a portent of disaster. Two snakes slithered out of nowhere once the victim was killed and started to consume the liver. When they were seen they immediately disappeared. The soothsayers' recommendation was to start the sacrifice all over again. On this occasion a careful watch was kept on the victim's entrails but once more, and a third time after that, the snakes came slithering up, tried the liver and vanished unharmed — or so the story goes. The soothsayers warned that this omen was threatening to Gracchus himself. He was urged by them to watch out for men hiding, and for secret plots. However, no foresight could alter his impending fate.

Livy, *History of Rome*, XXV.16

Gracchus and his companions were wiped out by the Lucanians who had been offered the chance to change sides if they handed over the Roman general.

The death of Agrippa

The death of Agrippa, who seemed by all accounts to have been designated by Augustus as his successor, in 12BC was considered to have been a disaster. Two hundred years later, Dio recorded the portents which were said to have surrounded this momentous event. The full range seems to be here: owls, comets, lightning, and crows.

Agrippa's death was far more than just a personal tragedy for his family, being a public one of such proportions to the Roman people that omens occurred on the scale they are inclined to before the greatest disasters. Owls persisted in flying around Rome. The house on Mount Alban where the consuls stay during the religious ceremonies was hit by lightning. A comet was seen for a number of days above Rome before eventually dissipating into flares, which looked like torches. Fire consumed a large number of structures in the city, including the hut of Romulus. It was set on fire when some crows dropped burning meat, which they had taken from an altar, on to it.

Dio Cassius, *Roman History*, LIV.29.7-8

The portents of the year 62

Tacitus recorded some worrying events in the year 62. As it turned out, of course, it was a portent for the town of Pompeii, which seventeen years later was destroyed forever by the eruption of Vesuvius.

In this year, the Gymnasium was struck by lighting and completely destroyed by fire and a statue of Nero inside it was melted down to a shapeless lump of bronze. An earthquake destroyed a large area of Pompeii, a densely-populated town in Campania. One of the Vestal Virgins, Laelia, went to meet her maker and Cornelia of the Cossi family was chosen in her place.

Tacitus, *Annals*, XV.23, for the year 62

Doom for Vitellius

During the civil war of 68-9, Vitellius was the third emperor to succeed after Nero. He was declared emperor by his optimistic troops in January 69. By July Vespasian was emperor. Vitellius was killed and his body flung into the Tiber. During his short reign he sought to curry favour with as many people as possible and issued optimistic victory coins. His expenditure on dinners, and his apparently fond memories of Nero began to cause concern. But his fate was already being marked out by omens, as Dio recorded more than a century later.

While Vitellius was conducting himself like this, there was a series of bad omens. A comet appeared and the moon, in unprecedented fashion, seemed to be eclipsed twice and was obscured on the fourth and seventh days. As well as these, two suns were seen: a weak and

pale one in the west, and a strong bright one in the east. On the Capitoline hill numerous giant footprints were seen, probably from some ghost that had come down. Soldiers barracked there that night said that the temple of Jupiter had opened by itself with a great noise, causing some terrified guards to faint.
Dio Cassius, *Roman History*, LXIV.8.1-2

Reading the signs

This might be considered a passage appropriate to religion. In a way it is, but the essence is really about bad omens and behaviour which was bound to have disastrous consequences. The anecdote comes from the life of Tiberius by Suetonius who began his tale by recounting the achievements and disasters of the emperor's antecedents, in this case a battle in 249BC.

Claudius Pulcher, through his contempt for religion, started a sea battle off the Sicily coast, despite the fact that the sacred chickens would not eat while he read the auspices. He threw them into the sea, saying they if they wouldn't eat they could drink. He was defeated and when the senate asked him to appoint a dictator he gave the post to his court summonser Glycias, as if he was poking fun at the danger his country was in.
Suetonius, *Tiberius*, 2.2

Nero's warning

In the latter part of his reign Nero toured Greece, and took the opportunity to participate in all its festivals. Wisely the respective organizers decided to appoint him the winner in every case, including a chariot race in the Olympic games despite having fallen out of his chariot and nearly being run over. He had even more grandiose plans.

Nero got it into his head to excavate a canal across the isthmus of the Peloponnese, and even started the project. But men shied away from it because when the first labourers started digging, the ground started bleeding, the sound of moans and rumbling could be heard, and lots of ghosts were seen. So Nero himself grabbed a tool and by starting to hurl out some of the earth gave the others no choice but to follow his example.
Dio Cassius, *Roman History*, LXIII.16.1-2

A lightning strike

Someone, some time, near Hadrian's Wall in Britain seems to have had a lucky escape from a bolt of lightning. We shall never know who he or she was, but that person commemorated the event on a single slab, found about one mile (1.6 km) west of *Onnum*, the fort of Haltonchesters, where in the fourth century the garrison may have been the first Ala (cavalry unit) of Sabinian Pannonians. The stone presumably marked the spot where the lightning struck.

The lightning of the Gods!!
RIB 1426

EARTHQUAKES

An earthquake disaster in the year 17

Many areas around the Mediterranean are prone to volcanic and earthquake activity. This has always been the case and remains so today. But the most devastating impact of earthquakes is felt in cities, and the development of great cities towards the end of the first millennium BC means that it was in the Greek and Roman world that earthquake catastrophes were first felt on an epic scale. In the year 17, during the reign of Tiberius, a major tremor caused destruction and panic in Asia.

In that same year 12 celebrated cities of Asia were destroyed by an earthquake. It came in the night, so that the damage was all the more surprising and terrifying. Even the normal method of escape by running out into the open countryside was not possible because the people were swallowed up by the gaping earth. It is said that huge mountains collapsed while what had been level ground was apparently pushed upwards and fires broke out amongst the debris.

The disaster hit Sardis worst and attracted the most sympathy. Tiberius promised the inhabitants ten million sesterces, and let them off paying taxes to the Treasury or the Imperial coffers for five years. Believed next most badly damaged was Magnesia, below Mount Sipylus. It was decided that the populations of Temnus, Philadelphia, Aegae, Apollonis, the Mostenians, and Hyrcanian Macedonians, as they were known, with the towns of Hierocaesarea, Myrina, Cyme, and Tmolus, would be exempted from tribute for the same interval. An inspector was to be sent from the Senate to examine their actual condition and to rehabilitate them. Marcus Aletius, an ex-praetor, was chosen, from a fear that, as the governor of Asia was an ex-consul, there might be rivalry between equals, and consequently embarrassment.

Tacitus, *Annals*, II.47

A coin to commemorate the disaster

Tiberius commemorated his munificence on a special issue of sesterces from the mint of Rome which carry his titles for the year 22-3. Such a specific design and legend was comparatively unusual at this date and reflects the importance of the event; perhaps the coins were manufactured in part for local distribution.

The Restoration of the Asian Communities. Tiberius Caesar Augustus, son of the deified Augustus, chief priest, with the power of a tribune for the 24th time.

Sestertius of the Mint of Rome, *RIC* (Tiberius) 19

A disastrous earthquake hits Antioch in 115

At the end of the war fought in Parthia Trajan retired to Antioch in Syria to pass the winter. Dio Cassius, admittedly writing long after an event which preceded his own birth by thirty-five years, provides a graphic account of the devastation wrought by an earthquake which rocked the whole region but which brought Antioch, packed with hordes of people attracted by the emperor's presence, almost to its knees.

When Trajan was passing the time of day in Antioch there was a terrible earthquake. Of the many cities damaged, Antioch suffered the most. Due to the fact that the emperor was wintering there and therefore crowds of soldiers and civilians had gathered there from all over the place to pursue court cases, embassies, business or just for tourism, no country or race escaped. In this way, in Antioch, the whole Roman world experienced a disaster. There had been a number of thunderstorms and ominous gales, but no one would have expected so much evil to follow.

To begin with there was a sudden resonant roar, after which there came a very powerful series of tremors. The whole ground was thrown upwards and buildings flew into the air. Some were swept upwards only to collapse and fall into rubble, while others swayed backwards and forwards as if they were in the sea and then turned over, spreading the broken pieces everywhere and even right out into the countryside. The thunderous roar of cracking and splintering timbers as well as roof-tiles and stones was absolutely terrible. An unbelievable dust-cloud was thrown up so that people were unable to see or hear anyone speaking.

As far as the people were concerned, a number of those out in the open were hurt by being grabbed up and thrown about with great force before being thrown down onto the ground as if they had fallen off a cliff. Some were severely injured and others were killed. In some places, even trees were wrenched out of the ground, together with their roots. It was impossible to calculate how many people were trapped and were killed because huge numbers of people were killed by falling rubble or were suffocated in the wreckage. Those who suffered the most were those who had limbs trapped under stones or timbers, because they had no chance of life but had no relief in a swift death.

In spite of all this, many people were saved which might have been expected considering how great a population was involved, but not all of them escaped without some injury. Many had lost a limb, others had their heads cracked open and others were coughing up blood. The consul Pedo fell into this category, and he died immediately. To sum it all up, the people suffered every kind of violent experience imaginable. While divine intervention kept the earthquake going for several days and nights, the people were in great danger and unable to help themselves. Some of them were crushed and expired under the weight of collapsed buildings, while others who chanced to have survived in a void where timbers had fallen making such a place or under the vaults of a colonnade, died of hunger.

When finally the terrible event was over, someone who tried his luck climbing over the ruins caught a glimpse of a woman alive. She was not alone, but had a baby with her. She had survived by using her own milk to feed herself and the baby. She was dug out and revived along with the baby and after that people searched the other mounds. But they could not find any other survivors except for a baby still suckling from its dead mother. As the bodies were pulled out no one could find any gratification at having survived oneself.

This is how great the disasters were that Antioch was overwhelmed by at that time. Trajan escaped through the window of his room. Somebody of exceptional size and strength had found him and showed him the way out so that he escaped with only a few scratches. While the tremors continued for the next few days he stayed out of doors in the circus.

Dio Cassius, *Roman History*, LXVIII.24.1-6, 25.1-5

An explanation for earthquakes

Until the dawn of modern science, 'scientific' explanations tended to derive from observations which failed to take everything into account. It was, for example, believed right up to the seventeenth century by some that all matter came from water. Jan Baptista van Helmont (1580-1644), a scientist in the Netherlands, found ample proof for this in the fact that he observed a tree to grow in weight by 164lb over five years, despite being only given water. Part of the reason for this sort of deduction was an occasionally slavish acceptance of statements by classical authors, especially those of Pliny the Elder. Here Pliny analyzed the cause of earthquakes and noticed that they were always accompanied by strong winds. Obviously, he concluded, winds caused earthquakes. Nevertheless, he did observe that structure with voids in their foundations were less likely to fall down though he did not understand the reason why.

According to the Babylonians, earthquakes and cracks in the ground (like all other natural phenomena) are caused by planetary forces from the three to which they attribute thunderbolts [Mars, Jupiter, and Saturn]. They take place when those planets are moving with the sun. If you can believe it, an astonishing and immortal incident of prophecy is attributed to Anaximander of Miletus, a natural scientist. It is said he warned the Spartans that an earthquake was about to take place and that they should protect the city and its houses. Next the whole city collapsed into ruins and a substantial section of Mount Taygetus (which stuck out like the stern of a ship) came away and collapsed onto the debris.

Another prophecy is attributed to Pherecydes (Pythagoras' tutor), which also turned out to be correct, when he told his fellow citizens that an earthquake was going to happen, having had a premonition while he was hauling water from a well. To what extent can men be considered different from the gods, even while they are alive, if these stories are true? Despite the fact that everyone should make his own mind up on this subject, I am absolutely certain that winds are responsible for earthquakes. Tremors in the ground never happen with the sea is calm and the sky so still that birds cannot hover because the air which supports them has been removed ....

Security against earthquakes is also found in wells because, like caves, they let the trapped breath out. This is also seen in whole cities. Where buildings have foundations cut through by numerous drainage channels, they are less shaken. Buildings standing over sewers are much safer, as can be seen at Neapolis in Italy. On the other hand, solid areas of towns are much more likely to suffer from this kind of calamity. The safest parts of buildings are arches, corners between walls, and posts. They spring back into place with each opposing force. Walls of clay bricks are also less susceptible to earthquakes.

Pliny the Elder, *Natural History*, II.192, 197

An earthquake's revelations

During the reign of Tiberius, an earthquake exposed fossil remains. They excited a curiously conditional interest.

Quite a few cities in Sicily and the Regium area were affected by the earthquake, and quite a few people in Pontus were shaken. Corpses of rather large sizes were exposed in the gaps that opened up in the earth. The people from that area were shocked and too frightened to move them, but they did send a tooth to Rome as an example. The tooth was not just a whole foot in length but actually even longer. The messengers showed it to Tiberius and asked whether he wanted the epic corpse brought along. Tiberius acted wisely by avoiding the impiety of robbing dead bodies but at the same time found out about its size. He ordered Pulcher, the well-known geometrician, and told him to reconstruct the face on the basis of the tooth's scale. Pulcher worked out what the proportions of the whole body and face would be from the tooth, and made a replica up quickly and brought it to Tiberius. Tiberius said he was quite satisfied by seeing that and had the tooth taken back to where it had come from.

Phlegon, *Amazing Stories*

VOLCANOES

Fumes, deadly for all except eunuchs

During the Parthian war, Trajan reached Babylon in 116 and saw the sights. In the epitome of Dio Cassius' work, prepared by John Xiphilinus in the eleventh century, comes an account of one remarkable local phenomenon, evidently volcanic.

Trajan also took a look at the opening out of which poisonous fumes come. They kill any land animal or bird taking in so much as a single breath from it. In fact, if this reached up or was spread all over the landscape the area would be uninhabitable but the fumes float about themselves and stay where they are. So animals that fly high enough over it or which graze nearby are safe. I myself saw another such vent at Hierapolis in Asia and, using birds, tested it. I also looked over into it and saw the fumes for myself. The opening is enclosed in a kind of cistern with a theatre built on top of it. It kills all living things except eunuchs. I do not understand why this should be so, I am only describing exactly what I saw and what I heard.

Dio Cassius, *Roman History*, LXVIII.27.1-3

Fires from volcanoes

In the Roman world there was no understanding of how a volcano functioned. The Latin description of a volcano means literally, 'mountain belching fire', and this is how the lava was perceived - as a form of fire.

Of the spectacular events connected with mountains, Mount Etna always glows during the night and supplies enough fuel such that its fires continue burning for a long time. This is in spite of the fact that the mountain is snow-bound in winter and the ash expelled is covered with frost. Etna is not the only place which Nature's fury threatens the earth with fire through. In Phaselis, Mount Chimaera burns all day and night with unceasing flames. Ctesias of Cnidus states that water makes the fire worse, but that soil or manure extinguishes it. In Lycia, the Hephaestus mountain range flare up with such force when a burning torch is put to them that stones and sand in the rivers glow. The fire is fuelled by rainwater. People from the area claim that if a man lights a piece of wood and draws a groove through the ground, fire follows in rivulets.

Pliny the Elder, *Natural History*, II.236

The eruption of Mount Vesuvius

Without doubt the single best-known disaster to have occurred in antiquity was the eruption of Mount Vesuvius, in southern Italy near Naples. It took place in the middle of the day on 24 August 79 in the short reign of Titus (79-81) and had a cataclysmic impact on what was a favourite beauty spot in the Roman world. That things were afoot in the area is obvious now from records of a destructive earthquake in 62, which was recorded by Tacitus (see above) and also Seneca (*Natural Questions*, VI.1). Not only were the towns of Pompeii and Herculaneum annihilated, but a host of smaller settlements, villas and other towns like Stabiae were devastated. More than a century later Dio Cassius recorded a general picture of how the catastrophe took place and its wider impact, though it is plain that what actually happened had become embellished by legend.

In Campania some frightening and astonishing events occurred. A great fire suddenly flared up at the very end of the summer. Mount Vesuvius, which lies close to the sea south of Naples, has in it inexhaustible fountains of fire. Once it had a symmetrical cone, and the fire leapt up from the center. The burning was confined to that area, and even now the outer parts of the mountain are untouched by fire. As a result, since the outer portions are not burned, while the centre is continually growing brittle and turning to ash, the heights around the centre are as high as ever, but the whole fiery portion of the mountain has been consumed over time, and has settled into a hollow.

Thus the entire mountain resembles an amphitheatre (if we may compare great things to small). Its heights support both trees and vines in abundance, but the crater is given over to the fire and sends up smoke by day and flame by night. In fact, it gives the impression that a great deal of all kinds of incense is being burned inside. This is the normal state of affairs, though with variations of degree. Often the mountain throws up ashes, as well, whenever there is extensive settling in the interior, and even discharges stones with a violent blast of air. It also rumbles and roars, as its vents are not obstructed but are open and free.

Such is Vesuvius, and these phenomena occur there year in, year out. But all the events which took place there in the past, however impressive (being unusual) they may have seemed to observers, would be reckoned trivial in comparison with what now happened, even if they had all happened simultaneously. What happened was this: numbers of huge men appeared, but bigger than any human, more like the Giants in paintings. They were seen on the mountain, in the surrounding countryside, and in the cities, wandering over the earth day and night, and also journeying through the air.

Then came a terrible dryness, and sudden violent earthquakes, so that the whole plain seethed and the heights leaped into the air. There were frequent rumblings, some underground, sounding like thunder, others on the surface, making a bellowing sound. The sea joined in the roar, and the sky added its peal. Then suddenly a dreadful crash was heard, as if mountains were collapsing in on themselves. First huge stones flew up as high as the mountain-top, then came a great quantity of fire and endless smoke, so that the air was darkened and the sun entirely hidden, as if eclipsed. Thus day turned into night and darkness came out of the light. Some thought that the Giants were rising again in revolt (for many of their forms could still be discerned in the smoke, and a sound as of trumpets was heard), others believed that the whole universe was being resolved into chaos or fire.

People fled, some from their houses into the streets, others from outside indoors, some from the sea to the land, others from the land to the sea. In their panic people regarded any place where they were not, as safer than where they were. All the while an inconceivable quantity of ash was being blown out; it covered both sea and land and filled all the air. Wherever it went it did a great deal of damage, especially to men and farms and sheep, and it destroyed all fish and bird life. Furthermore, it buried two entire cities, Herculaneum and Pompeii. In the latter the people were seated in the theater. So much ash was there that some of it reached Africa and Syria and Egypt. It also appeared in Rome, filling the air overhead and darkening the sun. In Rome the fear lasted for many days, as people did not know what had happened and could not explain it. In fact, they too thought that the world was being turned upside down, that the sun was disappearing into the earth and the earth being lifted up into the sky. The ash did the Romans no great harm at the time, though later it brought them a terrible pestilence.
Dio Cassius, *Roman History,* LXVI.21-23

Pliny the Younger watches Vesuvius erupt

By far the best-known record of the event is the eyewitness account by Pliny the Younger. The spectacle had attracted his uncle, Pliny the Elder (author of the *Natural History*), who was killed by the poisonous fumes. His nephew was asked by the historian Tacitus to furnish him with a description of the occasion to be incorporated into his *Histories* (which, apart from the period covering the civil war of 68-9 does not survive), and he responded with two letters.

Pliny to Cornelius Tacitus

You ask me to write you something about the death of my uncle, which you can leave to posterity as a reliable account. I am thankful, for I see that his death will be remembered forever if you record it.

He died in the destruction of the loveliest landscape, in a memorable disaster which affected peoples and cities alike, but this will be a form of eternal life for him. Although he wrote many long-lasting books himself, the indestructible nature of what you write will vastly add to his immortality. In my view the lucky ones are those who are born to do something worth writing about, or to write something worth reading. The luckiest, of course, are those who do both. My uncle will be counted amongst the latter for his own books and yours.

So with great pleasure I have taken up, or taken upon myself, the job you have given me. My uncle was at Misenum during his time in command of the fleet. On the 24 August at the seventh hour of daylight my mother alerted him to an unusually large cloud of strange appearance. At the time he was resting after dinner with his book, following some sunbathing and a cold bath. He had his shoes brought and then climbed up to where he could get the best view of the phenomenon. The cloud was rising from a mountain too far away to identify, but afterwards we discovered it was Vesuvius.

I can best describe it as looking like a pine tree rather than any other sort. It rose up into the sky on a very long 'trunk' from which 'branches' spread out. I suppose it had been pushed up by a sudden blast, which then lost its force, leaving the unsupported cloud to spread out sideways under its own weight. Some of the cloud was white, but other parts were dark patches of dirt and ash. The sight provoked my uncle's scientific instinct to see it from closer at hand. He ordered a boat to be got ready. He offered me the chance to go with him, but I preferred to carrying on studying (in fact he had himself set a writing exercise).

As he left the house he was brought a letter from Tascius' wife Rectina, who was terrified by the impending danger. Her villa lay on the foothills of Vesuvius, and there was no escape except by boat. She begged him to rescue her. He changed his plans. What had started out as a quest for information now needed a greatness of spirit. He launched the warships and boarded himself, prospective assistance for more than just Rectina, because that beautiful shoreline was heavily populated. He rushed to where other people were escaping and carried straight on into danger. It seems he had no fear, because he described everything and the shape of that evil cloud, dictating what he saw.

By this time ash was falling onto the ships, getting hotter and denser as they went closer. Next came bits of pumice, and blackened rocks, charred and shattered by the fire. Then they were on the shore, blocked by debris from the mountain. My uncle hesitated for an instant wondering whether to turn back as the helmsman was urging him. 'Fortune favours the brave [Terence, *Phormio* 203],' he said, 'make for Pomponianus.' Pomponianus was cut off at Stabiae by the width of the bay (which gradually curves round a basin filled by the sea) so he was not yet in danger, though it was obvious he would be as the catastrophe spread.

Pomponianus had already loaded his belongings onto his ships before the danger arrived. He intended to set sail the moment the wind [holding the cloud back] changed. The same wind brought my uncle right in, and he embraced the frightened man reassuring and encouraging him. In order to lessen the other man's fear with his own composure he asked to be taken to the baths. He bathed and dined, cheerfully or at least looking as if he was (which is just as impressive).

In the meantime great sheets of flame were lighting up many parts of Vesuvius. The light and brightness were all the more vivid against the darkness of the night. My uncle put it about that the fires came from farmhouses whose owners had fled without extinguishing the hearth fires, in order to calm people's fears. Then he rested, and looked to all account as if he was actually asleep. People passing his door could hear him snoring, which was rather resonant because he was stoutly built. The ground outside his room was rising so high with the build-up of ash and stones that if he had stayed there any longer escape would have been impossible. He got up and came out, rejoining Pomponianus and all the others who could not sleep.

They discussed what to do, whether to stay under cover or chance the open air. The buildings were being shaken by a series of strong tremors, and seemed to be shaking all over the place as if they had been ripped from their foundations. But outside, there was danger from the rocks that were falling down, even though they were light and porous. Weighing up the dangers, they plumped for the outside. As far as my uncle was concerned, that was a rational decision. The others just went for the option that frightened them the least. They tied pillows onto their heads to protect them against the shower of rocks.

Everywhere else in the world it was daylight now, but here the darkness was darker and murkier than any night. But they had torches and other lights. He decided to go down to the shore to see if there was any possibility of escape by sea. But it was still too rough and dangerous. Resting on a sail he took one or two drinks from the cold water he had asked for. Then came a sulphurous smell, warning of the approaching flames, and then the flames themselves. That sent the others into flight and roused him to his feet. Supported by two slaves he stood and then collapsed without warning. My understanding is that he was choked by the thick fumes blocking his windpipe which was weak by nature and often inflamed. When daylight returned two days after he died, his body was found untouched, unharmed, and still fully-clothed. He looked more asleep than dead.

All this time my mother and I were at Misenum but this has no historical interest and you only asked for information about his death so I will stop here. But I will add one thing, namely, that I have written down everything I did and heard at the time while my memory was still fresh. You will use which bits are important because writing a letter and history are two different things, as is writing for a friend or the public. Farewell.
Pliny the Younger, *Letters,* VI.16

Pliny to Cornelius Tacitus

The letter, which you asked me to write about the death of my uncle, has stimulated your curiosity to learn what terrors and dangers affected me while I remained at Misenum because I broke off just as my story started. 'Though my shocked soul recoils, my tongue shall tell [*Aeneid* II.12].'

My uncle having left us, I spent such time as was left on my studies (it was on their account indeed that I had stopped behind), until it was time for my bath. After that I had supper, and then fell into a brief and restless sleep. For several days earth tremors had been noticed but they didn't worry us much because that's quite normal in Campania. But they were so violent that night that everything around us seemed to be knocked over, not just shaken. My mother came rushing into my room, where she came across me getting up to wake her. We sat down in the forecourt of the house, which lay in a small place between the house and the sea. At the time I was still only seventeen. I don't know whether my behaviour at that precarious moment was courageous or foolhardy, but I picked up a copy of Livy and amused myself by browsing through his pages and even making extracts as I went just as if I was enjoying my usual leisure.

At that moment a friend of my uncle's who had recently joined him from Spain came up to us. Noticing me sitting beside my mother, and holding a book, he chided me for being so stupid and her for allowing me to be so. Even so, I carried on with my book. Though by now it was morning, the light was dim and faint. Buildings around us were on the point of collapsing and even though we were in open ground, it was too narrow and confined for us to stay there without imminent danger so we decided to leave the town. We were followed by a panic-stricken crowd (because to people driven demented by terror, any other prospect seems more sensible than what they come up with themselves), who shovelled us along as we came out by pushing hard behind us en masse.

Once we were beyond the houses we stopped, frozen, in the middle of a dangerous and terrifying scene. The carriages we had ordered brought out began running in different directions, even though the ground was flat, so that we could not steady them, even using large stones to chock them. The sea seemed to be sucked away and forced back by the earthquake. What is beyond doubt is that it left a much-enlarged shoreline and many marine animals were left high and dry. On the other side, a terrible black cloud, fragmented by swift and jagged flashes, revealing various shapeless sheets of flame behind it. They were like sheet lightning but much bigger. At this point our Spanish friend spoke up, even more anxiously, 'if your brother, your uncle, is still alive, he will want you both to come out of this alive. If he's dead, he would want you to survive him, so don't hesitate to escape!' Our response was that we were unconcerned about our safety so long as his was in question. He didn't wait any longer and raced off to hurry out of the danger area as quickly as he could.

Not long after this, the cloud sank down to the surface and obscured the sea. Already it had blotted out Capri and the Misenum promontory. My mother begged, implored and ordered me to escape however I could. A youth could get away, but she was slow and old and would die in peace if she knew she hadn't caused my death as well. I said that I would not escape without her and gripped her hand to pull her along more quickly. Reluctantly she agreed, but blamed herself for being the cause of slowing me down.

By now ashes were falling but not thickly yet. I looked about: a thick black cloud was approaching from behind, covering the land like floodwater. I said, 'let's get off the road while we can see where we are going otherwise we'll be knocked over and crushed by the crowd behind in the dark.' No sooner had we sat down to rest when it got dark. This wasn't the dark of a moonless or a cloudy night, but like the darkness in a closed room when the light is extinguished. Women could be heard screaming, babies crying, and men shouting. Some were calling for their parents, others for their children, or their husbands and trying to recognize each other from the voices that responded. People were bemoaning their fate, or that of their family. Some wanted to die to escape the terror of dying. Some raised their hands up to the gods but most were now sure there were no gods at all and that this was the final night at the end of the world.

Amongst these voices were some who made the real terror worse by imagining or inventing things. I recall that some said part of Misenum had collapsed, and another said it was ablaze. This wasn't true but they found some people who believed them. Some light returned now, which we thought meant a large burst of flames was approaching (as it turned out to be) rather than the restoration of daylight. However, the fire stayed some way from us so once again we were immersed in thick darkness. A heavy shower of ashes rained down on us, which we had every now and then to stand up to shake off, otherwise we would have been crushed and buried in the heap.

I could boast that, during all this scene of horror, not one groan, or expression of fear, escaped from me, had it not been for the fact that my miserable consolation lay in the thought that the whole human race was suffering the same calamity and that I was going to die with the world itself. Finally the darkness began to clear by increments, like a cloud or smoke. The real daylight returned and even the sun shone through but with a pallid light as it does when an eclipse is beginning. We were terrified by the sight of everything different, covered with deep ashes like a snowdrift. We went back to Misenum, where we refreshed ourselves as best we could and spent the night in anxiety and fear. It was mostly the latter because the earthquakes carried on while many terrified people ran up and down making their own tragedies and those of their friends seem ridiculous in comparison to what they were predicting would follow. However, neither of us had any intention of leaving, despite the dangers we had experienced and which still threatened us, until we heard what had happened to my uncle.

Naturally, these details aren't of any use to history and you will look at them with no concern for recording them. If they seem barely worth the trouble of putting in a letter, it is your fault for asking for them.

Pliny the Younger, *Letters*, VI.20

ECLIPSES

Lunar eclipse

Although astronomers of antiquity had a reasonable understanding of what caused solar and lunar eclipses, and were certainly able to predict them, such events still caused consternation amongst ordinary people.

The considerable confusion in the Vitellian camp under these circumstances was made rather worse during the night by a lunar eclipse. That the moon was obscured was less to do with that (despite the fact that such phenomena can make excited men frightened) than its blood-coloured and blackened appearance together with even more frightening colours. But in spite of this the men would not change their minds or give in. When it came to fighting with each other they came to blows enthusiastically, even though the Vitellians had no leader.

Dio Cassius, *Roman History* LXIV.11.1-2

Solar eclipse

Here, in a digression from tales of the events of the year 360, Ammianus Marcellinus attempts to explain how an eclipse of the sun occurred and, more to the point, why this phenomenon does not occur at every new moon. He is not entirely clear, because he did not fully understand the process. The moon follows a track in the sky at an angle to that followed by the sun. The moon's path crosses the sun's path at two points (on opposite sides) called the nodes. Eclipses, partial or total, occur only when the moment of new moon coincides with a node, and even then only where the narrow track of the moon's shadow falls. Most of the time the invisible new moon is above or below the sun as viewed from earth. The nodal points advance constantly around the paths which is why eclipses do not occur at the same time every year. Their brevity means that they can only be viewed from specific places.

All across the territories of the East the sky was seen to be covered over with dark mist, through which stars could be seen from the time of sunrise until midday. The hiding of the sun and its face completely removed from the sight of the world was an extra cause of terror. The fearful minds of men thought the darkening of the sun lasted too long. But the sun, diminished to the shape of the crescent moon reappeared, grew to the shape of the half-moon and was finally restored to its normal shape.

This phenomenon is never so clear as when the cycle of the moon's movements brings its monthly cycle back to the same start-point after a fixed period of time. That is, when the moon in the same sign of the zodiac [as the sun] is found in an exact straight line under the sun [i.e. exactly between the earth and sun] and for a short period of time stands still between the points which geometry calls the points of points [the subdivisions of degrees of arc].

Although the revolutions and movements of both heavenly bodies, as those who hunt for rational explanations had noted, after each monthly lunar cycle, end up in the same place at the same distance from each other the sun is not always eclipsed, but only when the moon (thanks to a kind of plumb-line made of fire) is directly opposed to the sun and placed between its form and our eyes.

In short, the sun is concealed and its light suppressed when it and the disk of the moon, the nearest of all the heavenly bodies, moving along together and each holding to its normal course and sticking to the height relationship between them and are in conjunction have come to the …. eclipse nodes.

Ammianus Marcellinus, XX.3.1-4

THE NATURAL WORLD

Remarkably vast trees

The largest of trees considered to have been seen in Rome right up to the present day, was one which Tiberius had put on show as a marvel on a deck which had been set up for a mock sea battle. The tree had been transported to Rome with the remainder of the wood used and survived until the time Nero's amphitheatre was built [in 59]. It was a larch log and it was 120 feet long and exactly two feet thick throughout its length. This made it possible to calculate the almost unbelievable height of the remainder of the tree by estimating the length to its top.

One especially unusual fir-tree was used for the mast of the ship which carried from Egypt, on the orders of Caligula, the obelisk erected in the Vatican Circus as well as four blocks of the same stone for its plinth. There has never been seen anything afloat which is as impressive as this ship. The ballast was formed of 150 cubic feet of lentils, and the vessel's length took up most of the left quayside in the harbour at Ostia. It was sunk there during Claudius' reign and used as a foundation for three moles which rose as high as the ship's towers which were placed on it. Puteoli cement, specially dug and transported there for the purpose, was used for the moles. Four men with linked arms were needed to circle the tree.

It is normal to learn that masts used for this cost 80,000 sesterces and that to built the rafts usually costs up to 40,000. The story goes that thanks to the lack of fir, kings of Egypt and Syria used cedar wood in their fleets. The greatest cedar is said to have grown in Cyprus, being chopped down to make a mast for a galley belonging to Demetrius with rowers arranged in teams of eleven. It was 130 feet long and took three men to span its circumference. German pirates sail in boats made from a single hollowed-out tree, some of which can accommodate up to thirty people.
Pliny the Elder, *Natural History*, XVI.200-3

A remarkable boy
It is fairly obvious that in the Roman world all sorts of physical handicaps might affect people. Accidents at work, violence in the streets or in the circus, war injuries, defects caused by dietary deficiencies, were all possible causes of individual tragedies. A broken leg or arm could be disastrous if badly set. Medical help was of course available, but mainly for those who could afford it. Its powers were limited and non-existent when it came to congenital defects. But necessity can be the mother of invention. Augustus was given a boy on a trip to Samos in 20BC, whose colossal handicap seems to have been overcome in a triumph of the human spirit.

A large number of delegations visited Augustus. The Indians, who had approached him before, now made a pact of friendship. They sent tigers as well as other things, and this was the first time the Romans had ever seen them, and the same applied, I believe, to the Greeks. They also gave him a boy who resembled our statue of Hermes in having no arms or shoulders. Nevertheless, in spite of his handicaps, he was able to use his feet to do every kind of task as if they were hands. Using his feet, he could pull a bow, fire missiles, and hold a trumpet to his mouth. I do not know how he managed this. I am only repeating what the records say.
Dio Cassius, *Roman History*, LIV.9.8-9

A terrible storm
After his great victory over the German tribes in the year 16, Germanicus prepared his troops to return to winter quarters. To speed things along he sent most of them by ship. It turned out to be a terrible disaster. When the fleet set out into the North Sea all looked promising.

With summer at its height, although some of the legionaries were sent back to their winter quarters on the overland route, Germanicus put most of them onto ships and took them down the Ems into the North Sea. To begin with, everything was peaceful, broken only by the sound of oars, and the billowing of the sails, of a thousand ships. But it was not long before hail started pouring down from thick black clouds, while at the same time waves, blown about by gales from all directions, reduced visibility to nil and made steering very difficult.

Meanwhile, our soldiers were terrified. Lacking any experience of maritime hazards, they neutralized the efforts of the professional sailors with their clumsy assistance or by obstructing them. After a time, the whole sky and sea became driven by the south wind. It drew strength from the soaked soil of Germany and its deep rivers. The unbroken expanse of cloud, made all the more forbidding by the proximity of the grim north, snatched and scattered the ships out to sea or amongst islands made lethal either by cliffs or underwater banks. Time and effort helped avoid these but when the tide changed to the same direction as the wind it became impossible either to ride at anchor or bale out the water which poured in. Horses, pack-animals, and baggage were all thrown over the side in order to lighten the vessels which were leaking through their sides while the water crashed over them.

Just as the open sea is stormier than coastal waters, and because Germany has a climate worse than anywhere else so did this disaster exceed all others in its extent and unprecedented nature. Around the fleet were either hostile shores, or a sea so vast and profound that it is considered to be the farthest-flung and deepest. Some of the ships were sunk and others were washed up on the remote islands. The troops, finding no trace of human life, died of starvation except those who lived off the bodies of horses washed up on the same shores.

Germanicus' galley was the only one to reach the land of the Chauci. Day and night, throughout that time, sitting on a cliff or promontory on that shore, he continued to declare the disaster had been his fault. Only with difficulty did his friends stop him from killing himself in the same sea. Finally, as the tide turned and the wind came around, the crippled ships started to arrive. Some had only a few oars left, others clothing used for sails and some of the worse-off in tow. These ships were immediately repaired and sent to explore the islands. Thanks to this foresight many of the troops were rescued, while others were revived by our new allies, the Angrivarians, who paid ransom money to recover them from the interior. Some were sent back by tribal chiefs from Britain where they had been blown. Everyone came back with fantastic stories: wild whirlwinds, birds never seen before, strange shapes which were half human and half beast. These were things which had been seen or imagined in an instant of terror.
Tacitus, *Annals*, II.23-4

Back from the dead

The writer on medicine, Celsus, produced a work which was one of those products of antiquity which sought to find out how things really were, and not what they seemed or were believed to be. In this passage he deals with how some people might query his summary of symptoms indicating impending death.

I know I might find myself being queried on this point: if imminent death is indicated by such sure signs, how can it be that some patients, given up for lost by their doctors, occasionally get better? There are rumours going about which claim that some people on their way to being buried have recovered. Indeed Democritus, a man whose reputation is justified, maintained that the absence of signs of life which doctors depend on is not completely reliable. Even more than that he would not accept that there were any sure signs of imminent death.

In response to these points I won't even insist that some signs, which don't fool experienced doctors, will fool inexperienced ones. For example, Asclepiades, meeting a funeral cortege, saw that the man being carried to his grave was still alive. Medicine is not at fault, when there is a fault on the part of one of its practitioners. But, more modestly, I put it that medicine is based on opinions, and it is in the nature of opinions that they provide answers more often but sometimes deceive.

Celsus, *On Medicine*, II.6.13-16

How bees reproduce

Pliny the Elder provides here some insights into the trouble of scientific examination in the ancient world. One of the advantages of lacking microscopes and chemical tests is that almost any theory will do, though Pliny shows that some are patent nonsense.

Amongst learned men there has been a lot of detailed discussion on how bees reproduce themselves, because no one has ever seen them having sexual intercourse. Most authorities subscribe to the theory that the young are formed in the mouth from a compound of the flowers of reeds and olives. Some believe they result from copulating with a male who is known as the king in each swarm, and which is the only male, and extremely large so that he is not exhausted. As a result, there would be no young without him so the females accompany him, not as their leader, but as if they were wives accompanying husbands.

Though there is much to recommend this theory it can be rejected by the production of drones. Why else would copulation result in some perfect young, and imperfect young? The first theory would look as if it was more accurate but for one reason: the fact is that, occasionally, larger bees are born in the remoter parts of the combs and they push out all the others. These troublemakers are called gadflies and how would they be born if they were formed [in the mouths] of the females? The only thing known for sure is that bees sit on their eggs just as hens do. The young which are hatched look to begin like white maggots, lying sideways and so stuck to the wax they look as if they are part of it.

Pliny the Elder, *Natural History*, XI.46-8

Plague

The ancient world was no less susceptible to plague than the middle ages or even our own world. Where there were densely-packed cities and ports for disease to be brought in, a viral or bacterial infection could wreak havoc in a population with no natural resistance. There was certainly no chance of inoculation or understanding of how the disease operated. This description of a disastrous Roman plague was echoed in Daniel Defoe's *A Journal of the Plague Year* (1722) about London in 1665.

This year [66], shamed by so many evil deeds, Heaven marked with storms and disease. Campania was devastated by a hurricane which wrecked villas, plantations and crops all over the place. Its devastating consequences reached as far as Rome where a terrible plague was wiping out people from every class, in spite of there being no evident disruption to

201

the atmosphere. But houses were filled with corpses and the streets with funeral processions. Age or sex was no protection from the threat. Slaves and freeborn people were struck down without warning amid the laments of their wives and children who, having been infected while tending the victims, were burned on the same funeral pyre. Senators and equestrians perished without discrimination, though their deaths were regretted less, in the belief that they had cheated Nero's cruelty by dying in an ordinary way.

Tacitus, *Annals*, XVI.13

Seneca is philosophical about calamities

Nothing lasts forever, whether for a single person or for a whole community. The fates of men and cities sweep ever onwards. Fear strikes amongst the most peaceful places and, without any upset to cause them, calamities occur in the most surprising places …. Consider how frequently cities in Asia or Greece have collapsed after a single earthquake, how many settlements in Syria or Macedonia have been swallowed up, how often this kind of calamity has wreaked destruction in Cyprus, and how often Paphos has fallen down on top of itself. Time after time we hear about the destruction of a whole city, and think how tiny a part of mankind are we who get to hear about it. So we should confront the troubles which circumstances bring and be conscious of the fact that rumours always make things out to be worse than they really are.

So a city [Lyons in Gaul] has burned down? This is a city which was wealthy and which was the very glory of the provinces of which it was a feature even though it stood apart sitting on a single modest hill. But time will clear away all the cities you hear about nowadays for their splendour and magnificence.

Seneca, *Letters* 91.8

9 Gods, spirits and demons

The Roman world lay across the paganism of prehistory and the Christianity of the medieval world. It was these ancient origins which helped the Romans regard almost all gods as variations on an infinite number of themes. There was no institutionalised sense of religious élitism, based on adherence to a single cult, until the coming of Christianity. When Rome captured a province the import and export of gods paralleled commercial trade. Local gods were venerated in Roman and local form, while more exotic cults like Isis from Egypt, and Mithras from Persia might find new homes in the cities and ports of the Roman Empire. There are, for example, temples to Isis known in London and Pompeii, while temples to Mithras are known in a variety of contexts but usually forts and ports such as Ostia.

The relationship with gods was not dissimilar throughout the ancient world. Deities were thought to have special powers over places or forces, and a believer would ask that god's or goddess's help in securing something or other. Subsequently the deity would be rewarded by the dedicant with a sacrifice or a gift. Where religious intolerance existed it was where it represented a political threat in refusing to acknowledge the divinity of an emperor or because it incited some sort of rising, as at Colchester in the year 60 (see Chapter 5). There was scarcely any sense that one cult need supplant another. This is so fundamental a difference between our world and theirs that it must be grasped before we can understand them.

Of course religion permeated all of Roman life so references occur throughout the whole of this book, both in official and private contexts. The passages included here help illustrate the background to beliefs and attitudes.

INTERPRETING GODS

Divine confusion

It is easy to believe that while ancient deities are confusing to us, this was not so in antiquity. But here Cicero discusses the impossibility of ever fathoming out the unlimited permutations and contradictions of myth and belief.

We also ought to reject the theory the gods who are deified mortals, and who are the subject of our most dedicated and widespread veneration, exist only in our imaginations and not in reality.... For a start, the 'theologians' list three different Jupiters, of whom the first two were born, according to them, in Arcadia, one being the son of Aether (who is also said to have fathered Proserpina and Liber) and the other being the son of Caelus, and said to have sired Minerva, the legendary patroness and inventor of war. The third one is the Jupiter of Crete, whose father was Saturn. You can see his tomb in that place ....

The sun's name, being Sol, you can work out from the fact that there is only one, the sole example, of his kind, but theologians have even come up with several Suns! One is the son of Jupiter, and grandson of Aether, another one was fathered by Hyperion, and the third was fathered by Vulcan, the son of the River Nile (it's this one whom the Egyptians say is lord of the city of Heliopolis). The fourth is reputed to be the one whom Acanthe gave birth to on Rhodes and the fifth is said to have sired Aeetes and Circe at Colchi.
Cicero, *On the Nature of the Gods*, III.53, 54

Life after death?

Pliny the Elder came to a conclusion about the afterlife which was a considered and rational approach. Whether one agrees with him or not is less important than appreciating his train of thought, which is of a type not usually associated with antiquity. Whether Pliny's views were widely reflected is unlikely. One need only bear in mind the attractive prospects promised by Christianity and the enormous increase in its adherents in succeeding centuries.

Various arguments concern the souls of the dead after burial. From their last day on, all men are as they were before their first day. After death, neither the body nor the mind has any sensation, any more than it did before it was born. However, it projects itself into the future out of wishful thinking and creates a false life for itself after death, sometimes by attributing immortality to the soul, sometimes by changing into a different form, sometimes by attributing senses to those below and worshipping phantoms and turning someone who has already stopped even being a man into a god. This is as if the way men breathe is somehow different from other living beings, or as if there were no animals known to live longer, for which no-one suggests a similar afterlife.

If we look at the soul on its own: what is its substance? What is it made of? Where does it think? How can it see or hear, and what does it touch with? What benefits do these senses provide, and what good can it experience without them? Next, where does it live, and how enormous are numbers of souls or shades from all past ages? These fantasies are like the prattling of children and belong to mortal beings greedy to live forever. The vanity for preserving bodies of men is just the same, as was the promise by Democritus that we will come back to life. That from a man who did not come back to life himself! Let there be a plague on this crazy idea that death renews life. What sort of ease will there be for future generations if the soul maintains permanent sensation in the upper world, and the phantom in the lower?

This blissful but credulous vanity certainly ruins the best thing in nature, death, and makes someone about to die twice as sorry at the prospect of the misery awaiting him.

This is because, if life is sweet, how can it be sweet to finish living? How much more simple and safer it is for each of us to trust in himself, and for us to find a scheme for future freedom by experiencing it before birth!

Pliny the Elder, *Natural History*, VII.188-90

Does prayer work?

In this passage Pliny the Elder explores the logic of believing in prayer by asking whether it had any discernible effect. If you believe that any one prayer does, he concludes, then you have no choice but to accept the premise that all have an effect.

Of the cures for ills which man has control over, the first raises a very important question, which is never resolved: do words and chants based on formulae have any effect? If they do, then credit rightly and properly belongs to the human race. But, as individuals, wise men do not believe in them even though the public as a whole trust in them the whole time. Not only that, but sacrificing victims is considered to be ineffectual if no prayer is said. Without one, it is thought the gods have not been consulted in the appropriate manner.

Besides, there are different forms of words for obtaining good omens, averting evil, and recommendations. We can see too that our magistrates pray according to standard formulae, and so that nothing is left out or put in the wrong place the wording of the prayer is dictated in advance by a reader. Other attendants are appointed to keep guard and to make sure silence is observed, and a piper plays so that no one can hear anything except the prayer. There are accounts of some astonishing occasions when both types of disruption took place. These are occasions when the sound of real ill omens ruined the praying or when an error in the prayer occurred, and when without warning the head of the liver or heart has vanished from the entrails, or doubled, when the victim was standing up ....

These days it's believed that our Vestal Virgins, using a spell, can lock a runaway slave to the spot so long as he is still within the city. But if we accept that as true, that gods listen to some prayers or are moved to act by certain forms of words, then the whole conjecture has to be accepted.

Pliny the Elder, *Natural History*, XXVIII.10-12, 13

WORSHIPPING THE EMPEROR

Emperor worship, or at least going through the motions, was a cornerstone of the Roman world. The elevation of the emperor and members of his family to posthumous, or even lifetime, divinity, was an important part of regarding the ruler as a representative of the pantheon. It took on several forms, including the posthumous deification of emperors such as Augustus and Vespasian, the veneration of the *numen* or 'spirit' of the emperor or emperors, and even the concept that the imperial lineage was itself sacred in the form of the 'divine house'. Naturally, the protocol was as much about hierarchy and form as anything else and it played a more important political and social role than a religious one. Some emperors rejected the privilege, and others were excluded from it after their deaths thanks to their notorious behaviour.

Tiberius' modesty

Tiberius, despite his gradual decline into decadence, refuted the concept that he be regarded as anything unusual. This included any idea that he might have divine qualities. Such was his posthumous reputation (see Chapter 4, for example) that the Senate and the Roman People had no trouble in granting him the mortality he so desired.

To begin with, Tiberius conducted himself as if he was a citizen of the old days, but he was even more unassuming than a private individual …. He forbade temples, flamens, or priesthoods to be set up in his honour. Next he forbade any statues or busts of him to be erected without his say-so. There was only one condition under which he did permit them: they could only be set up as embellishments in temples, not amongst statues of divinities. Proposals to swear an oath ratifying his actions, and another that September and October be renamed Tiberius and Livius respectively, were vetoed by him.

Suetonius, *Tiberius*, 26

The intermittent apotheosis of Claudius

The difference between real gods and divine emperors was that the latter could be demoted.

Claudius was buried with princely pomp and reckoned amongst the gods. This honour was ignored and eventually annulled by Nero but afterwards he was restored to it by Vespasian.

Suetonius, *Claudius*, 45

CULT PRACTICES

In the presence of a deity

Here, Seneca considers the evidence for the presence of deities. Like so many Romans, he was acutely affected by the sense that spirits and gods not only existed in the natural world but also in special individuals. Such feelings were reflected beyond the Roman world as well, and this was an important reason for Roman paganism finding itself at ease with the cults and beliefs of the provinces.

If you've ever found yourself in a thick wood of ancient trees which are exceptionally tall with thick layers of branches, one after another, shutting out any glimpse of the sky, then the scale of the forest, the loneliness of the place, and a sense of wonder at coming across such a deep unbroken gloom outside, will make you think there is a god here. Any cave with a mountain above where the rocks have been eroded deep into it, hollowed out into an impressively cavernous space caused only by natural forces and not human labour, will strike into your very soul a suggestion of something divine. Sources of important rivers are venerated by us. Altars are provided in places where great rivers suddenly escape from their hiding places. Hot springs are worshipped. Pools with water which is dark or bottomless has made them sacred.

If you ever find a man who is unworried by danger, unsusceptible to cravings, content in times of difficulty, at ease when a storm is raging, who watches mankind from up high and the gods on a level, then don't you think you'll probably find the feeling of veneration for him growing in you?
Seneca, *Letters* 41.3-4

On the source of the Clitumnus

Part of the Roman love of rural settings was a fancy for rustic shrines, sanctuaries sacred to woodland gods, river deities, or strange warrior gods. It was commonplace to visit these settings and deposit gifts in the form of altars, coins, written messages, jewellery, vessels - almost anything. So, an individual wants a service from a god, which might mean bringing a sick child back to good health or asking that a sworn enemy rot in hell. If the believer felt his desire had been adequately fulfilled he or she would donate an altar or other gift, suitably inscribed with a reference to the god, the dedicant's name and the formula *V.S.L.M.*, which expands to *votum soluit libens merito*, 'willingly and deservedly fulfilled his/her vow'. There was undoubtedly a deep veneration for the spirits within the landscape that was positively primeval and prehistoric. But the attraction was no less for the aesthetic appeal of places offering seclusion and beauty. Here Pliny the Younger records his own visit to such a place.

To Romanus

Have you ever seen the Clitumnus springhead? If not, and I think not or else you would have told me, see it as I saw it recently, regretting that I had left it so long.

At the foot of a modest hill, thickly wooded with ancient cypresses, the spring gushes out into several channels, all different sizes, before settling down and spreading out into a pool which is as clear as glass. You can count glistening pebbles and the coins, which have been thrown in, lying on the bottom. From here the river is carried on along more by its volume and vitality than the incline. It goes in an instant from being just a spring to being wide enough for boats to navigate, and for two moving in opposite directions to pass each other. Although the ground level stays constant the current is so strong that a boat moving downstream is bowled along with no need for oars, while one heading upstream can scarcely struggle along unless poles and oars are used together. Someone out for a pleasure cruise can trade hard labour for easy progress just by changing course.

The banks are covered with a thick blanket of ashes and poplars, the reflections of which can be picked out in the water as clearly as if that was where they were planted. The water is as cold, and as brilliant, as snow. Nearby is an ancient temple in which stands a statue of the god Clitumnus, dressed in the splendid robe of a magistrate. The oracles recorded here testify to his presence and the spirit's powers of prophecy. Around about are several little shrines to named cults with their own gods. Some of them even have their own springs, because as well as the main spring, there are a number of other smaller ones, which start out separately but later flow into the river.

The bridge across the Clitumnus separates the sacred waters from the general river. Upriver from the bridge only boats are allowed. Downriver, bathing is allowed as well. The deified Augustus gave the place to the townspeople of Hispellum and they run baths and a hostel, both paid for by the town. A number of villas, prettily set, lie along the riverbank. In fact, everything here will please you, and there is also plenty of reading material. You may examine the innumerable inscriptions written on every wall and pillar surface which honour the spring and the god. Some will impress you, others will make you laugh. But I know you are far too generous to laugh at such things. Farewell.
Pliny the Younger, *Letters*, VIII.8

According to custom

The catholicity of the Roman world was reflected in the maintenance of appropriate observations for different deities. Here Lucian recounts how different cults were treated. Underlying the various rituals though is the veneration for frenzy and dancing. This was a characteristic of some ancient religions and it is important to appreciate how much the state of drunkenness was regarded with some esteem, much as some people in modern times venerate the 'enlightenment' afforded by narcotic drugs (see Propertius in Chapter 4).

Bacchic dancing is taken especially seriously in Ionia and Pontus, even though it belongs to Satyric drama. It has so captivated people there that, at festival time, they forget about everything else and sit all day watching corybants, satyrs, and shepherds. People from the best families in top positions in the city dance without embarrassment and are proud of it .... Every town and region celebrates festivals of the gods according to the latters' individual rites. So, Egyptian deities are celebrated normally with laments, Hellenic by choruses, the non-Hellenic by noise of cymbal-players, drummers and flautists .... At Delos, not even sacrifices are offered without dancing. Choruses of boys are assembled and, to the sound of pipes and the kithara, some move about and others sing while the best dance in accompaniment. Hymns composed for choirs like these are called 'dances-for-accompaniment'.
Lucian, *On woodland pastures*

On the edge of Empire

This passage from Tacitus' description of Germany shows that classical gods were venerated there too. Mercury and Mars were particularly popular in northern provinces, often being conflated with local gods. Mars, for example, appears in dozens of manifestations in Britain, many of which are known from one or a handful only of locations. Nevertheless, recalling Seneca's observations above, they also perceived a more subtle divine presence in the natural world.

Mercury is the deity whom they chiefly worship, and on certain days they deem it right to sacrifice to him even with human victims. Hercules and Mars they appease with more lawful offerings. Some of the Suevi also sacrifice to Isis. Of the occasion and origin of this foreign rite I have discovered nothing, but that the image, which is fashioned like a light galley, indicates an imported worship. The Germans, however, do not consider it consistent with the grandeur of celestial beings to confine the gods within walls, or to liken them to the form of any human countenance. They consecrate woods and groves, and they apply the names of deities to the abstraction which they see only in spiritual worship.

Tacitus, *Germany*, 9

TEMPLES AND SHRINES

Dedication of a temple

Dedications to Roman gods in frontier provinces were part of provincial protocol. In Britain, some tribal leaders were well-disposed to being under Roman rule. Togidubnus, who ruled in southern Britain in the first century, adopted Roman forenames when made a citizen. He seems to have been created as a client king, a kind of puppet ruler whose reign provided a stage in the process towards full romanization. Damage to the inscription makes his exact status uncertain but the content otherwise provides a striking record of how classical religion was established in Britain within a few decades of the conquest.

To Neptune and Minerva, a temple, for the welfare of the Divine House, by the authority of [Tiberius] Claudius Togidubnus, [great king?] in Britain, given by the guild of smiths and its members from their own resources, the site having been donated by [Pud]ens, son of Pudentinus.

RIB 91, from Chichester (West Sussex) in southern Britain. Late first century

Pliny restores a temple

The gifts to the god Clitumnus reflected the contractual arrangement made with a god with respect to individual arrangements. For a landowner, the responsibilities ran deeper. Here, Pliny the Younger considers his duties with respect to a temple on his land.

To Mustius

The soothsayers inform me I must rebuild the temple of Ceres on my estate. It needs to be made bigger and its facilities improved. It's certainly too old and too small for the crowds which collect here on its feast day, when large numbers of people turn up there from whole area on 13 September. Lots of services are conducted and vows made and fulfilled. But there is nowhere around to get out of the sun or rain so, in my view, building a temple as well as I can with porticoes will be both generous and religiously respectful: the temple will be for Ceres, and the porticoes will be for the visitors.

So, would you please buy four marble columns for me of any type you consider appropriate, and marble to improve the walls and floors. As well as that we will need to have a new statue of Ceres made, thanks to age causing bits to fall off the old wooden one.

I don't have any suggestions about the porticoes yet, unless you can devise a plan for the location. They can't go round the temple because there is a road on one side and a river with steep banks on the other. On the opposite side over the road is a broad meadow where they would look good facing the temple, unless you have any better ideas based on your experience of dealing with sites where the lie of the land presents problems.
Pliny the Younger, *Letters*, IX.39

Restoration of a Pompeii temple

Religious observance was an important civic and social ritual. The earthquake of the year 62 at Pompeii caused considerable havoc, with many public buildings being severely damaged. This provided opportunities for families and individuals to do the 'right thing'. Here a six-year-old is credited with paying for the Temple of Isis to be rebuilt. The resultant temple structure itself is extant.

Numerius Popidius Celsinus, son of Numerius, rebuilt from its foundations at his own expense the Temple of Isis destroyed by the earthquake. In recognition of his munificence, the city council elected him as one of their number without charging a further fee, in spite of the fact that he was only six years of age.
Inscription from Pompeii, CIL.x.846, ILS 6367

Restoring a temple in Nicomedia

Of the many problems faced by Pliny in his time as governor of Bithynia and Pontus, and which he passed on to Trajan for a decision, was how to deal with an important city temple. The ancient temple of the Phrygian Mother Goddess Cybele (here called the Great Mother of the Gods) needed to be relocated but Pliny was anxious about offending religious proprieties.

Pliny to Trajan
Prior to my arrival, Sir, the Nicomedians had started building a new forum (next to their old one) in a corner of which there is an ancient temple dedicated to the Great Mother. This needs to be rebuilt or moved somewhere else largely because it is much lower than the new building which is now going up. When I asked in person whether there where any special provisions for protecting the temple, I discovered that the process of consecration is completely different from ours.

Would you consider therefore, Sir, if a temple unconsecrated according to our customs can be moved without affecting its holiness? If there are no objections on that score, moving it in all other respects will be very convenient.

Trajan to Pliny
You can, my dear Pliny, without tampering with religion, move the temple of the Mother of Gods to a more convenient spot if relocating it is what's wanted. You also need not worry if you cannot find any rules set by us for dedication because foreign soil cannot be consecrated under Roman law.
Pliny the Younger, *Letters*, X.49

An exotic eastern cult

Elagabalus (218-22), whose idiosyncratic rule is described above (Chapter 4), gained his nickname from his devotion to the sun god Baal of Emesa in Syria where he was brought up by his mother, Julia Soaemias, and his grandmother, Julia Maesa, sister of the wife of Septimius Severus. It was only one of several eastern mystery religions which spread across the Roman Empire. The Persian god Mithras, for example, found his way everywhere from southern Egypt to northern Britain and was often given a name associating him with the sun. The spread of these religions is interesting because of the element of mystery, and the tendency to considering one supreme deity. Christianity also benefited from this trend. Herodian provides this description of the cult of Baal in its home city.

A vast temple was built there. It was decorated richly with gold, silver, and precious stones. The cult was not only confined to local people. Every year regional governors of bordering territories, and barbarian rulers, tried to outdo each other in sending expensive dedications to the god. There was no artificial likeness of the god, like the ones Greeks and Romans set up. Instead there was a huge black stone with a rounded base and conical top capped with a point. This stone is venerated as if it had been a gift of heaven. Some small parts and marks on it, which protrude, are pointed out. The people like to believe these roughly represent the sun; at least this is how they regard them.

Herodian, *History of the Empire*, V.3.4-5

The festival of Laphria

The people of Patrai in Achaea in Greece acquired their sanctuary of Artemis Laphria thanks to Augustus. He donated the statue of Laphrian Artemis from Kalydon, Laphrios being attributed with having originally set it up. The gold and ivory statue depicted the goddess hunting. Appropriately, the annual ceremony in her honour (which Pausanias witnessed himself in c. 175) involved offerings of beasts from the forest. To us it seems breathtakingly vicious, but in some European towns to this day customs involving startling cruelty are only just falling out of vogue. In the Spanish village of Manganeses de la Polvorosa, for example, the local patron saint was traditionally celebrated until only recently by annually hurling a live goat from the church tower.

The Patreans hold an annual festival, the Laphria, to Artemis. They have a method of sacrifice only known to this place. Logs of wood, each 16 cubits long and still green, are set up round the altar in a circle. The driest logs are stacked up on the altar on the circle. When the time of the festival looms they build a smooth approach to the altar by placing earth on the altar steps.

The festival starts with a magnificent procession honouring Artemis. Last in the procession is the virgin priestess riding in a chariot drawn by deer. However, the sacrifice is not offered until the following day according to ritual. The festival is not just a matter of civic pride, but is very important to individuals as well. They throw live game-birds onto the altar along with all the other victims: wild boars, deer, and gazelles. Some people

bring wolf- or bear-cubs, and others the adults. They pile the altar up with fruit from cultivated trees. This was when I saw a bear and other animals forcing their way out at the first rush of flames. Some escaped as a result of their strength. But the people who threw them in, drag them back to the pyre. There is no record of the animals injuring anybody.
Pausanias, *Description of Greece*, VII.18.7

CHRISTIANS

There is perhaps something of a commonplace assumption that the Roman administration and general population, prior to the legitimisation of Christianity under Constantine I, were invariably proactively hostile to the new cult. In fact, this was not true. More often, Roman administrators and rulers were bewildered by a sect whose members refused even to go through the motions of offering allegiance to the emperor. It was this, much less than the worship of Christ, which caused problems. Nonetheless, there were periods of extreme intolerance. They frequently involved the popular belief that Christian ritual incorporated venial activities like human sacrifice. But at the same time, the Christians were as intolerant of paganism. Denouncements of Christians, masquerading as being in the public interest, could end up as witch-hunts and were just as likely to be motivated by personal grudges and animosity or even a desire to blackmail others. In our own time, political correctness has become a platform in which a few malicious individuals find it easy to dispose of personal enemies by the simple expedient of denouncing a colleague. In the Roman Empire, the legalising of Christianity provided a reciprocal forum in which to denounce pagans. So unpleasantness existed on both sides.

Dealing with Christians

This is one of the most famous letters Pliny the Younger ever sent. Here he seeks Trajan's advice (again) on how appropriately to enforce legislation against the Christians. He is less concerned about the nature of the cult than he is about their characteristic refusal to recant anything. Various problems of interpretation exist in whether it is just being a Christian, which was illegal, or the crimes they were accused of. There was a clear division between those to be tried locally and those who, as Roman citizens, had the right to be tried in Rome herself.

It is my custom, Lord, to refer to you every case where there is doubt. For, who is better able to govern my hesitations and to teach someone who is ignorant?

I have never attended an official enquiry into Christians. As a result I do not know the type or range of punishments to which they are normally subjected, nor the basis for starting an investigation and how far it should be taken. I am also uncertain whether they should be distinguished according to age, or whether young and old should receive the same treatment; whether someone recanting his faith should be rewarded with a pardon, or if he should gain nothing by doing so if he has once professed himself a Christian; or the name itself, if unconnected with the offences, or rather the offences associated with the name are punishable.

In the meantime those accused of being Christians brought to me I have treated in this way. In person I ask them if they are Christians. If they admit this, the question is repeated a second and third time, and they are warned about the prospective punishment. If they stand firm, I order them to be taken away and executed because whatever it is that they have admitted, it is their stubbornness and irrepressible obstinacy that I am sure should not escape punishment. There have been others with a similar madness who are Roman citizens, whom I have noted amongst those being sent to Rome [to trial].

Now the problem is being dealt with, as is common, the charges are becoming widespread and more varied. There is an anonymous paper going the rounds listing a number of the accused. From this lot I thought I should dismiss anyone who said they were not, and never had been, Christians once they had repeated after me a prayer invoking the gods and offered wine and incense to your statue (this I had instructed be brought into the court together with likenesses of the gods for this reason) and said bad things about Christ. My understanding is that no real Christian can be made to do any of these things.

Other people (whose names were provided by an informer) initially admitted the charge but then denied it, saying they had stopped being Christians at least two years ago and some as long as twenty years ago. All paid respects to your likeness and those of the gods like the other people, and said bad things about Christ. Also, they said that their guilt or wrongdoing amounted to no more than the following: meeting regularly on a set day before the sun rose to chant prayers amongst themselves in turn to revere Christ as if he was a god. They also took an oath to commit themselves, not for illegal reasons, but not to steal, rob or commit adultery, never to breach trust nor deny a deposit when asked to restore it.

Their practice, after the ceremony, was to split up and then get together again to share ordinary harmless food. But they had abandoned this practice, following my edict outlawing political societies, which was issued on your orders. This made me decide that getting the truth by torturing a pair of women slaves called deaconesses was all the more essential. All I uncovered was a decadent variety of cult, taken to rather extravagant lengths.

So, I have given up any more examinations and made haste to find out what you think. In my opinion the issue is one that seems to be worth you looking into, particularly because of the large numbers of people at risk. Many people, of all ages, all backgrounds, men and women, are being brought to trial. This is probably going to carry on. Not only the towns, but also the villages and countryside are being polluted by coming into contact with this vile religion.

However, I think that bringing it under control is still possible and diverted to a more profitable outcome. There is no doubt that the temples are starting to become crowded again after a long time in which they had been almost entirely abandoned. Sacred rituals, which had fallen out of use, are being performed once more. Sacrificial offerings can be bought everywhere, though until very recently there was practically no trade at all. From all this it can be easily concluded that many people could be reformed if provided with the chance to repent.

Trajan to Pliny

My dear Pliny, you have followed the appropriate procedure for examining cases of people accused of being Christians because an all-encompassing and routine rule could not possibly be set out. No one should seek out these people. If they are brought up before you and the charged proved, then punishment must follow. But, where a person denies being a Christian and shows that this is so by offering prayers to our gods he should be given a pardon due to his repentance, and regardless of what he has done in the past. Accusations can have nothing to do with pamphlets being circulated anonymously because they set the worst example and nor are they appropriate to this day and age.

Pliny the Younger, *Letters*, X.96-97

Gratuitous denouncements

A letter from Hadrian was said to have been sent to the governor of Asia, discouraging gratuitous trials of Christianity provoked by popular hostility.

Hadrian to Minucius Fundanus.

I have received a letter from your predecessor, his eminence Serennius Granianus. I believe that this should not continue without an enquiry, in order to prevent the harassment of individuals and giving assistance to mischievous informers. Consequently, if the provincials are able to draw up a solid case against Christians on this basis, such that they can plead it in an open court, let only this influence them, not just unfounded opinions or mere outbursts.

This is because it is much more correct for you to look at this if someone wants to make an accusation. So, if anyone does accuse Christians, and demonstrates that they are breaking the law, make a decision according to the type of offence, but in the name of Hercules, if anyone brings a case before the court for the sake of blackmail, look into this assiduously and make sure you impose penalties appropriate to the crime.

Cited by Eusebius, *Ecclesiastical History*, IV.9

Persecution in Gaul

This account of a persecution in Gaul in the year 177 during the reign of Marcus Aurelius arrived in the East where it was recorded. It illustrates some of the futile efforts made by the authorities. The futility came in two parts, firstly because violence is rarely effective in total suppression, and secondly, because violence was positively welcomed by Christians. They believed that life was no more than a miserable preamble to perpetual joy, and that to make that journey through torture in the face of brutality, made it all the more meritorious. Nonetheless it is interesting that some of the 'martyrs' were less than compliant when faced with real torture. Another interesting element is the hostility expressed in the court against Vettius Epagathus for his Christian sympathies. That he was a person of status and quality and yet a Christian was popularly felt to be proof of a betrayal of his own community.

The scene for these events was set up in the Gaulish provinces. Its regional capitals, Lyons and Vienne, through which the Rhone flows abundantly, are better known and more famous than others in the area. The pre-eminent churches of the region sent a paper describing the martyrs to the Asian and Phrygian churches …. and I will repeat what they say.

'The enormity of the persecution here, and the terrible anger of the pagans against the saints, and the sufferings of the blessed martyrs, are more than we can record accurately, and nor can they be described in words …. to begin with, they tolerated with dignity everything that the rabble dealt out to them, screams, whippings and being pulled along, rape, imprisonment and stonings, and all the other things which are liable to happen from the hands of a raging people against whom it believes to be its enemies. Next they were dragged to the forum by the tribune and city administrators. They were accused of crimes to which they confessed, and then they were banged up until the governor arrived.

'Next they were brought in front of the governor who did everything cruel to them that he could, until one of the brethren, Vettius Epagathus (consumed with the love of God and brotherly love) who had lived a life of such strictures that in spite of his youthful age he had a reputation equal to Zacharias the Older, intervened …. His personality prevented him from tolerating the injustice being meted out to us and, overcome with anger, he demanded that his defence of the brethren that they were not atheists or impious be heard. He was shouted down by everyone near the tribunal, for being a man of high status. The governor would not accept the just demands which Vettius had put forward and only asked if he, Vettius, was a Christian too. Vettius unequivocally confessed and was removed to the lined-up martyrs….

'The remainder were then separated. The first to be martyred were clearly prepared and they fulfilled a martyr's confession readily, but some of the others seemed not to be so prepared. Unable to withstand the ordeals of a tremendous conflict, their training and strength failed them. About ten gave in like those who were in the wrong time. This caused great sadness and mourning beyond measure amongst us. They compromised the dedication of others who had not been arrested ….

'Certain pagan slaves of some of our number were also arrested, because the governor had proclaimed in public that we should all be prosecuted. These people (whom Satan had seized), terrified by the tortures they saw being meted out on the saints, made false accusations about us of Thyestean banquets [Thyestes had eaten his children in his sleep], Oedipodean intercourse [incest], and other subjects which it would be wrong for us either to speak or think about or even to get the idea that such things ever take place amongst human beings.

'When this rumour started circulating, everyone turned against us like wild beasts, so that if any person had felt lenient towards use for the sake of friendship they now became angry and raged against us, and what our Lord had said was now fulfilled, "yes, the time is coming that whoever kills you will think that he is doing God a service " [*John* 16.2]. At last, then, the martyrs experienced suffering beyond all description, because Satan was trying his hardest to make them utter blasphemies….

'When the tyrant's tortures had come to nothing by Christ through the forbearance of those blessed saints, Satan thought up other methods, locking them in jail in a horrible pitch-black place, stretching their limbs on the rack, cranked up to the fifth hole, and other outrages which frenzied, devil-driven, warders are liable to perpetrate against prisoners. In that way the majority were throttled in prison, the group which the Lord had chosen to illustrate his glory by dying in that manner.

Eusebius, *Ecclesiastical History* V.1

Christian intolerance

Nearly a century after the legitimisation of Christianity by Constantine I, paganism retained a powerful grip on many communities. This was especially so in the cities of North Africa. Pagans took extremely unkindly to the legal proscriptions on public celebrations of their cults. This incident, described in a letter by St Augustine, at the time Bishop of Hippo (in modern Algeria), illustrates not only the pathological hatred felt by some pagans for Christians, but also the supercilious and self-righteousness of the Christian establishment. Augustine was incandescent to find that there appeared to be no will, at any level of society, to restrict or control pagan anti-Christian riots.

Defying legislation passed only a short time ago, a sacrilegious festival was held on the first day of June, a pagan feast-day, prohibited by nobody, and was so insulting and shameless that a troupe of dancers actually had the cheek to go down the same street past the church doors. Nothing like this even happened in Julian's reign! The church was stoned when the clergy tried to stop this highly illegal and insulting carry-on. Nearly a week later, stones were thrown at the church again after the bishop had pointed out the widely-known laws on the subject to the magistrates who were, for all practical purposes, getting ready to enforce the legal provisions.

On the following day, when our brethren wanted to file a protest in court, in order, so it seems, to fill those lost souls with fear, they found that their rights were withheld. On the same day, to see if they might not be distressed by dangers from heaven, a hailstorm answered their stonings. However, once the storm had passed, they immediately hurled another shower of stones, followed by fire, on the church roof and the people inside. One Christian who was in the area, and perhaps wandered into them, was killed by them. The others hid or escaped wherever they could.

Meanwhile, the bishop was hiding in a particular place, which he had crammed himself into. In here he could hear voices of people who wanted to kill him and were cursing themselves for allowing him to get away, and for committing such a terrible crime to no avail. This state of affairs lasted from late afternoon into the small hours. Nothing was done to control the situation, to instigate any rescue, by any of the people in a position to enforce any authority. Just one person, a stranger, intervened, thanks to whom a large number of God's servants were saved from those who wanted to kill them, and a great deal of property was also reclaimed from looters. The example of this man showed how easily the crimes could have been completely prevented, or at least stopped once they had begun, if only the people, mainly the leading citizens, had ordered them to stop either at the outset or once they had begun.

Augustine, *Letters* 91.8, in the year 408

10 Slaves, insurrections and masters

It is easy for us to condemn slavery. But we enjoy the luxury of machinery and there is no coincidence in the fact that laws against slavery started to become effective at around the same time as steam power became common. Similarly, the southern states of the USA maintained slavery until the end of the Civil War in 1865, reflecting its nature as the least developed and mechanised part of that country. The truth is that complex states depend on a great deal of reliable labour. Whether slavery was just that is another subject altogether. In antiquity, slavery was perceived everywhere and all the time as a natural way of providing the individual and the state with labour.

Slavery varied enormously. At the bottom were the slaves who were the spoils of war, condemned to vicious short working lives in mines, quarries and galleys. Ordinary civilians who were captured could find themselves put to the sword or sold as slaves. Many might have preferred the former. The sheer brutality of a slave's existence at this level became attributed to the slave, almost justifying his oppression, and creating a sense that there was a slave state of mind. There is a remarkable parallel here with the Nazi regime and the way in which they justified the use of slave workers by regarding them as lesser beings. Even the more enlightened slave owners spent much of their lives frightened of what their slaves might do to them, a fear enhanced by the belief that slaves lacked the ability to reason and the fact that perhaps a third of the urban population were slaves. The monumental growth in the slave population only exacerbated these fears.

At the other end slaves were valued members of households who lived in considerable comfort, were frequently provided with their freedom, and who remained as family retainers indefinitely. Freed slaves and their descendants could rise to high office and wealth. Unlike the post-Civil War United States, former slaves were not instantly identifiable by their colour, though it is probable that differences in mannerisms, use of language and behaviour gave them away. Those freed by wealthy owners were likely to enjoy social contacts and status not available to free men of low birth. Of course, slaves suffered from considerable legal restrictions. They were unable, for example, to own property. Anything given or left to them was automatically their master's. They could not, except under special circumstances, be recruited into the army. To be born into slavery meant automatic enslavement. In the end they were simply not free but because they oiled the wheels of the machine of Roman civilisation their use was not questioned. Except of course, that is, by the slaves.

REVOLT!

Spartacus

The revolt of Spartacus is the most notorious of all slave insurrections in antiquity. In our own time, its fame owes much to the celebrated motion picture, *Spartacus*, which has provided an enduring image of a complacent and arrogant ruling class confronted by a threat to the very foundations of everything they held dear. In Roman times the revolt was regarded as an appalling warning. It occurred during the late Republic in 73BC when military leaders like Crassus and Pompey were jockeying for power. The race was on to be the man who suppressed the revolt, and thereby reap a harvest of glory for saving Rome; as so often, political opportunism supplanted more worthy motives. But for the public at large, a slave insurrection cut right through the very heart of their lives; it quite literally threatened their whole world.

The uprising of the gladiators and the devastation of Italy, normally called the war of Spartacus, began at this time. One Lentulus Batiatus trained a large number of gladiators at Capua. Most of them were Gauls and Thracians who, through no fault of their own but thanks to their master's cruelty, were kept locked up for the purpose of fighting one another. Two hundred of them hatched a plan to escape, but word leaked out. Only seventy-eight realised early enough to pre-empt their master and stole from the cookhouse chopping knives and spits and made their way through Capua. They came across onto a number of carts that were carrying gladiatorial weapons to another city and took them for their own use.

Next, they occupied a strong place and elected three leaders, of whom Spartacus was the chief. He was a Thracian, from the nomadic tribes, who was not only inspired and of great physical strength but was also, which one would not expect from his position, highly intelligent and cultivated in the manner of a Greek rather than a Thracian. The story goes that when he was first taken to Rome to be sold, a snake was seen to be wrapped around his head while he slept and his wife, who came from the same tribe and was a prophetess possessed with Bacchic frenzy, said this was a portent which meant he would possess a great and terrible power which would end in no good. This woman escaped with him, and was living with him.

To begin with, the gladiators routed forces sent against them from Capua and, getting holding of proper military equipment in the process, threw away their own weapons because they regarded them as barbaric and shameful. The praetor Clodius was sent out from Rome against them with a force of 3000 troops. He besieged them in their position on a hill accessible only through one narrow and difficult path, which Clodius guarded, with sheer and treacherous precipices on all other sides. However, on the summit a very large number of wild vines grew. Cutting down as many of their branches as they needed, the rebels plaited them into strong ladders long enough to reach from there down to the bottom. By this method they all got down except one who stayed behind to throw down their weapons, and once he had done this, proceeded to save himself. The Romans were unaware of all this and therefore, by coming up from behind them, the rebels attacked them by surprise and seized their camp. A number of the strong and nimble shepherds and herdsmen that were there joined the rebellion, some being made fully-equipped infantry, and others were employed as scouts and light troops.

Now, the praetor Publius Varinus was sent against them. His deputy, Furius, with a force of 2000, was fought and routed. Next Cossinius was sent with a substantial force to advise Varinus and assist him in command. Spartacus tracked him and very nearly captured him while he was bathing near Salinae. Cossinius only just managed to get away while Spartacus captured all his baggage and then gave chase with much killing, assaulted his camp (where Cossinius was killed) and took it. After that Spartacus defeated Varinus himself in a series of battles, finally capturing his lictors and the horse on which he rode. By this stage, Spartacus had turned into a very substantial and terrifying power, but there was no sign that he was losing his judgement. Realizing that he could not expect to match the power of the Roman Empire, he marched his force towards the Alps. He planned that once he had crossed them, his army should disperse to their homes, some to Thrace, and some to Gaul. But, having become confident with their numbers and success, they would not heed his words and went about ravaging Italy.

This new danger added real fear to the shame and humiliation of the rebellion. The senate sent out both consuls off to fight what was expected to be a major war that would be extremely difficult to prosecute. The consul Gellius surprised a band of Germans, whose insolence and over-confidence had caused them to separate from Spartacus, and destroyed them. But when the other consul, Lentulus, besieged the rebels, Spartacus attacked him, joined battle, defeated all his senior officers and captured all his baggage. As Spartacus set off for the Alps, Cassius, then governor of Cisalpine Gaul, faced him with an army of 10,000. Being overwhelmed in the battle, Cassius had great difficulty escaping, and lost a very large proportion of his men.

When the senate heard the news they were furious with the consuls. Ordering them to have no further part in the affair, they appointed Crassus supreme commander of the war. Many of the other nobles volunteered to go with him, some because they were his friends, others for the glory. Crassus himself stayed on the borders near Picenum because Spartacus was now coming that way. He sent his deputy, Mummius, with two legions to march round a different way and told him to follow the rebels but not to get into a battle with them, or even any skirmishes. But as soon as Mummius saw what he thought would be a good opportunity for a battle, he engaged Spartacus and was defeated. Many of his troops were killed while many saved their lives by throwing away their weapons and making a run for it. Crassus severely rebuked Mummius, and re-equipping the soldiers, forced them to guarantee that in future they would keep hold of them. He divided the 500 who had started the flight and divided them into fifty blocks of ten, one each of which would die by lot. Thereby he restored the old Roman custom of decimation, in which ignominy was added to the penalty of death, which was savage and horrible and took place in front of the army, assembled as spectators.

When he had repossessed his men this way. Crassus led them against the enemy. But

Spartacus retreated towards the sea through Lucania. In the straits there he met with Cilician pirates and considered taking Sicily where, by landing 2000 men, he hoped he might revive the slave rebellion since the former one had only just died down and would take little to get going once more. But the pirates had struck a deal with him, and after receiving gifts and agreeing to the plan, let him down and sailed off. So Spartacus then moved inland again and established his army in the Rhegium peninsula.

It was there that Crassus came upon Spartacus. Taking into account the lie of the land, which itself suggested the idea, Crassus set about building a wall across the isthmus. This kept his soldiers busy and prevented his enemy from obtaining supplies. This large and difficult project he finished in a very short time, against all expectations, producing a ditch which ran from one sea to the other and was 40 miles long, 15 feet wide and deep, and overlooking it a marvellously high and strong wall. To begin with Spartacus sneered at these fortifications and disregarded them. But, as his supplies began to dwindle and he wanted to break out, he found he was walled in and that there were no more supplies where he was. Taking advantage of a night of storms and snow, he filled in a section of the ditch with earth and tree branches, and in that way got one-third of his army across.

This alarmed Crassus, in case Spartacus marched on Rome, but his fears were soon quashed when he saw that many of Spartacus' men had mutinied and left him, camping on their own by a lake in Lucania. This lake is reputed to change at intervals from being fresh to being so salty that it cannot be drunk. Falling on these men, Crassus beat them away from the lake but could not follow up the killing because Spartacus suddenly arrived and stopped them from running away. Crassus now began to regret that he had earlier written to the senate to tell them to recall Lucullus from Thrace, and Pompey from Spain. So, Crassus did all he could to finish the war before they arrived, knowing that the glory would go to those who had had to come to his assistance.

So Crassus resolved to attack first those under Caius Canicius and Castus who had mutinied and separated themselves from the others. He sent 6000 men in advance to capture some high ground as surreptitiously as possible. In order to do this, they covered their helmets but two women who were making sacrifices for the rebels spotted them. They would have been in terrible danger had not Crassus suddenly arrived with the rest and engaged in battle. This was the most viciously fought battle of all. Of the 12,300 men killed by Crassus' men, only two were wounded in their backs, the rest having all been killed in their positions as they fought bravely.

After this defeat, Spartacus withdrew to the mountains of Petelia while Quintius, one of Crassus' officers, and the quaestor Scrophas, followed closely in his tracks. But when Spartacus turned about and confronted his pursuers they were completely routed, dragging off with difficulty the quaestor, who had been wounded, into safety. This victory ruined Spartacus because the slaves became over-confident and refused thereafter to evade fighting battles and would not obey their commanders. Instead they surrounded the commanders as soon as they began marching and forced them to take them back through Lucania against the Roman army, which was just what Crassus was hoping they would do. News had already arrived that Pompey was on his way, and many people were already beginning to say that victory in the war would be his. All he had to do was come and fight the enemy and bring it to a close. Crassus was therefore very eager to fight the decisive battle himself and camped close to the enemy. Here, his forces began to dig a ditch when the slaves emerged and started fighting with the diggers. With Roman reinforcements arriving from every direction, Spartacus realised he had no alternative but to draw up in his troops in their battle positions.

To begin with, when he was brought his horse, Spartacus drew his sword and killed him, saying that if he was victorious the enemy had plenty of good horses he could use and, if he lost, that he would have no need of a horse. Then he made straight for Crassus himself, charging through the throng of weapons and wounded men but, although he did not reach him, he killed two centurions who attacked him together. Finally, once he had been deserted by his own men he stood, surrounded by his enemies, and fought to the last.

Crassus had been lucky and had also exhibited great military leadership, risking his own life in the conflict, but it was Pompey who got most of the credit in the war. The slaves escaping from the battle had run into Pompey's troops and been destroyed; thus Pompey was able to say to the senate that although Crassus had defeated the enemy in battle, it was he who had ended the war. Pompey was then honoured with a magnificent triumph for his conquest of Sertorius and Spain while Crassus did not go so far as to ask for a proper triumph, even though he would have liked one. Indeed he was thought rather less of for accepting the minor honour of a foot procession called an 'ovation', for a war fought against slaves.

Plutarch, *Life of Crassus*, 8-11

The strange case of the slave Clemens

Since Augustus was the first emperor, there was no precedent for his succession, which was complicated by him having no son living in the latter part of his reign. A son was thus acquired, by the simple expedient of marrying his stepson Tiberius to his daughter, by a previous marriage, called Julia. When he succeeded in 14, Tiberius placed Agrippa Postumus (Augustus' grandson, and earlier considered a possible heir but rejected on the grounds of his unsuitability) in exile on the island of Planasia [Pianosa] which occasioned a remarkable plot by one of the latter's slaves.

During that same year [17] the daring of a single slave, if it had not been swiftly checked, would have destroyed the nation through discord and civil war. One of Agrippa Postumus' slaves, called Clemens, having learned that Augustus was dead, dreamt up an un-slave-like scheme of going to the island of Planasia and rescuing Agrippa by fraud or force and taking him to the armies of Germany. A very slow cargo boat frustrated his bold plan. In the meantime Agrippa had been murdered so he turned his mind to an even greater and more dangerous exploit. He stole Agrippa's ashes and sailed to Cosa, a promontory in Etruria, and disappeared into hiding until his hair and beard had grown because his age and built were similar to that of his master. Then, through appropriate agents who knew his secret, the rumour was put about that Agrippa was alive, first as whispered gossip, then (as usual with forbidden subjects) in a rumour which started to circulate wherever there were fools with flapping ears, or the disaffected revolutionaries. Clemens himself went to the towns in the evenings, without showing himself in public or staying in the same place for long.

Rather, as he knew that truth grows stronger with publicity and delaying tactics, lies by haste and uncertainty, he either left his story behind him, or arrived before it did.

Meanwhile the rumour circulated throughout Italy, and Rome fell for it too, that Agrippa had been saved by the grace of Heaven. Already, large crowds welcomed Clemens at Ostia and he was met secretly in Rome itself when a dilemma began to plague Tiberius: should he use troops to destroy one of his own slaves, or let the rumour die down of its own accord? Tiberius' mind veered between shame and fear, thinking he must overlook nothing and then that he should not fear everything.

Finally, he passed responsibility for the affair to Sallustius Crispus, who chose two of his clients (some say they were soldiers) and ordered them to approach Clemens as would-be accomplices, offering money and promising their support whatever the danger. They did as they were told. Then, waiting for a night when Clemens was off his guard, they took with them enough force. Having bound and gagged him, they dragged him to the palace. When Tiberius asked him how he had turned himself into Agrippa, he is said to have replied, 'just as you became Caesar.' He could not be forced to tell who his henchmen were. Tiberius did not risk a public execution, but instructed that he be killed in a private part of the palace and that his body be removed in secret. Despite the fact it was said many of the emperor's staff, equestrians and senators supported Clemens with money and advice, no investigation was made.

Tacitus, *Annals*, II.39-40

The insurrection of Curtisius

Spartacus and Clemens might have been dealt with but Rome's vast increase in wealth during succeeding decades did nothing to increase her sense of security. On the contrary, men acquired more and more slaves to run their homes and industries. This provoked an accumulating sense of terror in spite of the fact that the Spartacus revolt had led to a more enlightened approach and less oppressive treatment of slaves. Rather than rule through the rod, the idea was to encourage slaves with the long-term prospects of freedom. Nevertheless, slavery was still fundamental to the system and many masters continued to be oppressive. Trapped in a cycle from which they could not escape, the wealthier Romans looked around themselves to see that they were being increasingly outnumbered by a seething mass of slaves who might turn nasty without warning. Some of them did, provoked either by insensitive masters, or by would-be troublemakers who spotted in the slaves an instant army of disaffected supporters. During the reign of Tiberius, only a lucky break prevented one such insurrection exploding.

During the same summer [of 24], a lucky accident crushed the seeds of a slave revolt in Italy. The man who instigated this was one Titus Curtisius, a former ordinary soldier in the Praetorian Guard. Beginning with clandestine get-togethers at Brundisium and nearby towns, and then with manifestoes openly published, he incited the wildest rural slaves in remote country districts to make a bid for freedom.

Divine providence led to three naval escort vessels coming into port. In the same region then too was the quaestor Curtius Lupus who, in accordance with time-honoured

tradition, was in charge of the woodland grazing areas. He assembled a force of naval troops and broke up the rebellion from its outset. Tiberius immediately sent the tribune Staius with a strong force, and he seized Curtisius and his most daring henchmen and dragged them to Rome. Here, people were already quaking in their boots at the thought of the vast slave population, which had grown immensely, while the numbers of free people diminished by the day.
Tacitus, *Annals* IV.27

Runaway slave

Slaves had no rights to speak of. 'Human rights' certainly did not exist in antiquity. We can assume that there must have been innumerable occasions when individual slaves fled. Many were caught and executed but others disappeared into the seething mass of humanity. Most presumably had the sense not to draw attention to themselves. In this curious incident, during the civil war of 69, one such slave put it about that he was a senator who had been murdered by one of Nero's slaves. Why he should have done this is a mystery. His fate was inevitable.

A man appeared calling himself Scribonius Camerinus, claiming that he had spent Nero's reign hiding in Istria, being a place where the old Crassi family had owned land, retainers and enjoyed popularity. In order to develop this farce he surrounded himself with human scum. Credulous rabble and a few soldiers, who either believed him or liked the idea of trouble, were quickly swelling his numbers when he was taken to Vitellius and interrogated about who he was. No one believed what he said. Once his master had identified him as a fugitive slave called Geta he was punished in the usual way for slaves.
Tacitus, *Histories*, II.72

SLAVE LIVES

Staying out of trouble

From a time long before most of the passages in this book comes a short soliloquy by the slave Messenio in one of the comedies by Plautus written around 200BC. But the plays remained popular and this speech will have been heard across the Empire for many centuries afterwards. Essentially, this is a short guide to surviving for a slave. Messenio paints a graphic picture of the consequences of behaving otherwise.

These, I think, are the marks of a good slave: he must take care of his master's affairs, look after them, and think about them. When his master is not at home, he needs to look after them just as carefully as if he was there, perhaps even more so. The slave needs to look after his back and legs more than his appetite and stomach. He will bear in mind, if he has sense, how masters reward lazy, dishonest and worthless slaves: whippings, chains, treadmill, exhaustion, hunger and bitter cold, suitable remuneration for idleness. So, being a good slave is much better than being a bad one. I don't mind being sworn at, but I do hate a real flogging, and I'd much rather eat corn than be the one who grinds it. So,

I obey my master's orders and carry them out with care and efficiently, which overall I think is to my best advantage. And it certainly pays! Others might think differently, but I intend to toe the line. If I stick to that, I won't get into trouble, and I won't have anything to fear if I'm ready for my master, whatever happens. It won't be long now before I get rewarded for my services. In any case, that's my version of service: taking care to see my back doesn't get hurt.

Plautus, *The Menaechmi*, V.4

Chores

In this excerpt from one of the comedies of Plautus, the oppressive master Ballio berates his slaves in a manner showing that he expected loyalty, devotion and hard work in return for abuse and brutality.

BALLIO: Well? Does that hurt? . . . . Now you lot stand here, members of a race born to be whipped! Listen to what I say. You man, with the jug, fetch the water and make sure the kettle is filled instantly. You with the axe, set about shopping the wood
FIRST SLAVE: But the axe is blunt.
BALLIO: So what if it is? You're blunted with stripes, but is that a reason why you shouldn't work for me? I'm ordering you to clean up the house. You know what your duties are, hurry up inside.

[First Slave exits]

BALLIO (to Second Slave): Now you, smooth down the couches. Polish the silver and set it out properly. Make sure that when I get back from the Forum I'll find everything done: swept, sprinkled, scrubbed, smoother, cleaned and set out right. It's my birthday today. You should all set about celebrating it. Take care — are you listening? — set out the salt bacon, brawn, collared neck, and udder in water. I'm planning to entertain some real gentlemen in the proper manner to make it look as if I'm rich. Get inside, sort these things out so that when the chef arrives there'll be no hold-ups. I'm off to market to buy some fish. You boy, go first: I have to make sure no one swipes my wallet.

Plautus, *Pseudolus*, Act I.2

Looks are less important than reputations

The only way to take precautions about slaves was to shop around and take advice. Here, Pliny the Younger discusses slave-buying with a friend much as we might approach buying a service today. It is interesting to see that his principal concern is honesty, reflecting the preoccupation with trust.

To Plinius Paternus

Just as I depend so much on your sound judgement, so I also depend on your critical eye, not because I think you have good taste (I don't want to puff you up), but because it matches mine although even that is a bit much. Jokes aside, I think the slaves you recommended I buy look fine. The only other thing I care about is that they are honest.

On this, I can only rely on their reputations rather than their appearance. Farewell.
Pliny the Younger, *Letters*, I.21

Trust and the household expenses
If slave-owners like Pliny remained in constant fear for their lives, it was not the only worry which slavery brought. Slaves were unconditional dependants; everything they consumed had to be provided, and that meant food and clothing. So far as Seneca was concerned, the fact that time had to be spent watching them for thieving only added to the inconvenience.

The household staff demand clothes and food. So many bellies of extremely greedy beings are to be cared for, clothes improved, the hand of the most dishonest watched, and use made of people weeping and swearing. How much happier is the man who gives nothing to anyone, except the one he denies most easily, himself! But since so much strength is not for us, our possessions certainly ought to be reduced, so that we might be exposed less to the injuries of chance.
Seneca, *On a Tranquil Mind*, VIII.8

A baker slave at Pompeii
Celerus, slave of Quintus Granius Verus, made this.
Stamped loaf of bread from Pompeii. PC 250

Library slaves
There were many types of slave. In spite of lacking their freedom, some seemed to have enjoyed fairly innocuous existences.

Cicero to Atticus, Antium April 56BC
It would be very pleasant if you come and see us here. You'll discover that Tyrannio has arranged my books in a marvellously good way, the remains of which are better than I had expected. But, I wish you would send me two of your library slaves for Tyrannio to use for gluing duties, and other menial work. Tell them also to obtain some good-quality parchment to make title pieces, which you Greeks, I think, call *sillybi*. But only do all this if it's not inconvenient for you.
Cicero, *Letters to Atticus*, IV.4a

Life in the mines
Like any developed state the Roman world depended on the extraction of metals. Silver and gold were the basis of exchange and the principal storage of wealth. Iron was the strongest everyday metal known, used for tools and weapons. Lead served as plastic serves us, and was used for plumbing and waterproofing. Copper, zinc and tin were all used in various forms of brass and bronze to make jewellery, furniture fittings, lamps and base metal coinage. Mines were operated by the state or by its lessees, but the actual labour was done by slaves.

Slaves who work in the mining system make their owners richer than can almost be imagined. But the slaves themselves are physically ruined. Their bodies are worn out by working day and night in the mines. Bad treatment means that many of them die. They have no chance to rest, or take a break, from their labours. Instead, the overseers use their whips to force them to put up with most frightful conditions. In this way, their lives are exhausted by misery.

Diodorus Siculus, *History of the World*, V.38.1

Teaching an owner a lesson

What is especially interesting about this account is the revelation that a brutal master, who treated his slaves with cruelty, had forgotten his own slave origins through his father. Thus, far from reflecting inherent brutality in the system it seems to amount to a classic example of someone who has come lately to wealth but without the education to know how to use it. Pliny was appalled at what had happened to this man, but knew the reason why.

Humanity is more about dealing with individuals than making much of one's position. In his anxiety to show his status, Largius Macedo, proved that he was not worthy of being considered 'a person of quality'. In spite of his more humane approach, Pliny felt no security. In this respect he illustrates the fundamental flaw of a slave-owning world. He believed that his slaves were inferior, lesser beings more inclined to brutality and who lacked reason.

To Acilius

The appalling treatment which Largius Macedo, a senator and ex-praetor, suffered recently at the hands of his slaves, deserves more publicity than just a letter. Even so, it can't be overlooked that he treated his slaves with cruelty and severity which showed that he barely remembered, indeed almost completely forgot, that his own father had once been a slave.

He was bathing at his villa in Formia when he was suddenly surrounded by his slaves. One grabbed him by the throat, another punched him in the mouth, while others trampled on his chest, stomach and other parts which I need not describe. When they thought he was all but dead they flung him onto the heated floor of the bath, to make sure he was no longer alive. There he lay, stretched out, and quite still, either insensible or pretending to be so, at which point they decided he must really be dead. So they brought him out like this, pretending that he must have been suffocated by the heat in the bath. Some of the more faithful slaves received him and his mistresses ran up, screaming hysterically. The noise of their cries, plus the fresh air, made him revive a little. He opened his eyes, moved his limbs and showed them (now that he knew he was safe) that he was not dead. The murderers fled immediately but most of them have since been caught, while the remainder are still being pursued.

Macedo was kept alive with great difficulty for a few days, and then he died. However, he expired having had the satisfaction of seeing himself revenged. So you can see the dangers, atrocities and insults which we face. There is no master who can feel secure because he is kind and considerate: thugs like this take up arms against their masters out of brutality, not rational thought.

So much for that story. What's the latest? What? Nothing, and if there was you would know all about it because I still have paper and the time (seeing as I am still on holiday) to spare for more. Actually, I can tell you one more thing about Macedo, which has just occurred to me. Once he was in a public bath in Rome when an extraordinary and portentous (considering how he ended up dying) accident happened to him. One of his slaves stepped out of his master's way and placed his hand gently on an equestrian. The equestrian turned round suddenly and hit, not the slave who had touched him, but Macedo, with such a violent slap that he nearly knocked him over. So, the bath turned out by increments to be fatal to him: first it was where he suffered an indignity, and then it was where he died. Farewell.

Pliny the Younger, *Letters*, III.14

Conditional magnanimity

This letter from Pliny the Younger to Plinius Paternus, possibly a relative, is a vehicle to console and reassure himself. Evidently, some sort of illness has circulated amongst his slaves and freedmen, causing a number of them to die, even some young men. Pliny congratulates himself at least for having freed some of them, so that he can feel better that they died free rather than in bondage. But he reveals to us that the privilege he accorded them of writing their own wills was still subject to some fairly severe restraints; the slaves had to leave their 'property' to someone else in the household which meant, legally, leaving it to Pliny himself. In the end then, slaves were slaves and however benign and humane the owner considered himself to be, his word was law and he owned everything they were or had.

To Plinius Paternus

The illness amongst my staff, causing the deaths even of some of the young men, have done for me. There's solace for me in two things, though they're not much at a time like this. First, I am always willing to free my slaves (for to be sure I don't appear to have lost them prematurely, now I have lost them as free men). Secondly I allow those who are still slaves to make wills which I treat as if they were legal documents. I treat their final wishes and conditions as orders to be obeyed and let them leave their possessions to whoever they wish, so long as the recipient is another member of the household. That's because to slaves, their household is like an autonomous nation of which they are citizens.

Although I get some comfort from these thoughts, the very tenderness which led me to grant them these privileges is overwhelming me. That doesn't mean I want to be tougher, even though I know most of the world would treat this kind of misfortune as just a reduction in capital. Thinking this way, they believe themselves to be better men and philosophers with it. Whether they are better or philosophers I do not know, but they certainly aren't humane. Part of having humanity is to experience grief and feelings, despite trying to resist them, and to be consoled and not be above being consoled.

But perhaps I have said more than I should, though I would like to have said more. There's some pleasure in expressing grief, especially crying on the shoulder of a friend who will approve of or sympathize with one's tears. Farewell.

Pliny the Younger, *Letters*, VIII.16

Public slaves

Pliny to Trajan

I beg, lord, that you guide me with advice on this stumbling block: whether I ought to guard prisoners in the provincial cities with public slaves, as done consistently up to now, or use soldiers. For I fear that public slaves are not faithful enough but this responsibility diverts too many soldiers. For the moment I have added a few soldiers to the public slaves. However, I see a danger to be that this might cause neglect by either party, when either one could blame the other for a fault perhaps committed by both.

Pliny the Younger, *Letters*, X.19

SLAVES AND THE LAW

Penalties for marrying slaves

Claudius proposed to the senate that women who married slaves should be penalized. It was decided that a woman who demeaned herself like this should be made slaves themselves if the slave-owner was unaware of the arrangement, and reduced to the status of freedwomen if he did.

Tacitus, *Annals*, XII.53, for the year 52

When a master is murdered by his slaves

The four percent tax on the purchase of slaves was remitted, but this was a fiction rather than a real benefit because, now sellers were obliged to pay it, they simply added it to the price .... Next the senate passed a decree which was both punitive and a precaution. When a master was murdered by his slaves, all those who were going to be freed under the terms of his will, so long as they lived in the same house, would be executed with his other slaves.

Tacitus, *Annals* XIII.31, 32, for the year 57-8

Recruits

The life of a Roman soldier might have been tough but it presented a more attractive prospect than a lifetime in slavery. Not surprisingly, escapees tried to hide themselves in the ranks. But even at a time when fingerprinting, identity cards and computerized records were non-existent, slaves could be identified.

Pliny to Trajan

Sempronianus Caelianus, an outstanding young man, has sent me two slaves found amongst his recruits. I have postponed a punishment for them so that I may take advice from you, the author of military discipline and its founder, on a suitable penalty. The main reason I am dubious about this, is that the men had sworn the oath of allegiance but not been allocated to a unit. Therefore, lord, I ask that you write with what course I might be obliged to follow, especially with this setting a precedent.

Trajan to Pliny

Sempronius Caelianus carried out my orders in sending those slaves to you, about whom it's necessary to find out if perhaps they deserve capital punishment. But what is important is, did they offer themselves as volunteers or were they conscripted, or were they even supplied as substitutes?

If they are conscripts, that is bad for the recruiting officer. If they were substitutes then those who offered them are guilty. If they came of their own accord, fully aware of their status, it will mean censure for them. That they have not been allocated to units is unimportant. For the truth about their origins ought to have been ascertained on the day on which they were first accepted.

Pliny the Younger, *Letters*, X.29-30

REALITIES OF FREEDOM

Looking at the Roman world from our perspective, its use of slavery at all seems appalling. But it is also worth considering it from a different point of view. It is not always appreciated that for many peoples beyond imperial frontiers, freedom of any sort was non-existent. Tribal chiefs had absolute power over their populations, able freely to oppress, murder, exact tribute, rape, and demand sacrificial victims. Freedom in some of these communities meant freedom for unregulated brutality, enjoyed by a few and suffered by many.

Law and order might not exist at all, and the chance to enjoy the fruits of one's labours no more than a dream. Wealth generated in such societies was diverted entirely for the benefit of the tribal aristocracy, while the greater mass just subsisted. Perhaps being a slave in a Roman household seemed a mild improvement, especially in a wealthy household where a certain amount of pride might prevail amongst the domestic staff. At least there was a chance of being freed one day whereas their former existences were life sentences. Here Julius Caesar describes the social order in Gaul in the mid-first century BC.

In all of Gaul there are two classes of men who have any rank or status. The rabble are treated as if they were slaves. They take no initiative on their own and are never involved in decision-making. Most of these people, if they have been reduced by debt or the great weight of tribute, or thanks to the misdeeds of more powerful men, give themselves up as slaves to the noblemen who have the same rights over them as masters do over slaves.

Caesar, *Gallic War*, VI.13

The passage is almost an epilogue for the rest of this book. Life for almost everyone in antiquity was enormously hard, and access to power, money and freedom (however defined) almost impossible. On the one hand we can reflect on the vast difference in what we take for granted, and how we have almost no sense any longer of the risks and brutality which confronted people in antiquity.

But we could bear in mind that we might have exchanged some forms of slavery for others. Caesar's observation of Gaul might have been about Rome, and about our world too. We live in an age when governments are gradually gaining more and more effective control over their citizens. Fear of unemployment and penury in old age drive people to work longer and longer hours. Regulations and restrictions on freedom abound and proliferate, illustrating a fear of civil unrest and disobedience which resembles the terror felt by the Roman ruling classes about their slaves.

Nothing, however, can deny a man or woman his or her personality and the freedom to roam within one's imagination. Tacitus reminded his readers of the transience of liberty. Like much of what has been included in this book his words serve to show that nothing changes and that we can find in the Roman world infinite reflections of our own.

A rare delight of the present time is that one may think as one wishes, and say what one thinks.

Tacitus, *Histories* I.1

Select glossary

Aedile. Magistrates who dealt with a variety of public services such as food doles, public order and district justice

Ambulatory. A walkway such as a covered verandah around a villa, or a temple

Amphorae. Large pottery container with a narrow neck and a pair of handles, used for distribution of goods such as wine, fish-sauce, olives, and grain

Amphitheatre. A public arena, elliptical in shape with concentric tiers of seats arranged around in ascending height. The first permanent example in Roman was the Colosseum built under Vespasian (69-79), and dedicated by Titus (79-81)

Apodyterium. The changing room in the baths-suite, where the bather began his sojourn through the chambers.

Atrium. The principal entrance hall of a Roman house. Characterised as a rectangular room from which other parts of the house opened off, with a central opening in the roof to let light in, and rain into a small central pool

Aureus. The standard Roman gold denomination, equivalent to 25 silver **denarii**

Auxiliary. Non-citizen Roman soldier, hired from the provinces and organised into cavalry, infantry or mixed blocks of troops which retained an ethnic title and special skills. Always used to bear the brunt of fighting and frontier garrison duties, the auxiliary was rewarded with citizenship for himself and his heirs on an honourable discharge, usually after 25 years

Basilica. An aisled hall used as civic centres across the Roman world. It was later adapted by the Christians for churches

Beneficiarius. A soldier detached from normal duties and assigned to the personal staff of an officer

Circus. Used for chariot races and athletic events. It consisted of a long track doubled around a central spine (*spina*) and was curved at one end. Spectators watched from ascending tiers of seats. The principal example was the *Circus Maximus* at Rome, but others are known around the Empire, for example Aphrodisias in Asia Minor (modern Turkey)

Cohort. A sub-division of a legion, made up usually of six centuries of 80 men (=480). The term was also used for **auxiliary** units of infantry

Consul. The most senior Roman senatorial magistrates, were elected in pairs annually. There were two to prevent one man assuming all the power. Each could veto the other. By the time of the Empire it had become necessary to increase the numbers in order to provide enough suitably-qualified candidates for other posts such as provincial governorships. As many as six consecutive pairs might serve for two months each in a year

Culleus. 20 amphorae-worth or 120 gallons

Curator. A catch-all term for someone in charge, for example a soldier in charge of supplies, or a supervisor of works

Cryptoporticus. A semi-subterranean tunnel with small high windows, often included as a feature of extravagant villas or houses. They provided cool retreats in summer

Denarius. The standard Roman silver coin until the early third century. Diameter about 17-20mm. In the first century a Roman soldier was paid the equivalent of 225 per annum, rising to 300 by the second century. Twenty-five denarii were nominally equivalent to one gold **aureus** but in practice silver and gold circulated at a value dependent on their purity. Purity tended to decline, especially of the silver, through the period with the result that older coin had a higher intrinsic value

Forum. The central market and commercial zone in a Roman city. Usually open air, with surrounding porticoes, it was filled with traders and customers, statues, honorific inscriptions and merchandise. Normally flanked by the **basilica** and the main city temples

Imperatorial province. The Empire was divided into senatorial and imperatorial provinces. The senate nominated the governors of the former (such as Greece) while the latter (such as Gaul and Britain) were governed by the emperor's personal delegates. Imperatorial provinces were technically the emperor's personal property and had been won by war

Iugerum. 2/3 of an acre (28800 sq ft)

Legate. The legate was a 'delegate' of the emperor, his personal nominee and representative to provincial governorships, provincial judicial administration, and the command of legions. Their numbers were drawn from the senators, and had to have served as **praetors** or, for the most senior posts, **consuls**

Legion. The backbone of the Roman army. The Empire never had more than about thirty of these, made up of around 5000 citizen legionaries

Lictor. An attendant. Magistrates such as **consuls** were supplied with these attendants as a mark of their status and importance. Thus the consul whose turn it was to take the lead was accompanied by his twelve lictors

Peristyle. A row of columns surrounding a building or space, such as a garden

Praetor. Normally 12-18 of these senatorial magistrates were elected annually. Under the Empire their duties included (at times) supervising the treasury and public games but for many of them most of the time the title was more honorific than practical. Men who had held praetorships became eligible for legionary commands and most provincial governorships though some special cases (like Britain) required men who had been consuls (**proconsul**)

Proconsul. A man who had served as a **consul** and was thus at the pinnacle of his senatorial career. He was eligible for governorships of senatorial provinces like Asia and special cases like Britain

Quaestor. Around twenty of these senatorial magistracies seem to have been elected annually under the Empire. Traditionally they had looked after the treasury and under the Empire they seem for some of the time to have continued in this role. They also served as secretaries to consuls, and also supervising certain public games

Senatorial province. See **imperatorial province**

Sestertius. The standard Roman unit of currency, represented in the Imperial period by a large brass coin which itself was no longer produced after the late third century. Its nominal value was equivalent to one-quarter of a silver **denarius**

Tablinum. A balcony or terrace, or a place where family archives were stored

Tribune. Magistrates traditionally appointed to look after the interests of the plebs, that is, the ordinary people. Their powers were strongly protected, and they could summon the Senate. By the time of the Empire the tribuneship was largely honorific, but most emperors also held the office as part of their Republican posture

Vilicus. A bailiff or overseer left in charge of , usually, a villa estate

Chronology

Principal (selected) events during the Roman Empire (from Actium to the death of Honorius)

31BC	Battle of Actium. Antony defeated by Octavian (Augustus)
26BC	Augustus takes supreme power, but casts it as a restoration of the old Republican order
AD9	The Varian Disaster in Germany: three legions lost
14	Tiberius succeeds Augustus
	Germanicus crosses the Rhine
33	Approximate date of Christ's crucifixion
37	Caligula succeeds
41	Murder of Caligula; accession of his uncle Claudius
43	Conquest of Britain begun
54	Death of Claudius; accession of Nero
64	Great fire in Rome. Nero begins his Golden House
68	Nero commits suicide; accession of Galba
69	January 2nd: declaration for Vitellius by troops in Germany
	January 15th: Otho's conspiracy, murder of Galba, accession of Otho
	April: Vitellius defeats Otho, Otho commits suicide
	July: Vespasian proclaimed in Alexandria, murder of Vitellius
70	Fall of Jerusalem
79	Death of Vespasian; accession of Titus
	August: eruption of Vesuvius
80	Colosseum dedicated
81	Death of Titus; accession of Domitian
96	Murder of Domitian; accession of Nerva
98	Death of Nerva; accession of Trajan
101-2	First Dacian War
105-6	Second Dacian War
111	Pliny the Younger appointed to govern Bithynia
113	Parthian War begins
117	Death of Trajan; accession of Hadrian
122	Hadrian's Wall begun
129	Hadrian reaches Athens
135	Jewish Revolt suppressed
138	Death of Hadrian; accession of Antoninus Pius

161	Death of Antoninus Pius; accession of Marcus Aurelius
162	Armenian rebellion
165	Plague reaches Italy
168-75	Marcomannic War
180	Death of Marcus Aurelius; accession of Commodus
186	Muitny in the army in Britain
192	December: murder of Commodus
193	January: accession of Pertinax
	March: murder of Pertinax, soldiers auction the Empire to Didius Julianus in Rome
	March: Pescennius Niger proclaimed emperor in Syria, Clodius Albinus in Britain
	June: murder of Didius Julianus
	June: Septimius Severus declared emperor at Carnuntum, makes Clodius Albinus Caesar
194	Severus defeats Pescennius Niger
195	Clodius Albinus challenges Severus
197	Clodius Albinus defeated at Lyons and commits suicide
208	Severus commences British campaign
211	Severus dies at York, accession of his sons Caracalla and Geta
212	Caracalla murders Geta
217	Caracalla murdered, accession of Macrinus
218	Murder of Macrinus, accession of Elagabalus
222	Murder of Elagabalus, accession of Severus Alexander
235	Murder of Severus Alexander, accession of Maximinus I
238	March: Gordian I and II proclaimed emperor
	April: Gordian II killed in battle, Gordian I commits suicide, proclamation of Balbinus and Pupienus
	June: murder of Maximinus I
	July: murder of Balbinus and Pupienus
	Accession of Gordian III
244	Murder of Gordian III, accession of Philip I
249	Philip I defeated and killed, accession of Trajan Decius
251	Decius defeated and killed by Goths, accession and death from plague of Decius' son Hostilian, accession of Trebonianus Gallus and his son Volusian
253	Aemilian makes a bid for the purple: murder of Gallus and Volusian followed by murder of Aemilian, accession of Valerian I and his son Gallienus. In Gaul, Germany and Britain the Gallic Empire starts with Postumus at its head
259	Valerian captured by the Persians
267	Goths invade Asia Minor
268	Gallienus murdered; Claudius II Gothicus succeeds. Postumus murdered.
270	Claudius II dies of plague; accession of Aurelian
271	The Aurelian Walls of Rome begun
273	Aurelian defeats the eastern revolt under Zenobia

275	Aurelian murdered; accession of Tacitus
276	Tacitus dies of exhaustion in campaign against Goths; accession of Probus
276-82	Probus suppresses revolts and expels barbarians on the Danube, Asia Minor and in Gaul
282	Probus murdered; accession of Carus
282	Carus murdered; accession of his sons Numerian and Carinus
284	Numerian killed
285	Carinus killed by Diocletian who succeeds with Maximian as Caesar
286	Diocletian splits the Empire between himself (East) and Maximian (West)
286-7	Carausian Revolt in Britain
293	Carausius killed; Allectus takes over in Britain
296	Allectus defeated and killed
305-24	Power struggle between the nominees and descendants of Diocletian, Maximian and their assistants ends up with Constantine the Great taking total control
313	Edict of Milan legitimises Christianity
337	Death of Constantine I. Struggle between his sons leads to Constantius II eventually winning supreme power
353-3	Revolt of Magnentius in the West
353	Constantius II in sole control of the Empire
360	Julian, cousin of Constantius II, proclaimed emperor in Gaul
361	Death of Constantius II
363	Death of Julian; accession of Jovian
364	Death of Jovian; accession of Valentinian I (West) and Valens (East)
367	Gratian appointed joint emperor with Valentinian I
375	Death of Valentinian I; Gratian rules in the West now with Valentinian II
378	Valens killed at the Battle of Hadrianopolis by the Goths; Gratian takes the East too
379	Gratian hands the East to Theodosius I
383	Revolt of Magnus Maximus in the West, Gratian killed
388	Magnus Maximus defeated by Theodosius I, Valentinian II restored in the West
392	Valentinian II murdered
395	Theodosius defeats Valentinian II's murderers, then dies himself
395	Arcadius succeeds to sole rule in the East, Honorius in the West
408	Death of Arcadius; accession of Theodosius II (d. 450)
410	Rome sacked
423	Death of Honorius

Classical authors

The following brief biographies provide some basic details about the more important sources of texts used in this book, and other authors who are mentioned.

Aelius Lampridius (fl. 395)
See **Aelius Spartianus**.

Aelius Spartianus (fl. 395)
One of the writers of the *Scriptores Historiae Augustae*, 'Authors of the Imperial Histories'. This collection of imperial biographies runs from the accession of Hadrian in 117 to the death of Numerian in 284, and includes usurpers and heirs who died before they had time to become emperors. They are of varying quality and it is unclear whether the attributed authors were authentic individuals or pen-names. The collection is thought to have been gathered together around the end of the fourth century. They include other attributed authors such as Julius Capitolinus, Aelius Lampridius and Flavius Vopiscus.

Ammianus Marcellinus (c. 325-95)
Soldier and historian from Antioch who nonetheless wrote in Latin. His history of the Roman world ran from the accession of Nerva in 96 up to the death of Valens in 378. His work is considered to be generally of high quality and broadly reliable though only its latter part (353-78) is extant. Aelius Lampridius after Capitolinus, and delete of Syracuse, thus: authors such as Julius Capitolinus, Aelius Lampridius and Flavius Vopiscus.

Augustine (354-430)
Born in North Africa, he worked as a teacher of grammar before going to Rome and Milan where he was exposed to Christian teachings and was converted in 386. Within a decade he was back in Africa and serving as Bishop of Hippo. His letters discuss a variety of subjects but provide illustrations of Roman life in the fourth century and some of the immense tensions created by the conflict between Christians and pagans, and amongst Christian sects.

Ausonius (c. 310-95)
Decimus Magnus Ausonius was a Gallo-Roman from Bordeaux who became a university teacher of rhetoric. He may have become a Christian but, if so, it seems to have been a matter of convenience. In later life he became a tutor to the emperor Gratian (367-83) who was promoted to Augustus when only seven years old. He wrote a variety of poems

in a self-consciously retrospective style. Like many of his time, he looked back to the literature of earlier centuries with admiration and used it as a model.

Caesar (102-44BC)
The most famous Roman of them all, Gaius Julius Caesar was a politician, egotist and military genius. He ruthlessly used all these attributes to gain absolute power. Fortunately for us he recorded his own account of the Civil War of 49-48BC and the earlier war in Gaul (58-52BC) which includes the account of the two invasions of Britain. They are distinctive for their straightforward, factual, qualities.

Cato (234-149BC)
Marcus Portius Cato was regarded in his own time and afterwards as the very model of upstanding Roman virtue and tradition. His *On Agriculture*, the only one of his books to survive, was regarded ever afterwards as a classic textbook on rural management.

Catullus (*c.* 84-54BC)
Gaius Valerius Catullus was born in Verona but came to Rome as a young man. His life is only really known from the poems which tell us that he served on the governor's staff in Bithynia, and far more vividly about his affair with 'Lesbia', in reality Clodia, wife of Quintus Metellus Celer. She was famed for her looks and power and the affair was a disaster thanks to her infidelity.

Celsus (fl. 14-37)
Aulus Cornelius Celsus had similar wide-ranging interests to **Pliny the Elder** which he compiled into an extensive general encyclopaedia. Only the section on medicine has survived, an intriguing thematic collection of descriptions which foreshadows modern medicine.

Cicero (106-43BC)
Marcus Tullius Cicero is best known as a philosopher, lawyer and orator. A great deal is known about him because a remarkable number of his prolific works have survived including speeches, discourses on various subjects such as public duties, old age, and religion, and a vast number of his private letters. In 51 he was made governor of Cilicia. His opposition to the rise of dictatorships and effective monarchical rule meant that he was one of many prominent individuals to be purged by the triumvirate of Octavian (later Augustus Caesar), Antony and Lepidus.

Claudian (fl. 395-405)
Claudius Claudianus came from Alexandria and wrote in Greek originally, apparently turning to Latin later in life. He mainly wrote poems which praised members of the imperial house such as Honorius (393-423) and other high officials, and which sometimes act as important source material for events which are otherwise unrecorded.

Dio Cassius (*c.* 150-235)

Dio Cassius Cocceianus, or Cassius Dio Cocceianus, was born in Bithynia but worked as a lawyer in Rome before proceeding through a senatorial career of provincial governorships and consulships. He wrote a major history of the Roman world from the beginning to his own times. The text has many gaps, parts of which are made good by summaries produced in late antiquity and the Middle Ages from the now-lost originals. Dio's works help fill the holes in **Tacitus** and form a vitally important source for imperial history, augmented for the latter part by **Herodian**.

Diodorus Siculus (fl. 40sBC)

Born in Sicily Diodorus Siculus wrote a history of various places such as Greece, Rome, Italy, and Persia which contained a variety of information trawled from other sources. He tended to include anything, however incredible it was, and believed it all usually at the expense of covering important historical events.

Eusebius (*c.* 260-*c.* 339)

Eusebius' origins are unknown but after 313 he was made bishop of Caesarea in Palestine, and took an active and prominent role in the various liturgical disputes at the great Christian councils of the era. He produced a large number of books on Christian affairs but is now best known for his *Ecclesiastical History* which was written from at least 311 onwards, perhaps earlier, though he revised it several times up until around 324.

Frontinus (*c.*35-103)

Sextus Julius Frontinus was a soldier and senator whose duties included governing Britain under Vespasian from about 76-8. He produced two important works: a military treatise on Stratagems, and a description of the Aqueducts of Rome. The latter was written as a result of his appointment to be supervise the water-supply to the city.

Herodian (*c.* 178 - post 238)

Nothing seems to be known about Herodian for certain and this includes where he came from, though the fact that he wrote in Greek makes it almost inevitable he came from the East. Certain clues are said to indicate he came from Alexandria or Antioch. Either way it is ironic that his imperial history of the years 180-238 appears to be the only Roman history which has survived intact. Although it includes part of the period covered by **Dio Cassius**, the texts provide confirmation and other information.

Horace (65-8BC)

Quintus Horatius Flaccus was the son of an ex-slave. Despite this inauspicious beginning his education and literary skills brought him into the circle of famous poets like **Virgil**. His friends provided him with the means to support himself and he also contributed to Augustus' campaign for power.

Jerome (*c*. 345-420)

Eusebius Sophronius Hieronymus, known to history as Jerome, was one of the first great Christian scholars. Born where Yugoslavia once was, his movements reflected the cosmopolitan nature of the Empire. Amongst his most important works was the Latin ('Vulgate') version of the Bible. His letters are models of passionate and sincere belief, as well as bigotry, intolerance and repression. He seems to have placed particular emphasis on controlling his female disciples, perhaps expressing feelings which he was unable to act on in a more normal way.

Josephus (*c*. 37-post 93)

Titus Flavius Josephus was a Jew who was sent for training as a priest and was a pharisee by the time he was 19. A visit to Rome, coupled with his intelligence, led him to realise that the revolt being planned in Judaea was a foregone conclusion. He nevertheless fought with his people but skilfully evaded committing suicide in a mass-suicide pact. Thereafter he sided with the Romans and was ever after regarded as a traitor by the Jews. His account, *The Jewish War*, of the revolt and its suppression by Vespasian and Titus includes powerful images of the Roman war machine in action.

Julius Capitolinus (fl. 395)
See **Aelius Spartianus**.

Juvenal (fl. *c*. 78-135)

Allusions in his works to Aquinum in Italy make it possible this is the Junius Juvenalis of an inscription found there which records a military career as tribune in the First cohort of Dalmatians, a unit known to have been stationed in Britain by the early second century. His Satires are amongst the best-known works of classical literature and were amongst those translated into verse by John Dryden in the seventeenth century.

Livy (59BC-AD17)

Titus Livius wrote his great history of Rome during the reign of Augustus. Like **Virgil** he was acutely conscious of the momentous change in his time and used his literary skills to bolster the new regime. He was famous in his own time as a writer and his work is characterised by its essential emphasis on style and patriotic rhetoric, rather than factual reliability and objectivity.

Lucian (*c*. 115-200)

Lucianus came from Samosata in Syria. Despite modest origins he trained as a lawyer but moved off to travel and study, producing a series of texts on a variety of subjects including biographies of philosophers, and essays on literary topics and dialogues on the gods. They are regarded as witty and observant.

Lucretius (*c*. 99-55BC)

Titus Lucretius Carus is known only for his monumental poetic exposition of physics, astronomy, the nature of life and its beginning, the soul, and sexuality known as *The Nature of Things*. His work seems to have earned the admiration of **Cicero** and his brother by the year 54. Assuming that it was published posthumously, which it is believed to have been, this provides an approximate cut-off point for his death. **Jerome** states that his work was corrected by Cicero, and that the death of Lucretius occurred in his forty-fourth year. There is some suggestion from Jerome that Lucretius was reputed to have been of unstable mind.

Martial (*c*. 40-104)

Marcus Valerius Martialis was a Spaniard who came to Rome and, despite a lack of independent means, joined a circle of upper-class educated men like **Seneca** and **Pliny the Younger**. His *Epigrams* provide a rich resource of witty observations on everyday Roman life.

Ovid (43BC - AD17)

Publius Ovidius Naso was a poet whose works and behaviour did not earn him the patronage of Augustus. Indeed, he was exiled to the East. His best-known work now is his *Metamorphoses*, an invaluable repository of myth but he also wrote a number of other poems, for example *The Art of Love*, of which Augustus disapproved.

Pausanias (fl. 150-80)

Pausanias came from Asia Minor, probably the city of Magnesia, and worked as a doctor. However, he is now known only for his *Description of Greece* which he produced after spending many years travelling in Greece during the reign of Hadrian. His work is an invaluable compilation of his own eye-witness accounts and material drawn from other books which are now long lost.

Phlegon (early 2nd century)

A freedman of Hadrian who wrote books on remarkable sights and phenomena, but only a few short passages have survived.

Plautus (*c*. 254-184BC)

Titus Maccius Plautus worked as a comic actor in Rome as a young man. Despite attempting a career in business he returned to the theatre but this time as a playwright, modelling his work on Greek originals which he adapted for a Roman audience. His works remained immensely popular and in later times he enjoyed the kind of reputation that some of the great English Restoration playwrights enjoy in our own time.

Pliny the Elder (23-79)

Like **Celsus**, Gaius Plinius Secundus was interested in almost everything and anything. His family came from northern Italy and held public and military posts in Germany, Gaul and Spain. He was prefect of the fleet at Misenum when his curiosity got the better of him during the eruption of Vesuvius and he died, apparently of suffocation, while attempting to rescue friends. His principal claim to fame is his *Natural History*, a monumental work which tabulates almost everything and anything from natural phenomena to freaks, minerals to astronomy, and trees to bees. A mix of credulousness and insight, it was treated as an invaluable resource by the early modern scientists.

Pliny the Younger (*c.* 61-113)

Nephew of **Pliny the Elder**, Gaius Plinius Caecilius Secundus was born in Como. His uncle adopted him as his son in his will. He held a series of public offices but it is his letters to his friends, acquaintances and colleagues which provide perhaps the most important resource for much day-to-day management of private Roman households, intellectual affairs, and the governorship of a province. The latter was recorded in a stream of letters to Trajan covering everything from family use of official couriers to the administration of corrupt and inefficient city government. Nevertheless, it is his two letters to Tacitus concerning his eye-witness account of the eruption of Vesuvius which are amongst the most memorable pieces of writing to have survived from all antiquity.

Plutarch (*c.* 45-117)

Plutarch wrote a series of biographies of great or terrible men from the Greek and Roman world in the form of matched pairs where he saw parallels in the way their careers had developed. Some of these provide useful accounts of great historical accounts. The life of Crassus, for instance, includes a detailed description of the great slave revolt of Spartacus. The celebrated motion picture of the episode ultimately depends, despite extensive embellishments, on this passage.

Propertius (*c.* 50-10BC)

Sextus Propertius was another of the first century BC poets whose works endured throughout antiquity. However, he was not preoccupied with the meaning of life, the founding of Rome or myth, but his love for his mistress Cynthia.

Sallust (86-*c.* 35BC)

Gaius Sallustius Crispus was a member of **Caesar**'s party. His account of the *Catiline Conspiracy* recounts how Lucius Sergius Catalina, a spectacularly corrupt and ambitious politician who routinely utilised murder and extortion, developed a plot to overthrow the state when his advance was thwarted.

Seneca the Younger (*c.*4BC-AD65)

Lucius Annaeus Seneca was a Stoic philosopher, lawyer and politician who spent much of his professional life in Rome dodging imperial opprobrium. He was noted for his treatises on subjects like anger and peace, and, in his later years, for his letters and his character assassination of Claudius. He served as Nero's tutor, having been recalled to the post by Claudius who had earlier sentenced him to death before exiling him. His association with Nero was not only dangerous but also damaged his personal reputation. He was obliged to commit suicide by Nero after a plot against the latter was uncovered.

Sidonius (*c.* 430-post 476)

Gaius Sidonius Apollinaris was a Gallo-Roman Christian from Lyons. By his middle years he was Bishop of Auvergne and acted as a leader in the resistance against barbarian attacks. In spite of the late date his letters are a mine of information on late-Roman villa life where monumental country estates functioned as proto-medieval fiefdoms with colossal local power and influence. In spite of this, and his Christian position, he looked back to the lives and literature of an imperial Rome that was around 500 years old.

Strabo (*c.* 54BC-AD25)

Born in Asia Minor, Strabo is now only known for his famous and invaluable description of the ancient world which includes accounts of architecture, government and politics based on his own personal observations.

Suetonius (*c.* 77-post 121)

Gaius Suetonius Tranquillus was well-placed to produce his almost legendary *Twelve Caesars*, a series of pen portraits of the first eleven emperors and their progenitor, the dictator **Caesar**. He was a correspondent of **Pliny the Younger**'s which helps place him in a literary and social context. He wrote other works too, for example the lives of famous men of literature, but it is his accounts of men like Caligula and Nero which have immortalised these remarkable emperors. At once informative and scurrilous they remain a delight to read.

Tacitus (*c.* 55-post 117)

Cornelius Tacitus is the most celebrated of all Roman historians. His two principal works, the *Annals*, and the *Histories*, covered the period from 14-68, and 68-96, respectively. Of the former, much is extant, but missing sections include the whole reign of Caligula and part of that of Claudius. Only the first part of the latter has survived taking us through the civil war of 68-9 into the year 70. His Latin is distinctive for its abrupt style. Although he used his works to carry sub-texts (the account of the reign of Tiberius is an implicit assault on Domitian) he remains the most informative historian of the period. His account of his father-in-law's life, the *Agricola*, is considerably more partisan but still vital to the history of the province of Britain.

Terence (*c.* 186-159BC)

Publius Terentius Afer was probably born in Carthage. He wrote a series of comedies, such as *The Eunuch*, based on Greek models and was well-known in his own time, often being cited by other authors. However, his influence also lasted well into modern times.

Tertullian (*c.*160-220)

Quintus Septimius Florens Tertullianus, from Carthage, was a convert to Christianity. He produced a number of works in defence of the new religion, as well as writing about women's excessive luxury and promoting the Greek cloak over the toga.

Varro (116-17BC)

Marcus Terentius Varro was a highly-educated man with a wide range of interests including history, science, language and agriculture. In spite of a vast published output only his works on agriculture and the Latin language are extant. He was a friend of Julius Caesar's and lived to a venerable age.

Vegetius (4th or 5th century AD)

Flavius Renatus Vegetius was a military writer under the Late Empire. However, he principally described earlier military techniques and equipment in a manual which was extremely popular in the Middle Ages and later.

Velleius Paterculus (*c.* 20BC-post AD30)

Gaius Velleius Paterculus was a senior soldier who served as a military legate under Tiberius. He wrote a workaday account of Roman history which, despite beginning with the Trojan war and having missing sections, nevertheless provides an important narrative for the later years of the Roman Republic into the early Empire. The work is admired for its efficient summarising of periods of what would otherwise be wholly lost.

Virgil (70-19BC)

Publius Vergilius Maro was the greatest of all Roman poets. He was to Augustus what Shakespeare was to the house of Tudor. His *Aeneid* provide literary and mythical foundations for Augustus' regime. His *Georgics* and *Eclogues* celebrated the Roman fantasy of bucolic purity. His works entered common Latin parlance in the way that Shakespeare's words and turns of phrase characterise modern English though many of us fail to realise it. Passages and quotes pop up across the Empire in space and time as children's writing exercises and spouted by circus crowds. **Ausonius** even composed a lewd poem entirely made up of juxtaposed lines extracted from all over Virgil's works. More ancient manuscripts of Virgil have survived than those of any other author.

Vitruvius (fl. late 1st century BC)

Marcus Vitruvius Pollio was an architect and civil engineer in the late first century BC. By the reign of Augustus he was supervising the construction of imperial military artillery. His work on architecture described everything an architect needed to choose sites, plan towns, orders of architecture, design and form, hydraulics, astronomy, and artillery. The work was one of the most influential to survive from antiquity and was largely responsible for the revival of classical forms which led to Palladian architecture in Europe and the developments by Thomas Jefferson and others in the United States.

Abbreviations and references

Bath = **Tomlin, R.S.O., 1988**, 'The curse tablets' in **Cunliffe, B., 1988**, *The Temple of Sulis Minerva at Bath. Volume 2, The Finds from the Sacred Spring*, Oxford University Committee for Archaeology Monograph no. 16, Oxford

CIL = *Corpus Inscriptionum Latinarum* (Berlin 1863-)

Davis = **Davis, William Stearns, ed., 1912-12**, *Readings in Ancient History: Illustrative Extracts from the Sources*, 2 Vols, Allyn and Bacon, Boston

ILS = **Dessau H., 1892-1916**, *Inscriptionum latinae selecta*, Berlin (three volumes). These inscriptions are now available on the Internet at http://gnomon.ku-eichstaett.de

OGIS = **Wittenberger, W., 1903-5**, *Orientis Graeci Inscriptiones Selectae*, Leipzig

PC = **Ward-Perkins, J., and Claridge, A., 1976**, *Pompeii AD 79*. Exhibition Catalogue. Imperial Tobacco Ltd., Bristol

RIB = **Collingwood, R.G., and Wright, R.P., 1995**, *The Roman Inscriptions of Britain*, volume 1, second edition, Stroud (with revisions and addenda by R.S.O. Tomlin). The texts of these inscriptions are also available on the Internet at http://www.romanbritain.org.uk and http://www.bedoyere.freeserve.co.uk

RIC = **Mattingly, H., Sydenham, E.A., Sutherland, C.H.V., and Carson, R.A.G., (Eds)**, *The Roman Imperial Coinage*, London

SP = **Hunt, A.S., and Edgar, C.C., 1988**, *Select Papyri*, Loeb Classical Library, Harvard and Heinemann (three volumes)

SHA = *Scriptores Historiae Augustae* (see Aelius Spartianus and Julius Capitolinus under **Classical Authors** above), a series of imperial biographies from Hadrian to Numerian of varied attribution

Tab. Vindol. = *Tabulae Vindolandenses*, most readily accessible in **Bowman A.K., and Thomas, J.D., 1994**, *The Vindolanda Writing Tablets*, British Museum Press, London

Further reading

There is a vast wealth of books covering aspects of society, culture and history of the Roman Empire. The following is a selection of some of the more useful. M. Cary and H.H. Scullard's *A History of Rome* (third edition, Macmillan 1975 and 1979) is a work in the old school of basic chronological narrative. Despite having been around since the 1930s in various forms it is still an immensely useful work of reference with a vast amount of basic information, which is often difficult to locate in more modern works. Having said that, even older textbooks such as William Ramsay's *A Manual of Roman Antiquities* (for example, fourth edition, Charles Griffin 1901) can provide details about magistracies and technical details which modern books seem to find it convenient to omit, leaving the reader none the wiser.

Colin Wells' *The Roman Empire* (Fontana, second edition 1992) is a lively and readable account of imperial history with a very substantial descriptive bibliography to which the reader is referred for a colossal number of recommendations. Martin Goodman's *The Roman World* (Routledge 1997) covers the period 44BC to AD180 in rather more detail and has sections dedicated to regions of the Empire as well as religions. A more thematic exploration of the Roman world can be found in *Experiencing Rome. Culture, Identity and Power in the Roman Empire* (Routledge and the Open University 2000), a selection of essays edited by Janet Huskinson.

For the texts there is no more accessible source than the Penguin Classics series of paperback translations which includes most of the principal authors. Especially recommended are the editions of Pliny the Elder, Suetonius and Tacitus. Most of the introductions to these texts are also excellent. However, the only comprehensive source of the texts themselves is the Loeb Classical Library (Harvard and Heinemann) which combines translation with original texts. Unfortunately the significant cost of these books puts them beyond the reach of most readers, though they can often be found in second-hand bookshops. Anthologies can be found in Naphtali Lewis and Meyer Reinhold's *Roman Civilization. Sourcebook I: the Republic* and *Sourcebook II: the Empire* (Harper Torchbooks, various editions), as well as Jo-Ann Shelton's *As the Romans Did* (Oxford 1998).

Although large format illustrated books of the Roman world abound there is no better combination of images, maps and text than Tim Cornell and John Matthews' *Atlas of the Roman World* (Phaidon 1982) which provides history, geographical descriptions and pictures alongside a wealth of maps and charts. Further colour and detail is to be had from Martin Henig's (Ed.,) *A Handbook of Roman Art* (Phaidon 1983) which contains a series of essays by experts on different aspects of Roman art and creativity.

The Internet is also now a fertile source of supporting material. At the time of writing, the pages at http://www.fordham.edu/halsall/ancient/asbook.html are an immensely useful resource with dozens of links to texts and other data covering the whole of the Roman world. A site dedicated to Roman texts resides at http://www.geocities.com/Athens/Forum/6946/literature.html . Inscriptions are available at http://gnomon.ku-eichstaett.de and the editor's http://www.romanbritain.org.uk (also available at http://www.bedoyere.freeserve.co.uk) . One of the disadvantages of the Internet is that these links are liable to change in time. However, use of the search engines will normally locate alternatives or revisions.

Index

Names are indexed under their most familiar form, thus Agricola, Gnaeus Julius, appears under A. The Index is divided into two: sources, and general.

Index of sources

General Index